Winning Strategies
for Business

Winning Strategies
for Business

Rajat Kanti Baisya

Response
Business books from SAGE
Los Angeles ▪ London ▪ New Delhi ▪ Singapore ▪ Washington DC
www.sagepublications.com

First published in 2010 by

Response Books
Business books from SAGE
B1/I-1 Mohan Cooperative Industrial Area
Mathura Road, New Delhi 110 044, India

SAGE Publications Inc
2455 Teller Road
Thousand Oaks, California 91320, USA

SAGE Publications Ltd
1 Oliver's Yard
55 City Road
London EC1Y 1SP, United Kingdom

SAGE Publications Asia-Pacific Pte Ltd
33 Pekin Street
#02-01 Far East Square
Singapore 048763

Published by Vivek Mehra for SAGE Publications India Pvt Ltd, typeset in 11/13 AGaramond by Tantla Composition Pvt Ltd, Chandigarh and printed at Chaman Enterprises, New Delhi.

Library of Congress Cataloging-in-Publication Data
Baisya, Rajat K.
      Winning strategies for business/Rajat Kanti Baisya.
            p. cm.
      Includes bibliographical references and index.
      1. Strategies planning.   2. Success in business.   3. Corporations—Growth.   I. Title.

HD30.28.B333   658.4'012—dc22   2010   2010032555

ISBN: 978-81-321-0442-1 (PB)

The SAGE Team: Qudsiya Ahmed and Anupam Choudhury

This book is dedicated to my wife, Susmita, son, Rishabh and daughter, Deepshikha, for their encouragement and support while writing this book.

I would also like to specially dedicate this book to the memory of my daughter, Deepanwita, who has always been a great source of inspiration for me in whatever I try to do.

Contents

List of Tables

List of Figures

List of Abbreviations

ABC	Activity Based Costing
AMUL	Anand Milk Union Ltd
B2B	Business to Business
B2C	Business to Customer
BCG	Boston Consulting Group
BEC	Break Even Capacity
BIFR	Board for Industrial & Financial Reconstruction
BMC	Bombay Municipal Corporation
BOP	Balance of Payment
BPR	Business Process Reengineering
BSC	Balanced Scorecard
BSE	Bombay Stock Exchange
CAP	College of American Pathologists
C&FA	Clearing & Forwarding Agent
CEO	Chief Executive Officer
CII	Confederation of Indian Industries
CKD	Completely Knocked Down
CMM	Capability Maturity Model
COQ	Cost of Quality
CRM	Customer Relationship Management
EPS	Earning Per Share
ERP	Enterprise Resource Planning
EU	European Union
EVA	Economic Value Added
FDI	Foreign Direct Investment
FICCI	Federation of Indian Chambers of Commerce and Industry
FMCG	Fast Moving Consumer Goods
GCMMF	Gujarat Cooperative Milk Marketing Federation
GDM	Global Delivery Mechanism
GDP	Gross Domestic Product
GDR	Global Depository Receipt
GIS	Geographic Information System

GNI	Gross National Income
GNP	Gross National Product
GP	Gross Profit
GRI	Global Reporting Initiative
HRD	Human Resource Development
HRM	Human Resource Management
HUL	Hindustan Unilever Ltd
HVO	Hydrogenated Vegetable Oil
ICT	Information and Communication Technology
IMF	International Monetary Fund
IPL	Indian Premier League
IPO	Initial Public Offer
ISO	International Standardisation Organisation
JIT	Just-in-Time
KDCMPUL	Kaira District Cooperative Milk Producers Union Ltd
MGI	McKinsey Global Institute
MIS	Management Information System
MNC	Multinational Corporation
MRP	Maximum Retail Price
NABL	National Accreditation Board for Testing and Calibration Laboratories
NASDAQ	National Association of Securities Dealers Automated Quotation System (American Stock Exchange)
NCAER	National Council of Applied Economic Research
NIFTY	National Index For Fifty
NRI	Non Resident Indian
NTB	Non Tariff Barrier
OECD	Organisations For Economic Co-operation and Development
OSDC	Off shore Software Development Centre
OTS	Open Top Sanitary Can
P/E	Price Earning Ratio
PAL	Purpose, Agenda and Limit
PDC	Proximity Development Centre
PERT	Project Evauation Review Technique

PESTEL	Political Environment Social Technological Economic and Legal
PPP	Public–Private Partnership, Purchasing Power Parity
PSU	Public Sector Undertaking
ROI	Return on Investment
RTE	Ready to Eat
RTS	Ready to Serve
SAARC	South Asian Association for Regional Cooperation
SBU	Strategic Business Unit
SCM	Supply Chain Management
SDC	Soft Drink Concentrate
SME	Small and Medium Enterprise
SP	Strategic Planning
SPU	Strategic Planning Unit
STR	Stock Turnover Ratio
SWOT	Strengths Weaknesses Opportunities and Threats
TEMPLES	Technology, Economy, Politics, Law, Environment and Society
TFP	Total Factor Productivity
TPM	Total Productive Maintenance
TQM	Total Quality Management
UB	United Breweries Group
UNGC	United Nation Global Compact
WTO	World Trade Organisation

Foreword

NEVER BEFORE have we experienced so much uncertainty about the future. Familiar milestones and goalposts seem to be no longer able to guide businesses to plan and steer organisations to achieve their objectives. On the one hand, knowledge explosion, Internet and Information and Communication Technology (ICT) revolution have forced organisations to innovate the ways to run businesses, and on the other, increased expectation of customers and shareholders, as well as the society at large, have created greater pressure on businesses to perform. To top it all, forces of globalisation and competition have opened up many new business opportunities to explore. Managing a business in the new economy, therefore, requires a different kind of approach and strategy. The old rules of the game seem to be no longer working well. Innovation and sustainability are now the keys to success. Delivering better value faster than competition will determine who will win in the end.

India is one of the most dynamic business environments on earth. From the small *kirana* stores to the giant conglomerates, India's business people are smart, hard-working and enterprising. Indian managers are also considered as most sought-after talents globally and are able to produce and demonstrate good results in challenging environments, both in India and abroad. There are many challenges to doing business in India, but still, India is a fast-growing economy and Indian entrepreneurs are emerging as winners. Some companies have done remarkably well and have emerged as global leaders from humble origins. Firms like Infosys, Reliance and Amul have become global leaders. Rajat Baisya has cleverly distilled the key strategic drivers that have helped these companies prosper in the global marketplace and finally emerge as leaders.

The book deals with identifying new challenges of market and environment and suggesting a framework to analyse the key issues to be addressed by an organisation, and within the given resources and constraints, how organisations can create strategic action plans to emerge out winners and still survive challengers' onslaughts.

The author has developed this into a strategic toolkit that allows a. manager to develop a winning plan for her/his company. Through examining the new challenges faced in the modern marketplace, he explores strategies for survival supported by numerous real-life examples to illustrate the points. With the 'downside' covered, he then helps the manager develop growth plans to gain competitive advantage, thereby allowing the business to win. This rigorous approach to forming a strategy for business is essential for most businesses.

It is worth asking a few questions. Are the current strategies working for you in the current market? Is your growth trajectory looking different now, forcing you to look for newer markets and to exploit newer opportunities? Is your current winner product fast becoming obsolete because of technological advancement taking place outside your business? These and other related questions will make you think for a new strategic direction that can ensure that the rate of change within your organisation will happen faster than the rate of change taking place outside your organisation. This alone can help you finally emerge as the winner.

Amid these turbulent times, the threats to business are sizable, but the opportunities are also enormous. If you don't capture these opportunities, someone else will. Rajat Baisya's disciplined approach to strategy should help you and your business navigate a winning path in these challenging and exciting times.

London

Charles Wilson
Chief Executive Officer
Booker Group Plc
UK

Preface

BUSINESSES ARE now required to perform in a highly dynamic environment. Rapid technological changes coupled with global competitive forces make the business environment all the more complex. We are, therefore, passing through a phase of 'survival of the fittest'. Businesses have to learn to survive in the ever-changing business environment. To achieve this, we need different strategies. Old rules of the game do not seem to be working any longer.

Strategies are developed to cope with the competitive environment. A given strategy is not likely to work in all markets with an equal degree of effectiveness. The core strategies of a firm are thus organisation-specific in a given market and competition. When market environment is highly dynamic and is changing very fast, it is necessary for businesses to constantly monitor competitive behaviour and make course correction wherever necessary to ensure success. In an open market economy, organisations have to consider the whole world as a potential market opportunity. Even the small scale industry has to integrate its business with the rest of the world and build networks and collaborations to survive. In the new economy, being big and resource rich will not be the criteria for success. Even a small company can challenge a large player and can emerge as a winner at the end of the game. Technology will be the key driver for growth and success. Managing technology to create new products and enter the market first will be a key success factor for growth and even for survival. Organisations will be required to benchmark themselves constantly with the leader in the category as well as with the best in class in terms of business practices to improve their business processes and to be competitive. Organisations will also be required to create incremental value in the entire value chain of their businesses to survive and will have to focus only on those activities which they can do better than others. Many new businesses will emerge out of the new concept of providing services by taking a view that all businesses, in one way, exist to provide service. The business model will undergo drastic changes. Virtual organisations and small, lean and mean organisational structures will replace the large hierarchical organisation models.

The life of a corporation is believed to be about 35 years. Those organisations which have survived longer have constantly adjusted with time. In the new economy, this has reduced considerably, and now, organisations are either seen to be making it big in just five years, or even disappearing in a span of 12 to 13 years. The organisations that can quickly re-adjust to these changes and to the new realities will survive. Rest will gradually decay.

Some of the articles included in this book have appeared in leading financial and economic newspapers and dailies including *The Economic Times*, *Business Standard* and *Observers of Business & Politics*, etc. Those articles have been updated, revised and then incorporated in the chapters wherever they were found relevant. The book is intended for students and teachers of management as well as for practising managers and corporate planners in the industry and researchers in the areas of strategic management.

New Delhi   **Rajat Kanti Baisya**

Acknowledgements

A LARGE part of the work included in this book was written and published in leading economic and financial dailies while I was in the industry. The book, therefore, contains many experiences that I have gathered while working in specific functions. I have had the good fortune to work with some of the best-known and successful Indian and global corporations and with the best-known and respected leaders of the industries in this competitive world. Because of close association and opportunity of working very closely with these industry leaders to see how they take key investment, policy and business decisions, and because of my diverse background of working in all corporate and business functions, I was able to take a holistic view of the business to understand what will and what will not work. And, on this issue, I was greatly benefited from my association with those leaders of the industry, some of whom are no more. I would thus like to particularly acknowledge the association with Mr Ramesh Chauhan and Mr Prakash Chauhan of Parle-Bisleri Group of Industries, Late Vittal Mallya and Mr Vijay Mallya of United Breweries Group, Mr M. McDonald, the then Managing Director of Corn Products India Pvt. Ltd (now known as Best Foods International—a Unilever group company), Mr Yousef Jameel, Chairman of the global conglomerate— Jameel Group of Companies and Late H.P. Nanda of Escorts Group. I would also like to acknowledge the association of Mr Anil Nanda of Escorts Group. Together with him, I have worked to bring to India some well-known joint venture partners—like Helmut Nanz of Nanz Gruppe, Germany, in food retailing, and started the first modern food retail chain 'Nanz' in the country during the late eighties when we were still in the old economy—while Mr Nanda was the Managing Director of Goetze India Ltd (a joint venture of Escorts and Goetze Germany). While working with Mr M. McDonald, I was able to gain access to his wealth of knowledge and well documented information in the areas of finance and marketing. While I have lost touch with him after he moved to his homeland—Scotland—I gratefully acknowledge the kind of knowledge that he tried to impart to me.

Mr Jameel financially supported many technology product ideas in universities in Europe and elsewhere till those were commercialised successfully, and therefore, was a great risk taker.

Late Vittal Mallya was a true visionary in the sense that he single handedly built the empire that is now emerging as a global enterprise. He was a man of few words and was a great listener. I had the opportunity of working with him to see how he takes crucial investment decisions. When the prohibition order against alcohol was promulgated in several states including Haryana and at a time when the liquor industry was closing down, he was picking up this closed industry for a song. He had foreseen that prohibition would not be sustainable and, therefore, put the UB Group in a greatly advantageous position when prohibition was withdrawn in later years.

The final shape to the manuscript of this book was given while working at the Department of Management Studies, Indian Institute of Technology (IIT), Delhi. I would like to thank all my faculty colleagues in the department for their encouragement and help while working on this book. The IIT system encourages research and academic writing and is conducive enough to motivate the faculty to write books, which has greatly helped me to complete the work in spite of heavy work load, for which I am grateful to Professor Surendra Prasad, Director, IIT Delhi and Professor V.S. Raju, former Director of IIT Delhi.

I would like to thank Mr Charles Wilson, CEO of Booker Group Plc, UK, for writing the Foreword for this book.

I acknowledge the untiring and unconditional support that I have received from my family members—my wife, Susmita, daughter, Deepshikha, and son, Rishabh—while working on this book. My father, Late Dr Rabindra Kumar Baisya, would have been very happy to see this book. But it is my misfortune that he died prematurely. My mother Mrs Vidyut Prava Baisya always asks me whether I am writing and researching. I have received their blessings in abundance which I gratefully acknowledge. I also gratefully acknowledge the support of my two maternal uncles, Mr Haripada Purkayastha and Mr Amitabha Chaudhuri, while I was still a student at Calcutta University and Jadavpur University.

Finally, SAGE Publications has taken this up as my second project with great challenge. They always do a meticulous job in publishing.

The title of the book has undergone changes a couple of times. The present title 'Winning Strategies for Business' is the outcome of my joint interactive discussions with the marketing team of SAGE. I gratefully acknowledge the tremendous efforts of the publishers in releasing the book on time.

Introduction

GLOBALISATION AND liberalisation have changed the rules of the game—the way businesses need to be managed today. Trade barriers and geographical boundaries are gradually disappearing, integrating the geographical territories and markets. Information and Communication Technology has further integrated societies and markets by making faster communication and information flow possible. Technology development cycle has reduced drastically which in turn has reduced the product life cycle. Businesses are required to consider the entire world as their market. Even small companies will have to integrate their business globally. It will be increasingly difficult to keep the local niches if the global vision is missing. Internet has opened up new possibilities to do business. The traditional business model will no longer be relevant. New models of business are emerging. Organisations will even work from virtual locations and still remain connected 24X7 with customers, employees and partners. The familiar milepost will no longer guide the business decisions. Businesses will be facing more uncertainties and challenges and more regulatory pressures. The businesses, therefore, have to be more flexible in their approach and functioning.

Making profit alone will not be the sole purpose of existence of any organisation. There will be a greater role of the businesses and industry in relation to their stakeholders. And more importantly, businesses have to recognize their role in the wider context of society and community. Without the support of society, business will not survive and, therefore, will have to be more responsive to the society's need and welfare. There will be growing concern for environment, safety, health and hygiene. People will be more health conscious and there will be increasing demand for health and nutrition and natural products. With growing education and knowledge, customers will be more discerning and demanding about their rights and privileges. Product liability cost will increase. Product not likely to meet the global standards and specifications will, therefore, be risky to roll out.

Consumers will not accept product failure and promising after sales service will be considered as a failure in terms of the product's performance. Hence, products for the new order economy will have to be designed in a way that they do not require any service during their useful life. The products and services will be required to deliver the promises marketers make while promoting the product. Superior quality or pure claim will gradually be losing its relevance in terms of product differentiation. All products will be required to deliver the required quality which will be defined as meeting the customers' requirement and committed specification. The products in the market available for sale will be assumed to meet the stated and expected quality standards. Products not meeting those criteria will have no reason to be there in the market and will, therefore, inevitably end up as failures.

Organisations will become more lean and mean. There will be emergence of global managers who will learn to service and take care of global customers and work in a global business environment. People and talent will move freely from various parts of the world—just like goods and services. People will start working from home and distant locations—this would be feasible as long as they stay connected and report the progress on the given assignment. This phenomenon will trigger the emergence of virtual organisations which will connect employees based in distant locations of the world. There will be no permanency in the job. People will lose their jobs if they are not adding value to the business or are no longer relevant to the organisation. Only those who perform will be able to retain their jobs. There will be numerous opportunities for people to work in many other sectors including social and development sectors. Those jobs will also be very remunerative.

Just being big and having access to resources will not be sufficient reasons to survive in business. Businesses will, thus, lose fortune in a much shorter period of time. At the same time, new players will come up from nowhere within a short period of time. The industrial landscape will, therefore, change very fast because of the appearance of new players and the closure of many established businesses. Governments will be increasingly focusing only on regulations and controls and allowing the businesses to participate in all sectors, leaving only the essential services and the defense sector. There will be more outsourcing of jobs, functions and manufacturing allowing corporations to focus on their prime activities.

There will be more acquisitions, mergers and strategic alliances taking place for the businesses to realign and gain from new strategic initiatives by drawing on the synergies from each other. There will be many global acquisitions. India and China will gradually emerge as powerful global economies. There will be flow of capital from developed economies to these countries to create facilities for manufacturing goods and developing services which can be marketed to the rest of the world. This will lead to the emergence of global Indian corporations.

In order to make their products and services globally competitive, organisations will be seen to be shifting their manufacturing base to countries where they are likely to incur the least cost for the products to be sold into the global market.

Indian companies were caught unawares when all of a sudden they were exposed to the open market economy. There were, therefore, various kinds of reactions that we have witnessed. Some have realigned with the global players, forming joint ventures, whereas some others have sold their businesses to the global players. Some of them have continued fighting and have eventually emerged as winners. They have changed their business models and have upgraded themselves in the value chain to put up a fight against their MNC counterparts. There are corporations that have gone ahead and acquired global companies whereas there are also MNCs that have failed in the Indian market and there are still some who have had to close down their business or have even decided to try new business proposals. The reaction, therefore, has been mixed.

In the 'new order economy', organisations will be facing global competition and, therefore, will be required to follow new strategies to survive and grow. When old rules will not work, organisations will have to learn new methods and processes to survive. This book is intended to discuss some of these survival strategies and is structured to provide an understanding of the strategy development processes taking an organisation-wide effort.

In this book, we have discussed generic strategies as well as offensive and defensive strategies. We have also discussed acquisitions, diversification, mergers and joint ventures as various avenues for delivering growth. This book also discussed competitive benchmarking and ways to protect one's own market share and pricing strategies. In addition to this, the book also deals with innovation management and risk management as well as with issues related to corporate social responsibility and corporate governance.

The above mentioned are spread out over the eleven chapters of this book, out of which the last chapter deals with some Indian case studies wherein the companies started small but later made it to the top and have earned a position and secured a place for themselves on the global map. The cases have been summarized to highlight the major and key strategic drivers which helped these organisations to not only survive the competition but to also grow and eventually emerge as global Indian players.

Strategy Development Process—Basic Approach

Why Do We Need Strategy

THE ENVIRONMENT is the key factor. It changes the rules of the game in business. Changing market, technology, buyer behaviour, socio-political conditions and, most importantly, competition require different strategies to survive in the marketplace. The life and success of an individual depend on his innate capability to cope with the environment. The survival and success of a business firm depends on its innate strength to adapt to the environment. The traits, skills or the resources in command do not mean anything if the individual or organisation cannot cope with the changing environment. In this competitive environment even leaders fade away. Eighty per cent of Fortune 500 listed companies of 1970 do not appear in the list of 1997. Many names which were famous once do not trigger any enthusiasm now. And, companies not coping with the changing business environment won't stay in business for long.

In 1923, the eight wealthiest people in the world met. Their combined wealth exceeded that of USA. Twenty-five years later,

- President of the largest steel company, Charles Schwab, died bankrupt.

- President of the largest gas company, Howard Hubson, went insane.
- Greatest commodity trader, Arthur Cutton, died insolvent.
- President, NY Stock Exchange, Richard Whitney, was sent to jail.
- President of Bank of International Settlements, Leon Fraser, committed suicide.
- The greatest stock broker of Wall Street, Jessis Livermole, committed suicide.
- President of one of the greatest monopolies, Ivan Kreuger, committed suicide.
- Member of president's cabinet, Albert Fall, was sent to jail.

To survive in the ever changing market we, therefore, need strategy.

Business Environment

The key challenges of the business environment are:

- Increasingly inconsistent environment.
- Familiar landmarks no longer serve as guide posts.
- Competitors, partners, suppliers and customers (increasingly unpredictable).
- Firm-level micro decisions influenced by national level macro parameters.

Organisations need to carefully consider the environment as it will have an impact on their performance. The environmental factors greatly influence an organisation's strategic direction. Broadly, factors that impact all businesses equally are called macro factors/ and those that influence a specific business are called micro factors (Figure 1.1).

FIGURE 1.1: MACRO AND MICRO ENVIRONMENTAL FACTORS

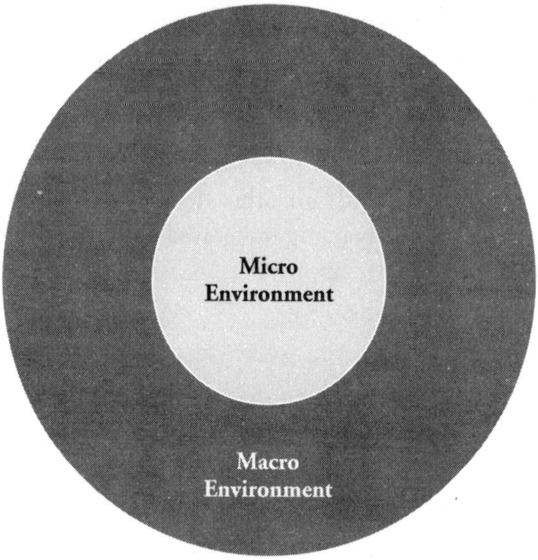

Source: Developed by author.

Emerging Trends

Some of the emerging changes can be classified as follows:

- Globalisation
- Liberalisation
- Privatisation
- Regional Economic Grouping
- Mergers and Acquisitions
- Strategic Alliance
- Emerging Rural Markets
- Consumerism

Post liberalisation, entrepreneurs have the freedom to enter any industry, trade or business. Government controls and licensing have been removed. Foreign direct investment (FDI) has been made easier in many industry categories. Import–export norms have been simplified and liberalised. Rupee is convertible on current account. Many reforms have been introduced in the capital market. The state is to act in a market friendly manner to ensure smooth functioning of the market economy and to provide legal framework and ensure stability of the market. It is not the business of the government to do business and, therefore, government is selling nonperforming PSUs to private players as a key initiative towards privatisation. The government is also diluting its holding in profit making PSUs by offering it to the public to generate funds for other developmental activities. The Indian market is gradually being integrated with the global economy. In many cases, automatic approval is granted for foreign direct investment.

Future Trends

- With growing competition, product differentiation and positioning will become more important.
- Class marketing/niche marketing will grow in importance and there will be a decline in the relative importance of mass marketing barring a few exceptions.
- The growing competition will also increase the importance of the augmented product.

Businesses that have failed to recognize the change in the environment have suffered losses. For example,

- Swiss watchmakers dominated the global market for long but they ignored the emergence of quartz watches and, therefore, lost out to the Japanese.
- IBM was synonymous with the computer business but it ignored the growing PC business and networking, and is now struggling for survival.
- Few market leaders in the US and the USSR focused on Defense Equipment Manufacturing and Supply. Changing political environment forced them to go bankrupt.
- There was a time when the owners of cinema theaters enjoyed big advantages but the advent of cable TV has triggered the closure of these theaters.

As indicated in Figure 1.2, businesses are facing a rapid change in the socio-political as well as economic and competitive environment.

FIGURE 1.2: FIRM'S POSITION IN THE CONTEXT OF ENVIRONMENT

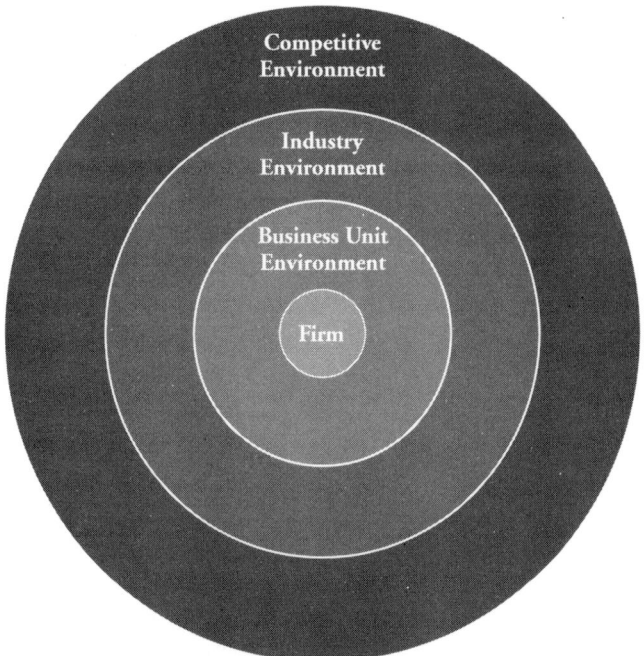

Source: Developed by the author.

The purpose of strategy, therefore, is to:

- Build a successful business plan in a competitive environment.
- Face the challenges of competition.
- Create situations for avoiding competition in a monopoly situation.
- Ensure that a corporation survives by helping it adjust with the changing business environment.

The objective of survival strategy is to understand the pressures involved in building a successful corporate strategy.

Strategic Management—Basic Approach

Business decisions are undertaken and strategies are adopted to win at the end of the game and not on the basis of win some and lose some. But the reality is that we don't have a winner in every product that we launch. Fact of the matter is that 90 per cent of new launches fail in the marketplace. In these days, when the competition is extremely intense, one needs to compete with the expert in the business category which one owns.

All organisations will have to face specific identified competitors and also have specific market segments as their customers in the marketplace. To formulate any meaningful strategic plan, these two players (competitors and customers) have to be understood with as much clarity as possible. And, the third player is the corporation itself. The Chinese war strategist Sun Tzu has said in his book *The Art of War* (1995), written two and a half thousand years ago, that:

> If you know the enemy and know yourself, you need not fear the result of a hundred battles. If you know yourself but not the enemy, for every victory gained you will also suffer a defeat. If you know neither the enemy nor yourself, you will succumb in every battle. Knowing the enemy enables you to take the offensive, knowing yourself enables you to stand on the defensive. Attack is the secret of defense; defense is the planning of an attack.

Attack is thus a form of defense.

Corporation, customer and competitor are, therefore, strategic three Cs (Figure 1.3). Collectively, we can call them the strategic triangle (Kenichi Ohmae 1982).

Your own corporation as well as your competition are trying to offer the same set of customers a differential value by either offering the same benefit at lower cost or better benefit at the same cost. The fight among competitors, therefore, is on delivering better value to the customer. Two or more competitors competing in the marketplace are fighting for market share by offering a differentiated product and service and, therefore, offer a different value to the customer. It is the decision of the corporation whether to create multiple products

FIGURE 1.3: THE STRATEGIC TRIANGLE OF THREE Cs

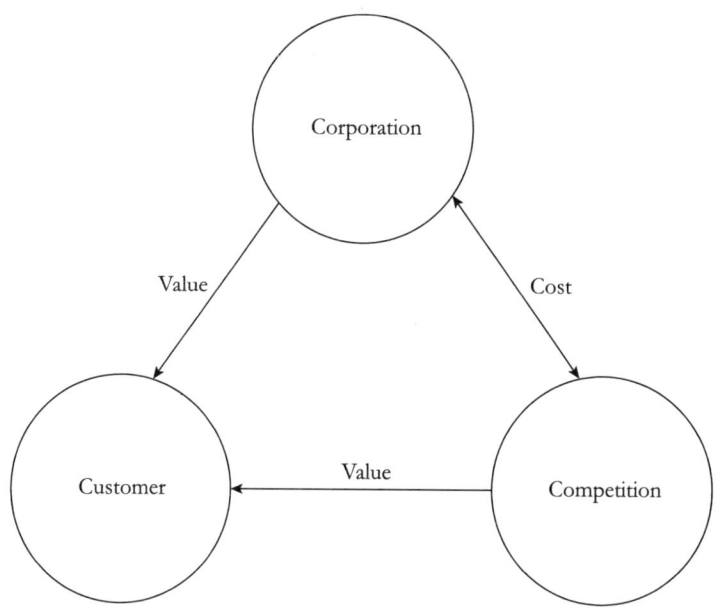

Source: Ohmae (1982).

and proposition for multiple market segments or to focus on a key targeted segment.

The basic objective of any strategic plan is to achieve superior level performance in relation to the competition. The key performance criteria will be determined by the ability of the business to create superior value and deliver it faster than the competition. In order to achieve that, business strategists have to ensure that strategic formulation captures the strengths of the business and product offerings in relation to the needs of the market in the context of what the competition has to offer. Strategy formulation also has to make an attempt to exploit the identified weaknesses of the competition.

As the environment is constantly changing, it becomes essential to be abreast of the changes. Businesses should thus:

• Identify new openings and opportunities
• Identify dangers and problems
• Identify whether there is any need to change

SWOT (Strengths, Weaknesses, Opportunities and Threats) analysis and TEMPLES (Technology, Economy, Politics, Law, Environment and Society) analysis can be made for the business and environment to identify problems and opportunities available in the medium term and long term.

Techniques for Environmental Analysis

Corporations have to understand the implications of business environment on their own business. The various approaches for doing this are as given below:

- Verbal and written information
- Reports and analyses by business analysts
- Search and scanning
- Spying
- Seminars and conferences including expert seminars
- Forecasting
- Formal Studies (organisation's own study or through engagement of a research agency)
- Market intelligence

It is possible to use various models and frameworks to initiate information gathering in a given market. A few of those are discussed below.

The PESTEL framework

The most important aspect of the environment is often referred to as the macro-environment. This consists of broad environmental factors that impact to a greater or lesser extent on almost all organisations. In a given category, macro-environment normally impacts all organisations in a similar manner. However, it is important to identify these issues and particularly those that are likely to have a differentially large impact on a specific organisation. And, since the PESTEL framework looks at the way in which future trends in the political, economic, socio-cultural, technological, environmental and legal (PESTEL) environments might impinge on organisations, it provides a summary of some of the questions to ask about key forces at work in the macro environment.

It is particularly important that PESTEL is used to look at the future impact of environmental factors, which may be different from their past impact.

POLITICAL FACTORS
- Business cycles
- GNP/GDP trends
- Interest rates
- Money supply
- Inflation
- Unemployment
- Disposable income

ECONOMIC FACTORS
- Government stability
- Taxation policy
- Foreign policy
- Trade regulations and trade policy
- Social welfare policies

SOCIO-CULTURAL FACTORS
- Population demographics
- Income distribution
- Social mobility
- Cultural diversity
- Lifestyle changes
- Attitude towards work and leisure
- Consumerism
- Levels of education
- Skilled manpower availability

TECHNOLOGICAL FACTORS
- Government spending on research and development
- Government and industry focus on technological efforts
- New discoveries, innovations and development
- Speed of technology transfer
- Rates of obsolescence

ENVIRONMENTAL FACTORS
- Environmental protection laws
- Waste disposal regulations
- Energy consumption and production
- Competition law

LEGAL FACTORS
- Monopolies legislation
- Employment law
- Health and safety
- Product safety and liability regulations
- Exit Policy

SWOT analysis

A SWOT analysis summarises the key issues from the business environment and the strategic capability of an organisation that are most likely to impact on strategy development. The aim is to identify the extent to which the current strengths and weaknesses are relevant to and capable of dealing with the threats or capitalising on the opportunities in the business environment.

Strategy Development Process

A different set of customers and competitors are required for large businesses with multiple business portfolios. Each business group will, thus, have separate strategic triangles of Cs where corporation will be the common thread. Under such a situation, how the strategic plan has to be formulated will depend on the organisation itself. One way of doing this is to formulate the divisional strategies for each SBU (strategic business unit) and then integrate them at the organisation level. However, the organisation has to answer the question about how many SBUs the corporation can have to be able to make the presence in the marketplace sufficient to help it enjoy a respectable market share, growth and profit.

The strategy formulation for each such SBU can be termed as Strategic Planning Unit (SPU). The Strategic Planning Units are best established where each unit can freely address all related issues across functions which can help create either differentiation or incremental value for its customers which have been identified as having similar needs.

The strategic planning process, therefore, has to encompass all functional areas of the business to understand how maximum value can be realised within the business to deliver superior value to its target customers. The value delivery process can be understood from Figure 1.4.

The creation of incremental value is not enough. The value so created needs to be captured, integrated and assimilated within the business and finally delivered to the customers for superior performance. The way it needs to be capsuled and delivered requires a

FIGURE 1.4: THE VALUE DELIVERY TRIANGLE

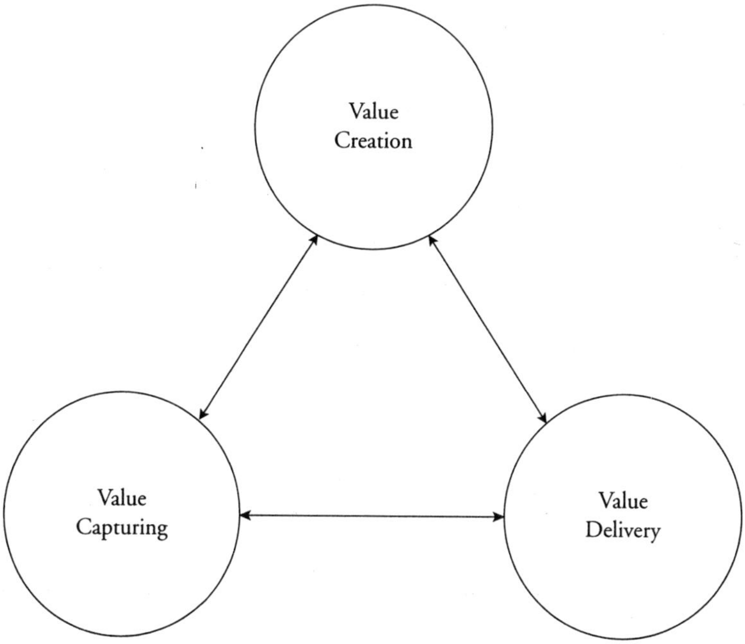

Source: Bowman and Ambrosini (2002); Wolfgang (2001).

strategic approach. Value creation is an organisation wide phenomena and effort. Each business function within the corporation has the scope of creating incremental value for the business. How the value so created is to be captured and used for the organisation's advantage is the key issue. All businesses do not have the similar capability.

Michael Proter (1985) had said that organisations can have cost advantage or quality advantage delivered through superior technology against its competitors. But it is no longer either cost or quality in the context of today's competition where each business has to face global players with enormous resources at their command. It is, therefore, necessary to combine both cost and quality for competitive advantage. It is imperative for all businesses that initiatives on value delivery be directed across functions to reduce cost by eliminating all non value adding activities in the business processes, adding value by upgrading quality of goods by incorporating new and superior technology and through process and product innovations. This will necessitate having the ability to manage knowledge and innovation in the business.

Strategy formulation, therefore, needs a very clear understanding of the organisation's internal capabilities in the context of external business reality including understanding the competition, technology trends, customers' expectations and general macro and micro economic environment. These internal and external environments need to be analysed in context of the corporation's vision, mission, objective, goals and milestones to determine the strategic options available for action. Schematically, this approach of strategy formulation can be shown in Figure 1.5.

The strategies can be formulated either for:

- Growth
- Survival
- Consolidation of business
- Or even combination of these separately for different strategic business units (SBUs)
- Achieving some strategic objective—short term or long term

FIGURE 1.5: STRATEGY DEVELOPMENT PROCESS

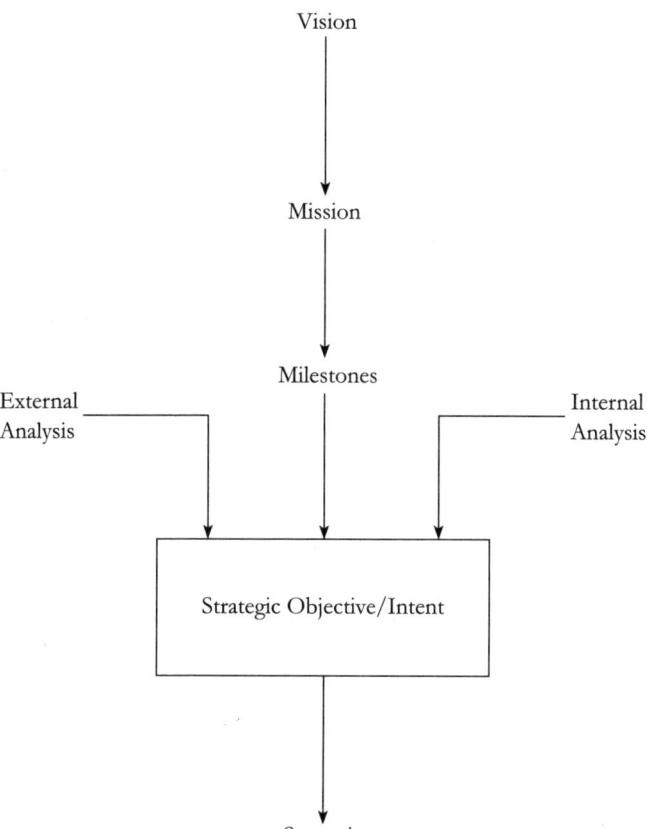

Source: Developed by the author.

Strategic Planning

The strategy development process, therefore, has three major components, namely, strategic objectives, strategic analyses and strategic choices, as depicted in Figure 1.7.

To develop organisational strategies, there are three distinct steps and phases. The first task is to decide upon the objective and goal of the organisation in terms of short-term, medium-term and long-term objectives that the firm wants to achieve. This needs to be analysed

FIGURE 1.6: STRATEGIC PLANNING PROCESS

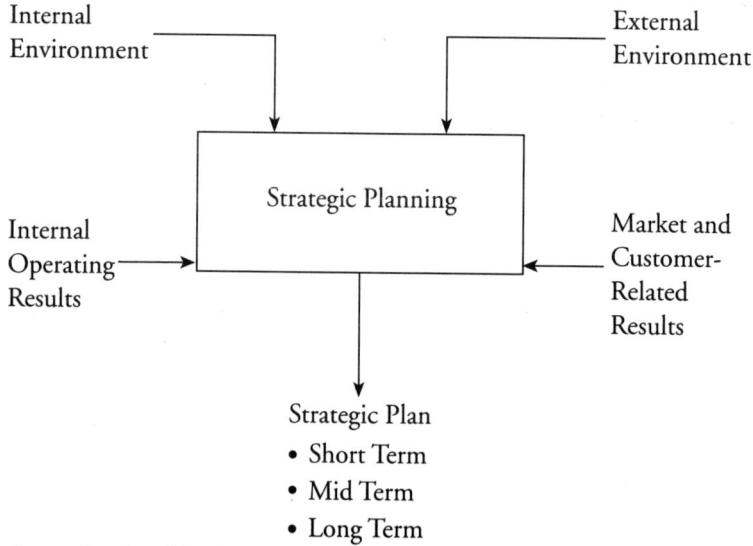

Source: Developed by the author.

FIGURE 1.7: STRATEGY DEVELOPMENT TRIANGLE

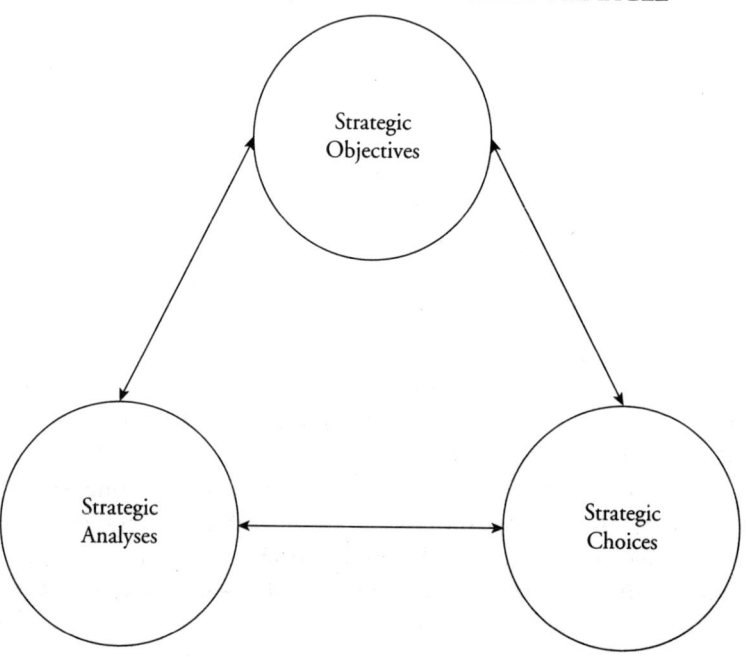

in as much detail as possible and the milestones should be clear, measurable and achievable in a given business environment. The basis of the objective is normally derived from the firm's vision and mission. This has to be seen in the perspective of opportunity and competition. If one does not capture an opportunity, someone else will do so; hence, the organisation has to see the opportunities available in the context of its own ability to capture them for its growth and survival.

It is necessary to identify obstacles in the way of achieving objectives and to assess whether they are removable or not. If necessary, one should modify the objectives.

Strategic analysis is the phase of information gathering from all available sources. This includes the firm's internal performance, capability and resource analyses including human and financial resources. Also, external analyses covering competitor analysis, business environment, socio-economic and political environment analyses and regulatory frameworks.

Strategic choices and options will emerge from strategic objectives and strategic analyses. The choice can even include the option of pursuing the current strategies if those are found to be relevant in the current context, which means no change in the strategic direction. There can be multiple strategic options and a firm needs to select only those choices which are feasible for the organisation to implement.

As shown in Figure 1.8, strategic analyses actually lead to the strategic direction that an organisation should pursue.

Strategic Options

Strategic options in the same business environment for different businesses could be different and that is dependent upon the organisations skills and resources, structures and systems as well as its own culture and leadership (Figure 1.9). As these vary across organisations, the options that will emanate will also differ from organisation to organisation. This means that, at any given time, the options that work in one organisation may not work in another.

From careful strategic analyses, many options or strategic choices can emerge which a firm should consider carefully to clarify each

FIGURE 1.8: FIRM'S STRATEGIC DIRECTION

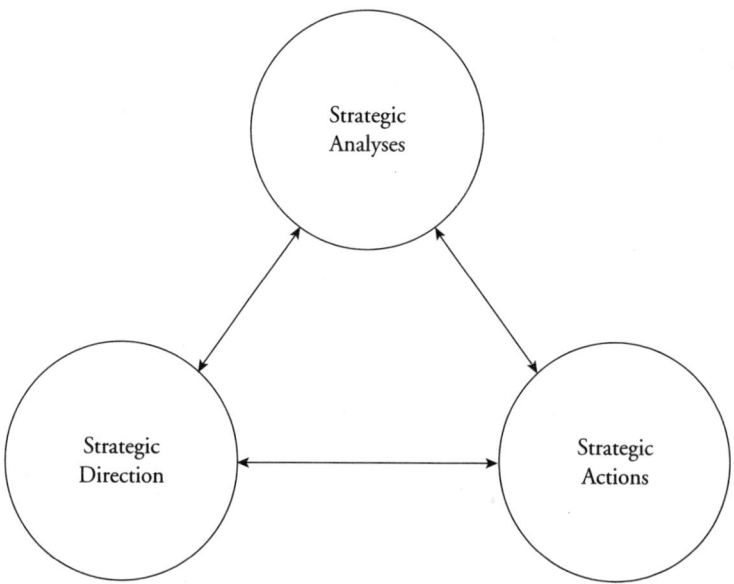

Source: Developed by the author.

option in terms of its feasibility and impact on the business. One should think creatively to arrive at possible strategic options.

The options could be:

- Change nothing
- Concentrate on existing processes, products and methods
- New product development
- Enter new market
- Development of existing market
- New innovations
- Integration—horizontal/vertical
- Diversification—related/unrelated
- Turnaround
- Divestment
- Liquidation
- Merge business units and divisions
- Acquisition

FIGURE 1.9: FACTORS INFLUENCING STRATEGIC CHOICES

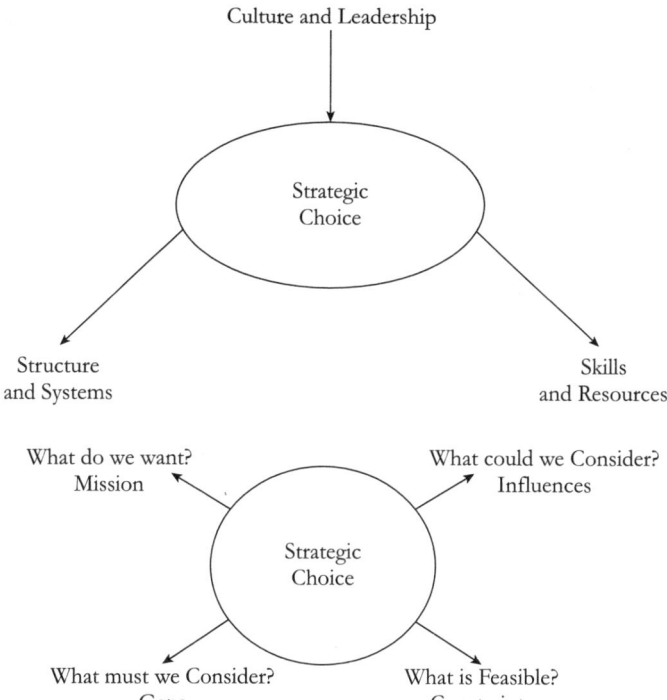

Source: Developed by the author.

Under each such option, one has to think about possible gains and problems.

The typical criteria for selection of strategic options are decided based on the following factors (Michael Porter 1985b):

- Impact on the business
- Competitiveness
- Compatibility
- Feasibility
- Risk
- Controllability

Figure 1.10 shows the various factors that need to be studied to evaluate the feasibility of strategic options.

18   Winning Strategies for Business

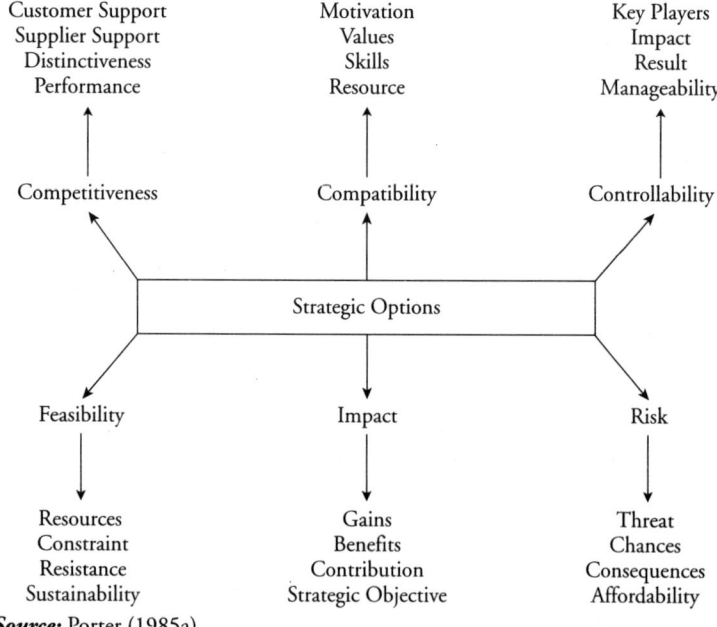

FIGURE 1.10: EVALUATION OF THE FEASIBILITY OF STRATEGIC OPTIONS

Customer Support	Motivation	Key Players
Supplier Support	Values	Impact
Distinctiveness	Skills	Result
Performance	Resource	Manageability

Competitiveness   Compatibility   Controllability

Strategic Options

Feasibility   Impact   Risk

Resources	Gains	Threat
Constraint	Benefits	Chances
Resistance	Contribution	Consequences
Sustainability	Strategic Objective	Affordability

Source: Porter (1985a).

Strategy and Tactics

Table 1.1 compares and contrasts strategy and tactics.

TABLE 1.1: STRATEGY VS TACTICS

Strategy	Tactics
Generally has long-term implications	Generally, they are short-term measures and approaches to achieve an immediate objective
Requires approval and support of the top management	Can be initiated at any level but normally implemented by the lower level managers or line managers
Generally, srategies are few in number	Tactical approaches can be large in number
Provides the broader direction to business	Tactical approaches and directions normally emanate from each broader strategy

Source: Developed by the author.

Formulating a Winning Strategy

Winning strategy

Meaning of a winning strategy will be different for different corporations even if they are operating in the same domain area. The term winning strategies refers to evolving such strategies which, when implemented properly, make the corporations winners at the end of the game. Firms have different objectives keeping their current status and stage in mind as well as the resources available to support those strategic objectives. Normally, strategies are formulated either for growth, survival or even for consolidation of the business depending on the current stage or phase that a business is passing through, according to which the meaning of winning also changes.

COUNTRY AND FIRM-LEVEL STRATEGY

The winning strategies can have two dimensions, namely, country-level perspective or firm-level perspective to generate a set of winning strategies for both. Firm-level strategies depend on the country-level strategies but the reverse is not necessarily true. Country-level strategy can change the business environment in which individual firms are required to operate and, therefore, firms or corporations very much depend on the country perspective.

It is the responsibility of the country to provide a level playing field for the industry to compete in the global arena. For example, if a product is energy intensive and if cost of power is much higher and power is in short supply, then at the international level, there is no way that the local players can compete with it. For energy intensive products, local players will then require subsidies to become competitive.

NO UNIFORM PRESCRIPTION WILL WORK

One cannot have a uniform set of strategies applicable to all firms. Strategies are formulated following a process of assessment of a firm's internal strengths and weaknesses as well as the commitment to make resources available to achieve those objectives in the context of the external environment and the opportunities. While the external environment and the opportunities remain the same for all types of organisations, their implications on the businesses and the organisation's ability to exploit those opportunities will never be the same. Hence, we cannot have a set of strategies which will help all organisations come out as winners at the end of the game. Therefore, strategies would have to be organisation specific. But we can learn from others' experience.

INDUSTRY CATEGORY DEPENDENT

Strategies also change depending on the industry category or domain that an organisation belongs to because industry category competitiveness and domain specific strategies largely influence the firm level strategies. Thus we need to consider domain specific issues to suggest the winning proposition for any firm.

FIRM-LEVEL STRATEGY

As far as firm-level strategies are concerned, one should appreciate that the list will be long. Besides, not only the strategies but also the tactical approaches that a firm takes are important including the successful implementation of strategic initiatives.

Products or services win or lose in the marketplace depending on their value proposition. To win, we will have to offer superior value in relation to our own competitive set. India is a country that is considered to be a low cost producer which is largely attributable to our low cost of manpower. But in due course of time this advantage may no longer be there. What will then be the sustainable winning strategies that will cut across the industry category?

GLOBAL OPPORTUNITY

The most important point that we need to keep in mind is that irrespective of size and industry category, businesses have to consider the whole world as their market and, thus, we need a global strategy considering the opportunities that are available to the businesses for exploitation in the short term as well as the long term.

LARGE MARKET

India has a distinct advantage in that it has a large captive market which is not the case with the developed economies. They only are eyeing fast developing markets like India and China. Local businesses know our market much better than the MNCs coming and setting up operations here. Remember that India creates one Australia every year in terms of population.

BIG IS NOT ENOUGH

Just because MNCs have deep pockets and staying power, one cannot necessarily assume that they will win. There are many MNCs that did not succeed. For example, Sara Lee is a 35 billion US dollar company. It operated in India for three years in food products, introduced bakery products and then left. Nutricia acquired business from Hindustan Unilever Ltd (HUL), did not succeed and sold the same to a local industrialist in Indore (Ruchi Industries Ltd). Heinz, a global leader in food products, is still struggling after acquiring Glaxo's food business in India. Just because an organisation is big is no guarantee that it will succeed. Wal-Mart operated for eight years in the German market, lost money and then decided to exit that market where local players were growing and flourishing. Thums Up still sells more than Coke.

ACQUISITION

For large businesses, acquisition could be a better strategy for faster growth. It gives dual advantage in the sense that it eliminates a competition as well as offers faster growth. We are already seeing this trend and this strategy will continue.

NEW STRATEGIC INITIATIVES

Businesses have taken many new strategic initiatives because of fast changing consumer behaviour triggered by change in technology as well as by competitive forces arising out of globalisation of economies.

From the beginning of nineties, many new strategic initiatives have been undertaken by the forward looking and progressive organisations. It started with ERP, Business Process Reengineering, Benchmarking, Balanced Score Card and Core Competency in addition to the various types of industry specific quality certifications and the concept of Total such as Total quality, Total Customer Satisfaction, Total Productive Maintenance as well as flexibility in the form of Flexible Enterprises. All these are undertaken with the sole objective of improving the value delivery and thus becoming more competitive. Now, no one thinks that these can deliver above average performance.

These days, businesses do not get very much enthused if we talk about these initiatives. Now, the key mantra is innovation. You need to innovate the way you carry out business and that includes product and process innovation. But if you are not a profitable company, you cannot afford to have a future, and if you are not innovative, then also you have no future. As Peter Drucker said, there are only two revenue centres in a company—marketing and innovation—the rest are all cost. In Peter Drucker's words, 'Because the purpose of business is to create a customer, the business enterprise has two— and only two—basic functions, i.e., marketing and innovation. Marketing and innovation produce business results; all the rest are cost' (Drucker 1992) You need to be profitable to be innovative and innovative to remain profitable. Constant innovation, thus, has to be the core strategy of our corporations. There are a lot of innovations that marketers can create for the success of the business.

Large MNCs have resources but financial resources alone will not guarantee success. Best example in the current context is the IPL teams of 2008. The Jaipur team was formed with youngsters at the least cost. In fact, the Kolkata and Bangalore team was costing their owners double the amount that Jaipur had spent but what we see at the end is that Jaipur has finally emerged as the winner.

The winning strategy will, thus, create a culture for constant innovation within the organisation. The normal performance management culture which organisations practice to measure performance against set targets is not enough. The organisations will have to allow their people to think out of the box. Winning strategies should, therefore, come from the radical way of thinking.

COUNTRY STRATEGY—INDIAN PERSPECTIVE

The key country specific issues can be summarized in the 4Es, namely Energy security, Environment, Education and Employment. The oil reserves and other traditional sources of energy are not enough to meet the world's energy requirement which is constantly increasing with technological development. The entire world is looking for a solution to this problem by exploring alternate sources of energy such as hydrogen. As per predictions, the next 50 years will be a difficult period and businesses will, therefore, have to look for alternatives and more sustainable forms of energy. Sustainability will, thus, be a key issue.

The other country level strategic imperative in India is to bring all sections of the society into the mainstream development process. The fruits of liberalisation and globalisation have not reached the underprivileged 300 million of our population who are still below the poverty line. If we fail in our efforts, the whole process of new economic policy will be unsustainable.

Due to the impact of globalisation, we cannot produce anything which does not have any import component in it. Dr Ashok Mitra, a well known economist and former Finance Minister of West Bengal, while talking about the Indian Strategic Dilemma, cited the example of IPL and said, 'Even in games like cricket and football, we have an imported component. In the beginning of nineties, our import bill was to the tune of USD 90 billion and today it is over USD 750 billion. Our forex reserve is high but so is our import content' (Mitra 2008).

Providing quality education is another key imperative which will solve and help to nullify the impact of social disparities.

The last strategic issue at the country level will be protecting the environment. It has been reported that in Mumbai, builders have grounded over 25,000 trees and as per law, they are supposed to deposit Rs 2,500 per tree and also plant three trees in place of one tree and take back the deposit after three years after giving a report that the three trees that were planted have survived and are healthy and growing. Otherwise, they will lose their deposit. The Mumbai Municipal Corporation (BMC) has so far collected over Rs 90 million which will give an impression that none of the builders have planted any trees and have decided to opt for getting their deposit forfeited than nurturing three trees for three years for every uprooted tree.

Key Success Factors

The success of the enterprise will depend on the following factors:

- Understanding the consumer better than the competition
- Delivering the customer requirement better than the competition
- Projecting and delivering superior values

- Constantly upgrading products and services to remain aligned with the technology
- Delivering the product where customer wants
- Speed of action and delivery

Chapter Summary

This chapter attempts to define strategy and its purpose giving reasons why do we need strategy to run a modern day business. We have discussed many cases to illustrate that if we don't adjust chances are that we will not survive in the ever-changing business environment. Size and resources of the enterprise would mean nothing if businesses do not evolve constantly to counter the forces of change.

The various frameworks such as SWOT, PESTEL, etc., are discussed to scan the environment to understand the forces of change as well as to understand the organisation's own capabilities and limitations in order to take appropriate action plan for growth and survival.

We have then discussed the various approaches to the strategy development processes. Following the established process will help organisations to arrive at several strategic options that a firm has to consider in order to decide on the strategic direction. Several strategic options are then tested against a set criteria which ideally suits the organisation. Hence, all firms in the same business in a given market will not have similar strategies because their strategies need to be organisation specific.

II

Impact of New Economic Policy on Business

Survival Strategies to Counter Competition in the New Economy

IF THERE is no competition, there will be no need for a strategy. In a monopolistic business environment strategies are not that important as they are, in reality, in a sellers' market. But since the nineties we have been facing global competition. We have been seeing signs of it ever since the then congress government in power initiated steps towards economic liberalisation in 1991.

Our small scale sectors will no longer enjoy the various concessions, reservations and support which they earlier received from the government. They are still enjoying some preferential treatment in select sectors but the same will be withdrawn in phases. Subsidies on petroleum based products as well as on fertilizers will be gradually reduced and will finally have to be withdrawn completely in years to come.

Fertilizers and steel have already been decontrolled and import policy has been further liberalized. Because of International Monetary Fund (IMF) pressure, import duty has been drastically reduced, in phases, which will permit foreign goods to be freely available in India at a competitive price.

In industrially developed countries, the market is matured and more saturated. These countries are, therefore, looking for new markets.

They will sell their goods and services and set up new joint ventures in India, creating competition for local companies. Foreign investors have been very active in our capital market from the time the earning per share (EPS) and price earning ratios (P/E) became favourable and the share price came down to its realistic level.

In the 1990s, we have, thus, seen more acquisitions and changes of management happen than before. If the management is not competent, it is likely to lose control of the company. The board of directors will be more actively participating in the decision making process of the companies which will no longer be able to afford to have only hand picked yes-men on their boards. Listed companies will have to appoint independent directors on their boards, and corporate governance practices will now be more frequently questioned by the shareholders, particularly after the much debated Enron and now Satyam episodes.

It is generally believed that India has cheap labour but if labour productivity is taken into consideration, Indian labourers are not that cheap. This does not mean that Indian labour cannot generate higher productivity. Our trade union activity is responsible for the present state of affairs. Trade unionism also needs to undergo a total metamorphosis. Some indicators of change in that direction, particularly related to labour policy, have already been implemented. Cost of labour will drastically increase which will be a major deterring factor in engaging a large workforce in the industry.

Availability of Indian managers, who are considered to be one of the brightest and most capable managers in the world, will be a problem. There will, thus, be a scarcity of efficient and capable business managers. Large multinational companies will try to grab them at a higher price. Managers will be required to work in a highly dynamic global environment with lesser support staff in a lean and mean organisational structure. They will be increasingly dependent on technology since the Internet has now redefined the way we do business.

In the context of the above mentioned changes, we need to develop strategies for survival and growth in a highly competitive environment.

Since 1960, Japan has been steadily increasing its share of world market from five per cent to 20 per cent and has overtaken both US and Germany. This was possible because Japan made real value addition in its manufacturing sector and continues to lead in manufacturing technology. All new products and inventions are being conceived in Europe or USA, but the Japanese have consistently demonstrated superior ability in translating concepts into marketable products by using those technologies. Japan, of course, in the later years suffered from lack of entrepreneurship which has a reflection in the downturn in its economy. It has also registered a decline it its competitiveness index.

Europe was all set to become the largest single world market during the 1990s, but it is not clearly known whether it will develop tendencies to protect its own industries against the threat of external competition. The much talked about European Union (EU) has yet to make its bigger presence felt in competition with the US economy emanating from the leadership struggle.

Worldwide, there is a growing concern about environmental safety, pollution, declining environmental quality and depletion of natural resources. Motorcar designs are now determined by environmental considerations. Future cars will have to be designed in conformance with zero emission norms. To this effect, there is already legislation in the US and Europe has adopted the same. Many other countries, including India, have evolved their auto emission standards. These countries are now introducing labeling systems for environmentally friendly products. These tendencies will see an increase even in India like they are doing in other western countries. The demand for chloro fluro carbon (CFC) free aerosols, unleaded petrol, phosphate free washing powder, etc. will increase.

Most of these environment friendly products will be more expensive. Customers, by and large, will be willing to pay the price of perceived value of the product but competition will keep the price and quality at a reasonable and affordable level. Innovation will, therefore, be the name of the game. Increasingly, better products and environment friendly products will be available at reasonable and affordable prices. Competition will make that possible.

The manufacturing company in the twenty first century will be required to be watchful for the ways of legislation on the one hand and changing customer preferences on the other. The market is expected to develop rapidly for high value domestic and industrial products. The products of new WTO regime will, therefore, be based on knowledge, innovation and technology.

The improved quality of life will result in growth of quality consumer goods, healthcare, leisure, travel, security systems, convenience goods and environmentally acceptable products and services. Products will increasingly be judged by the costs for their useful life. Consumers will increasingly become more conscious about the quality of the food that they eat. People will increasingly switch over to environment friendly organic and natural products. There will be increased growth of traditional and ayurvedic and natural remedies.

Reliability will become even more important, while for domestic goods, after sales service will be regarded as an unacceptable failure of the product. Products will, therefore, be required to be designed and manufactured to provide trouble free service during their useful life. To attract customers, goods and merchandise will be given longer term warranty by their producers. These indications are already visible in the marketplace. Consumer durables manufacturers are now providing warranty for up to five to seven years covering the useful life of the product, which is a major departure from the earlier practice of giving one year's warranty for any manufacturing defects. Some automobile companies now give four years or up to 80,000 km running warranty covering critical parts including engine performance.

The decision to manufacture must be part of the overall strategy of the company. The starting point is to know what benefits will accrue to the business only by manufacturing the product. All businesses must be considered as services. The product is, thus, only the means to deliver the service. How that product has to be acquired depends upon the nature of the business. The decision to manufacture must be based on competitive advantages. Outsourcing of product and services will gradually gain momentum and will increasingly be the preferred option. The concept of preferred suppliers as opposed to multiple supply sources will gain momentum and accordingly marketers will choose to work with the select supply base for mutual benefit.

In some cases, the most critical factor for deciding about the manufacturing process and technology is price and, in other cases, price may be less important than quality and reliability or even sustainability. Other important factors are speed of delivery, range of choice that can be offered to the customer and, most importantly, the flexible manufacturing system, etc., because of the flexible nature of the demand of the product and services. These factors will guide the decision whether to manufacture and, if so, what manufacturing processes will be chosen. These are strategic choices for a company and they must be taken in the context of the overall plan of the company and not as an isolated decision. Businesses in the same category will realign for, both, cooperation for mutual benefits as well as for competing for the market share and growth.

Competitive advantage through new product innovation will be the prime driving force of manufacturing industry in the current scenario. The prime focus of the business would be customer satisfaction through innovation or through innovative business practices.

The main emphasis will be on producing products which have greater functionality at lower costs so that they can deliver higher value to the customer. Companies will be more flexible and will be doing continuous benchmarking of competition and of best practices for cost, quality, time and sales growth. Innovation must, therefore, be a continuous process and should be happening in the organisation as a routine and not by accident. Industries are born or reborn and provide a step-function in competitive advantage. The PC industry resulted from the microprocessors—prior to that no market existed. The compact disc reshaped the industry for recorded music which had existed for 70 years. Compact discs have also replaced floppy discs which are considered to be unreliable and to have low storage space. Now compact discs will also get replaced by smaller devices with higher storage capacity.

The traditional principles of fragmentation of tasks, separation of departments and technologies, and specialisation of skills which have supported the industrial endeavour in the past are no longer acceptable. The organisations of today are smaller, leaner and more transparent and permeable. Matrix type virtual organisations are now evolving. It does not matter from where you are working as long as you are connected and task oriented.

Today, the need is for multidisciplinary engineers with a business understanding. In the new industrial environment there cannot be any partition between development and production departments, the production and the logistic functions and the logistic distribution and the marketing activities. The boundaries between departments and functions are gradually disappearing. The businesses will have to be managed as an integrated holistic unit. In the new economic order what we need is the manufacturing systems engineers who can take a holistic view of the entire supply chain process. The current concept of supply chain management (SCM), in fact, covers all functions from procurement to production, to quality control to services, logistics and distribution management.

The essence of manufacturing during the next decade will be on flexibility. Factories will need to cope with volume fluctuations, avoiding the tendency to build stocks to cushion changes. There will be more frequent model changes on the line and more variants at any given point of time. Quality will be in the hands of operators on the line, and as the workers will be more knowledgeable, product improvement will also often come from them. The new designs with improved features and aesthetics will be initiated by the shop floor operators which will be perfected by the designers and R&D engineers. This change will require them to be multi-skilled. To understand their role in the organisation and in the manufacturing process, continuing education, training and retraining will be required to fulfill this task for a career.

New initiatives in design change and product innovation will not necessarily be top management driven. The growing importance of teamwork in the workforce and the requirement for communication among the members will make interpersonal relationships a much important training need in the future. Personal selling skills will be replaced by team based organisational selling efforts and relationship marketing will replace the traditional marketing function. Customer retention and loyalty programmes will gain increasing attention of the businesses in a highly competitive environment. Organisations will now be seen realizing the life long value of the customer by focusing on customer relationship management (CRM) to build long term relationships.

Good quality means that the customer always gets what he wants and that is possible if zero defect is the only acceptable standard in the organisations. These demands will call for high levels of training, education and experience from the managers. Manufacturing companies will have to respond favourably to environmental pressures and new legislations and the processes must be matched with the marketing strategy of the company.

Integrated logistics aimed at controlling materials, processes and services within the business will be imperative in the future. The workforce of the future will be multi skilled and total quality will be the central driving force behind improvement and motivation for a company's success. The success of the corporation will depend on its ability to adjust to the emerging changes in the marketplace. There will be more public-private partnership (PPP) to ensure the survival and growth of the enterprise. Many large investments will be seen in the PPP mode.

The fortunes of the companies will change much faster, and businesses will be seen exploring acquisitions as a faster way to grow. The business portfolio will be more frequently revisited and recreated. And finally, there will be fewer organisations in each category that will demonstrate their ability to operate on a global scale. The organisations, big or small, will have to consider the whole world as their market and, thus, will no longer work within small protected niches. They will, therefore, be required to operate on a global scale. This will be true even for the SME sector. Hence, in course of time, there will be the emergence of a global market with a global customer mindset. And, in that environment, the traditional marketing model will not work and, hence, a new marketing model, like e-marketing, will emerge.

Strategic Alliances—Fallout of Liberalisation

One of the effects of liberalisation of our economy, as we can see, is that established Indian business houses are either having strategic alliances or completely surrendering to the global players who have come here to capture the Indian consumer goods market. For example, Godrej had entered into a strategic alliance with Procter & Gamble by offering the latter its manufacturing and distribution capabilities, whereas Parle had virtually surrendered to Coke. It's a different matter that Godrej–P&G alliance, in subsequent years, has fallen through due to an intrinsic difference in their business objectives which the alliance could not serve.

The reason for both is apparently the fear of losing market share to global players who have enormous resources at their command. The thinking, therefore, is that it is better to sell the business to MNCs as long as the going is good rather than wait to be wiped out. Multinationals, on the other hand, are looking for distribution infrastructure and marketing channels for their goods. They are not interested in the Indian brands. Sooner or later, they will gradually convert popular Indian brands, which they have acquired, to their own brands. In the coming years we will, therefore, witness the disappearance of established Indian brands of consumer products.

As per the Parle–Coke agreement, Thums Up and Gold Spot will be replaced by Coke and Fanta, respectively but Limca will possibly continue as Coca Cola does not have any cloudy lemon-lime drink in their product portfolio. But Thums Up is such a strong brand that in spite of the sustained effort from Coke, the brand is still going strong. And, therefore, Coke has to support this brand. Reality is that Thums Up sells more than Coke even now.

Business houses will try to protect the value of their business first rather than wait to face the inevitable. Parle fought Coca Cola till 1977 and played a key role for their ouster from India. Parle also successfully fought Pepsi when it could not stop the latter's entry into India. But when Coke made its second entry into India, Parle realized that it now had to fight two giants. The obvious choice was, therefore, as they say, 'If you cannot fight your enemy–join them'.

What has actually led Chauhan brothers' decision to sell their business to Coke? To understand this we will have to go into the background history of Parle.

When The Coca Cola Corporation was operating in India earlier, Parle was their sole rival. In the face of stiff competition from Coke and against all the multinational muscle, Parle was able to keep its flag flying high with about 20 per cent market share. Although Parle could not establish any cola brand against Coke (both Parle Cola and Pepino failed), it could establish two popular brands, namely Gold Spot in orange segment and Limca in lemon-lime segment which kept the entire organisation going.

Till 1977, Parle, was, therefore, a non-cola company. It had over 40 bottlers in India and couple of them also in the Middle East. Its

Maaza brand of ready-to-serve (RTS) fruit beverage was so popular that it finally had to open a bottling plant in the US with a concentrate plant located in Singapore.

Parle fought Coke in the earlier days, both at the trade level as well as at the political level, and finally during the Janata rule, when Coke left in 1977, Parle was quick enough to launch Thums Up. The only competitor of Thums Up was Double Seven of Modern Foods and Campa Cola of Pure Drinks. They were no match to Parle's distribution infrastructure and marketing skills.

Soon Thums Up captured the entire cola market, and Parle's market share saw a growth of 60 per cent. Till recently, Parle was the market leader and Thums Up was the largest selling cola. Things were going very well for Parle till Rajiv Gandhi's government formed an independent Ministry of Food Processing Industries to attract foreign direct investment (FDI) in this sector and also to give this sector a special thrust.

The initial contribution of this new ministry was to grant entry to Pepsi which Parle opposed tooth and nail. Having failed to stop the entry of Pepsi into India, Parle decided to fight their opponent face-to-face in the marketplace. Because of its established brands and leadership position, Parle was definitely in an advantageous position.

Most importantly, their bottlers were wholeheartedly with them. In the soft drink industry, distribution is the name of the game which only franchise bottlers can provide. By that time, Parle had 50 highly experienced franchise bottlers in their fold. Although Pepsi was initially perceived as a threat by Parle, the former could not really make any significant dent in Parle's already established market.

After the exit of Coke from the Indian market, many companies tried to enter this field, for example, McDowell entered the category with their brands of Thrill, Rush and Sprint. Others who attempted an entry into the beverage market include Cadbury with their brand name Appela and Crush (orange beverages), Lipton with their brand name 21 and later on Tree-Top. But most of them withdrew their brands from the market having failed to survive the fierce competition, particularly from Parle's brands.

So what went wrong which led to the Chauhans' decision of selling Parle, an enterprise which they had built brick-by-brick and which was reigning supreme till recently. Initially, the Chauhans had dialogues with both Pepsi and Coke to find whether any kind of alliance was possible. They realized that fighting two big multinationals may not be that easy a task if not impossible, particularly because bottlers were not so confident this time and were inclined to switch sides.

Parle made public statements to the effect that there was no question of its joining hands with either Coke or Pepsi because it had the ability to fight any player in the market. Possibly, it was true. But this time their bottlers did not take their side. Some of the important bottlers even directly contacted Coke, at Atlanta, to take Coke's franchise. This weakened the Chauhans' base in the marketplace and also their confidence.

Parle, thus, had no other alternative but to continue the dialogue directly with the foreign companies and later on with professional help from McKinsey, it finally managed to strike a deal. According to the deal, the Coca Cola Corporation got direct entry into the market and access to the distribution network of Parle bottlers but the latter had to pay a hefty amount for this. Several reports have come out in the press on the amount of money that Parle got from Coca Cola.

In addition to the lump-sum payment, the Chauhan brothers were able to retain the bottling plants of Bombay and Delhi which together contribute 25 per cent of the total carbonated beverages sales in the country, Bisleri mineral water business and Parle Agro's Frooti business. Other salient parts of the deal stated that Coca Cola Export Corporation will develop the fruit beverage business and brands for Parle globally and Limca will continue as a brand. Some section of the press has reported that the Chauhans have got Rs 16 billion in the deal by selling practically nothing. The question that may arise is that who has gained more in the deal—Parle or Coke? It is a million dollar question, but Parle has definitely struck an excellent deal for itself.

In the later years we have observed that Thums Up continued to be a leading Cola brand in the country. Its sales, in fact, are more than coke. If Parle could visualize this before, it would not have sold this brand to Coke. But, in business, one can only take a right decision which is valid at that point of time. And, no one will deny that Parle took the right decision.

Strategies to Stay Ahead in the Race

Goods and services are normally designed, packaged and delivered to meet identified consumer needs. And, business is all about transferring those goods and services from one set of people to another, at a certain consideration, till they reach the ultimate consumer. This whole chain is complete once agreed transfer value is realized and the product is consumed by the end consumer. In this whole chain of doing business, there is always an agreed standard that the products or services are supposed to conform to—a measure of its quality. Quality, therefore, can be defined as the set criteria and specifications or expected performance standards that a product or service has been designed to meet. For example, a motor car has been designed to deliver specific fuel efficiency, engine power, safety and comfort and other features at an acceptable cost and as long as there is total conformance to this agreed standard, quality can be said to have been delivered.

As such, by quality we should not mean anything superior or better but only conformance to the agreed standards of transactions. These days, a lot of dust has been kicked off the ground in the name of Total Quality Management (TQM) and various quality gurus are tying to give various definitions to TQM. Seven guiding principles which outline organisational commitments and expectations for TQM include commitments to: (1) full customer (both internal and external) satisfaction, (2) quality first, (3) continuous improvement, (4) reliable processes and methods, (5) everyone involved, (6) superb work-environment and (7) continuous elimination of all forms of waste.

As technology changes, product life cycles become shorter and shorter and the consumer expectations and needs also change. Therefore, the quality specification of the product also changes. A company can afford to remain in a monopolistic market without upgrading the quality of its product, in line with the technology changes, till the time a competitor enters the market with better quality standards, which forces the first player to change its earlier quality specifications. If, however, the original player wants to remain in the leadership position, it should constantly upgrade its quality to avoid being pre-empted by any possible competition with a better product. But, in reality, it rarely happens. Quality, therefore, is the outcome of competition.

The general perception is that better quality means higher cost but it is not necessarily so. Although a Rolls Royce cannot be delivered at the Ambassador's price, quality improvement is definitely possible without any increase in cost. It can even be possible at a lower cost. Look at the computer and electronic goods industry. Prices are falling every day for high performance machines as a result of which, industries have to recover the development cost within a very short product life cycle. Hence, reality is that better quality of products and services can be offered at a lower cost. Cost, in fact, is attached to non adherence to quality, which leads to rejection, penalty and rework.

That quality is the outcome of competition can be best exemplified with the gradual improvement in the services of Indian Airlines when private airlines started setting new standards of service quality at the same cost. If Indian Airlines does not improve, sooner or later it will be out of business. 'Air India', the new name given after the merger of the then Indian Airlines (domestic operator) and Air India (International operator) both owned by the Government of India, is now struggling to remain relevant and profitable in the ever growing competitive aviation industry. The Jet Airways and Sahara Airlines, which was acquired by Jet in later years and renamed as JetLite, and other private airlines have set new rules of the game which forced the state owned Indian Airlines and now Air India to think differently and improve standards.

The other example of quality upgradation in the face of competition is Hindustan Motors (HM), a company which was established in 1942 in Baroda. In 1947, it shifted its operations to Uttarpara, 20 km away from Kolkata. The company initially entered into a collaboration agreement with Morris Motors, UK and Studebaker Corporation, US to manufacture passenger cars and commercial vehicles. During 1950s and 1960s Hindustan Motors had a monopoly, controlling about 65 per cent of the total passenger car market in the country. It started with a model called Ambassador Mark I and went on to introduce the same car as Mark II, Mark III and Mark IV without practically losing any market share. During the peak period of Premier Padmini's Fiat in the 1970s, Ambassador was still enjoying 50 to 55 per cent market share because premier Padmini was technically not a superior car and Ambassador was still favored as a spacious family car. This situation continued till Maruti appeared on the scene with a small, fuel efficient and more functional car.

Maruti also expanded the passenger car market in the country and in an expanded market HM's market share started falling and finally almost disappeared. Competition from Maruti forced HM to tie up with Isuzu Motors Ltd. Japan, which was in force till April 1993 to manufacture fuel-efficient petrol engine cars. Starting assembly and testing operations in 1987 from completely knocked down (CKD) kits imported from Isuzu Motors, it introduced Contessa cars with an 1800 CC engine after discarding the model that had earlier been unsuccessfully introduced with a 1500 CC Ambassador engine. During the same period, Ambassador's Nova model and later on Ambassador with an Isuzu engine with improvement in both the interiors as well as the exteriors was introduced. Ambassador with the Isuzu engine and the Contessa had a good demand. With these introductions, they were able to stabilize the cars sales in the later years and have been able to improve their financial performance

The comparative figures of Ambassador and Contessa, regarding the number of cars sold were as follows: In 1992–93, the company sold 19,565 Ambassadors and 2,484 Contessas and the total sales value was Rs 71 million. In 1993–94, 22,552 Ambassadors and 3,518 Contessas were sold and the net sales value was Rs 870 million. In 1994–95, 22,369 Ambassadors and 3,769 Contessas were sold and the total sale value was Rs 940 million. But, in the later years, the auto industry took a completely new turn with many new global players introducing their new range of cars. HM failed to respond to these changes and has, therefore, just been fading away from the scene.

Although, because of competitive pressure, HM demonstrated considerable improvement in the car's quality, it still had miles to go. It subsequently made an investment of Rs 1,000 million to upgrade the manufacturing facilities. Implementation of cost reduction programmes through the re-engineering route, improvement of interior, front suspension and steering geometry in the Ambassador car in collaboration with ADC of UK and ISO certification were among the other initiatives taken by HM.

Finally, in the face of competition, when all kinds of international car models are hitting the Indian market, HM has entered into a technical collaboration with General Motors for introducing the Opel Astra model in India. It was a petrol car with 1600 CC and 1300 CC models and was launched in the first quarter of 1997. Opel Astra was launched as scheduled under General Motors. Subsequently, GM also introduced Corsa. And, recently GM, in the US, filed a bankruptcy application.

The fortunes of a corporation change very fast in new economy and the size and past performance is no guarantee for the survival in future. In the changing environment, the organisations have to constantly evolve if they are to survive.

Chapter Summary

This chapter deals with the new challenges of the 21st century. How technology and forces of globalisation and liberalisation have changed the face of the business and its structure has been discussed citing numerous examples to prove the point. This chapter also highlights how the technology and trade policies, coupled with the forces of globalisation, have drastically changed the fortunes of a company. The chapter also discusses many cases to explain how companies are going for strategic alliances to survive the new rules of the game in the marketplace. Organisations are formulating numerous new strategic initiatives to stay ahead in the competition. Companies are becoming much leaner and meaner in structure and flexible in their approach to enable them to make quicker changes in their functioning and decision making processes to survive the competitive forces. New global players with better knowledge and much higher resources at their command are coming and competing with the local players forcing Indian players to adjust and to become more competitive.

III

Core Strategies for Survival

Generic Strategies and Industry Structure

EVERY CORPORATION has to pursue some generic strategies in order to survive the onslaught of the competition in the marketplace. The generic strategies are:

- Cost Leadership
- Differentiation
- Focus

The focus can be on both cost as well as differentiation. In cost focus, firms try to seek a cost advantage in their preferred target segment(s) whereas in differentiation focus, firms seek differentiation in their primary target segment. To succeed in the market, products need to differentiate themselves from the competition either on a tangible platform or even on intangibles as two products in the same category cannot occupy a similar position in the prospects' mind. Marketers, therefore, have to create some differentiation in the product to give consumers a reason to buy the product. The corporations which do not have any competitive advantage in their pursuit of generic strategies are, in fact, 'stuck-in-the-middle'. Firms can pursue more than one generic strategy simultaneously if they have pioneered one major innovation or when the competitor is stuck-in-the-middle (Porter 1985a).

Having cost leadership has a significant competitive advantage and if this is sustainable, firms can produce above average performance. Firms want to derive cost advantage by remaining focused on few product lines, improve productivity and reduce costs by eliminating non-value adding processes from the business. For example, Akai—a company focused on CTV had six models in three product categories and sourced them at cheaper rates from East Asian countries which had overcapacity. It has low overheads (0.7 per cent of sales), no R&D cost, very low inventory (five days), low dealer margin (2–3 per cent), zero waste, low distribution cost and low freight cost as their factory is located near to the port (Porter 1985a). In addition to product focus, focusers can also decide to have buyer focus, channel focus or trade focus.

Sustainability

A generic strategy does not lead to above average performance unless it is sustainable vis-à-vis the competitors. The pitfalls of generic strategies are that they are easily imitated and are, therefore, not sustainable. Even if they are not sustainable and are imitated, the collective actions of the players in an industry category can improve the industry wide category profitability.

If a firm can achieve overall cost leadership then it will be an above average performer in the industry provided it can command prices at or near the industry average prices.

In the differentiation strategy, firms focus on uniqueness in their product or service offering in some specific dimension that is valued by the buyers. Focus essentially rests with very narrow competitive scope within an industry. Focusers normally select a particular segment or even a group of segments within an industry and then tailor their strategy to serve this segment to the exclusion of the other segments or sub-segments.

Industry attractiveness

Michael Porter (1985a) suggested a five force model to decide about industry attractiveness or profitability which is a function of rivalry amongst the players, bargaining power of the buyers and suppliers, potential new entrants and threat of the substitute.

Industry profitability also depends on the industry structure. If an industry category is structurally unviable and unattractive, no amount of strategies can really help.

Industry structure

Broadly, the industry category can be divided into the following classes:

- Fragmented industry
- Emerging industry
- Matured industry
- Declining industry
- Global industry

Industry structure constantly evolves due to evolutionary forces that drive the changes in the structure of the industry. These forces can be outlined as follows (Porter 1985a):

- Category growth
- Changes in competition
- Changes in buyer segment
- Buyers' learning
- Reduction in uncertainties
- Diffusion of proprietary knowledge
- Accumulated experience of industry players
- Expansion or contraction of scale
- Changes in input cost
- Currency fluctuations
- Product innovation
- Marketing innovation

- Process innovation
- Technological upgradation
- Structural changes in the industry that provide input
- Government policy changes
- Entries and exits

Forces that determine industry attractiveness, as postulated by Michael Porter (1985a), are given in Figure 3.1. Competitive forces and players involved in support functions collectively determine

FIGURE 3.1: FORCES THAT DETERMINE INDUSTRY ATTRACTIVENESS

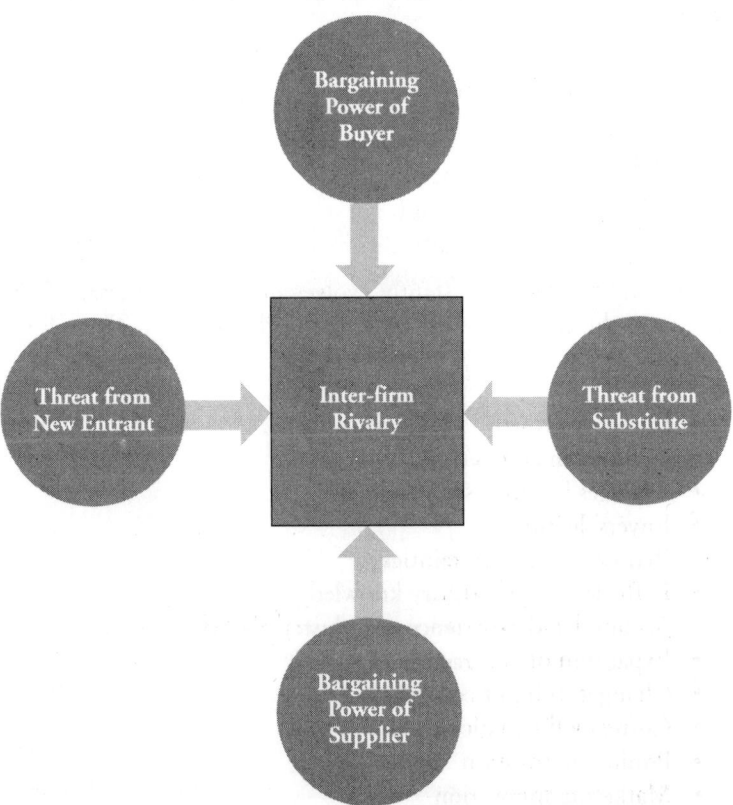

Source: Porter 1985a.

industry attractiveness. The category growth is also largely dependent upon the marketing expenditure of players in the category and the technology changes and new product introduction in the marketplace. The way the players compete will, therefore, have significant influence in the category attractiveness. For example, too much price war in a given category by the players involved might ruin the profitability prospect of the category altogether and finally reduce the category to a commodity.

Industry structure and its attractiveness can also be measured from the perspective of barriers to enter and exit the category. An industry where the entry barrier is high and the exit barrier is low is considered to be the better category to enter as it will be more profitable and will have fewer competitors. This has been discussed in the subsequent section.

Upgradation in Value Chain through Quality

As the competition is increasing, the old ball game is no longer working. We need to change with the changing business environment in order to derive competitive advantages to fight the onslaught of global competition. And quality assumes a significant importance in deriving that advantage.

As per Michael Porter's postulation, industries can derive competitive advantage either through price and cost leadership or through quality and technology leadership. During the 1970s and the 1980s, the Indian organisations, even those with very limited resources, were trying to derive competitive advantage by following the first route. An example in point is Nirma against Surf.

As against that, the large Indian corporations and MNCs were trying to take competitive advantage through quality and technology leadership by distinguishing their product—both in price and quality—delivered though superior technology, and both were thriving.

The ball game today is totally different. In every category, we have similar competition from several equals and many of them are global players who are setting new ground rules. In today's context, we need quality at a reasonable or affordable cost delivered through superior technology.

However, quality no longer has the same definition that it used to have. For example, one cannot compare the quality of an Ambassador car with that of a Rolls Royce, BMW or Mercedes. The customers of Ambassador do not need a fridge, a bar, a TV set, a mobile telephone, and for that matter sliding wind shield and controls on push buttons, etc., which the Rolls Royce customers will expect. Hence, such comparison is irrelevant today. Quality is, therefore, defined as product or services conforming to a set of design or process standards to meet the customers' requirements.

Further, quality is no longer the forte of a set of quality controllers working under the umbrella of quality inspectors, quality assurance, quality audit and quality control departments. It needs the commitment of everybody, starting from the top management to the assembly line operator, to deliver quality. Thus, quality extends the boundaries of one's own organisation and is an organisation wide phenomenon that is usually deeply ingrained in the value system of the organisation.

One of the leading exponents of the quality movement, Philip Crosby (1993), suggested that the cost of quality (COQ) always needs to be measured as a percentage of sales and should be budgeted for improvement.

He further said that 'there is no cost attached to delivering quality and the cost is actually attached to non conformance'. He has also advocated that COQ should be reported regularly and reviewed like all other operational costs and performance.

The cost of quality can be divided into three broad categories. These are prevention cost, appraisal cost and failure cost. The last one can be an internal or external failure in the sense that failure can be detected inside the factory before the product moves to warehouse for delivering. It can also occur in the marketplace or after a consumer has bought the product and even while consuming or using the product or even after consuming the product. In today's context when consumer protection and product liability insurance laws are becoming more stringent, external failure may become a very costly affair to manage even if we do not consider the question of losing the customer permanently and the loss of image to the organisation.

The prevention costs include all activities undertaken to prevent defects in design and development, purchasing, production, etc., for creating a product. For example, preventative maintenance, quality audits, drawing, checking, design review, specification review operators' training, supplier evaluation, participating in seminars, etc., can help prevent a possible product failure.

The appraisal costs are those incurred while conducting inspections and tests to determine whether a product conforms to the set standards. Examples include receiving, inspection and tests, production sample analysis, packaging, inspection, status measurement and reporting, etc.

The failure costs are associated with the product not conforming to the standards such as rework, scrap, service and repeated service, product liability, consumer affairs, etc. A prudent company makes certain that its product and services are delivered to the customer by a management system that does not condone rework, repair, or waste on non-conformance of any sort. These are expensive problems and have consequent repercussions. They must be prevented from occurring and re-occurring.

Depending on whether the loss is taking place in the manufacturing area or service area, actual measurements could have several indices. Cost can be reported as prime cost, manufacturing cost, processing cost, sales loss as loss of income and service as man-hour or labour wage loss, etc. Ultimately all such costs have to be expressed as percentage of sales and budgeted for improvement (Crosby 1993). By following this practice of measuring the COQ budgeting for improvement, one can see that as quality improves, COQ actually reduces. Quality improvement, therefore, is possible with the cost of quality coming down.

In a competitive environment, the success of any organisation will depend on its ability to deliver superior value for its customers faster than the competition. While value has several connotations, what we need for improving the business performance is to improve the economic value of the products and services. Continuous upgradation of quality is one of the surer ways of going up in the value dimension provided the perceived value of the increased quality is less than the cost of delivering it which consumers are asked to pay. In a competitive environment, businesses have to continuously upgrade the quality to ensure survival.

Managing Cost Structure

Lower cost provides immense advantage to the business in terms of better value delivery to the customer. If the cost structure is lower in comparison to competition, products can be sold either at a lower price or the consumers can be given better benefits. In either case, the value of the total proposition will improve and so will the success rate. Although businesses are most often described as profit centres or even as strategic business units (SBU), everything we do inside an organisation is only a cost. Organisations can, therefore, be considered as huge cost centres. The profit is actually external to the organisations. It is obtained or derived by transferring cost of goods and services with a margin to the prospective customers. However, today's customers are very discerning and are not prepared to pay for organisational inefficiencies. In a competitive environment, therefore, to maximize profit, one has to minimize cost as we cannot possibly push the price of the products to cover the increased organisational costs in a highly competitive environment.

There are only two ways in which one can reduce the cost and they are either through cost prevention or through cost reduction by resorting to cost cutting through elimination of all non value adding activities and processes in all business functions within the organisation. Cost prevention is always a better way to permanent cost savings. For any meaningful cost reduction exercise, one has to know the components of all costs that have gone into the product. For this purpose, Activity-based Costing (ABC) serves a useful purpose to understand the value adding and non value adding activities incurring costs. And, it is the non value adding costs that need to be removed from the business processes. This is what we call Business Process Reengineering (BPR). Without the active participation of the work force in the process, it is almost impossible to implement any meaningful cost cutting measures. Cost cutting normally does not get support from the work force because, to them, it actually means laying people off. But cost prevention can be expected to get support of the work force because controlled costs mean better and secured jobs (Drucker 1980). And employees really know where exactly the excess cost is. With participation and involvement of employees, one can eliminate non value adding cost from the system.

There are various elements of cost and one of them is employee cost. The general belief is that if the employee numbers are reduced, cost comes down. But a study of the wage bill of various organisations will reveal that, in absolute terms, despite a cut in the workforce, wages do not always come down. Besides, people are complaining about tension and fatigue because of being overworked in a leaner organisational structure. Also, while workers at lower levels are being reduced, the higher management is increasing its salaries and perks neutralising the impact of the reduction of cost from reduced labourers. There were days when a CEO used to have a salary ceiling which has been removed. Today, a CEO's salary can be anything but businesses should not lose sight of the fact that all costs have to be paid by the customers in the ultimate analysis.

How do we then attempt to reduce the employee cost? It should be accomplished by doing things differently so that it requires less people to do the same work. For example, reception and pantry services can be mechanized or mail distribution system can be reorganised to eliminate the requirement of a receptionist, peon or a mail boy. These services are to be reorganised in such a way that they become self managing (Drucker 1986). But if without making such operational changes receptionists, mail boys and peons are sacked, it will be a nightmare for the administration manager.

The other way of reducing employee cost is by eliminating redundant jobs. Non performers and nonfunctional jobs like executive assistants, manager special projects, marketing coordinators and similar jobs should be eliminated. All duplications should also be avoided. It is often found that the same set of data is referred to by more than one department, each run on a different computer with a different programme. Some organisations are even known to duplicate the entire research and development activity by creating research laboratories, scientific staff and technicians in two or more different locations (Drucker 1986).

The most effective way to cut costs is to eliminate an undesirable operation totally which will produce permanent cost savings. For example, if a business has multiple divisions and some of those business divisions are not doing well or are incurring losses, then it is better to close down the loss making and unprofitable operations all together.

Other significant cost elements in an organisation are inventory costs and process costs. Manufacturing process selection will have to be efficient resulting in high yield and low wastage. More process loss (unconverted material) means not only a direct cost but disposal of waste is an additional indirect cost which has to be incurred. Inventory cost can be reduced by making the whole procurement and distribution chain more efficient. Some of the companies in Japan have now reached a stage where production is done only against daily sales ordering quantity (Just-in-Time) (JIT) so that there is no idle inventory cost. In India, the inefficient infrastructure, poor transportation and communication facilities and unforeseen events such as flood, earthquake, riots, etc., make the concept of 'Just-in-Time' almost impossible to implement. But organisations can definitely improve upon the production planning system. As infrastructure improves, the logistics issues will also improve and a couple of years later the situation will not be as bad for Indian companies to manage trade level inventory.

The stock turnover ratio (STR) in most of the manufacturing organisation in India varies between six and 10. But the best performing companies in the world are reported to have achieved an STR as high as 40. There is, therefore, tremendous scope of improvement. On the procurement front, the earlier concept of having multiple sources of supplies is gradually losing ground. Now it is considered that a supplier is also a partner in the value chain. Hence organisational involvement in assisting suppliers to reduce their cost so that they can supply at a competitive rate is considered to be a much better way to manage procurement cost. But suppliers should understand the honest intention of the buyer in this process and not consider him as an intruder in their system. This can be overcome by having longstanding relations and ongoing dialogue.

Finally, every company should have short, medium and long term cost savings targets and plans to achieve that. A cost audit system should also be in place to see that these are progressing as per plan. Having cost advantage over the competition is a great source of competitive advantage. If there is significant cost advantage, businesses can price the product strategically to make the proposition attractive to the buyers.

Resorting to Cost Cutting

With the rising inflation, cost of products increases but marketers cannot pass on the same to the consumers fearing a drop in sales. When cost increases, the profits come under a squeeze and companies struggle to deliver on shareholders' expectations. Marketers, therefore, resort to cost cutting to cover fast rising costs. Products are still priced the same as firms fight to cover incremental costs. Major food marketers are quietly altering their recipes on candy, dairy products and chocolates by adding fillers and substituting costly ingredients with relatively cheaper ingredients to cut costs.

Hershey has substituted vegetable oil for the costly cocoa butter used in some of its chocolates without sacrificing the taste. Organisations are working closely with the ingredients manufacturers and suppliers for reformulation of products and recipes in many cases. The leading spice producer, McCormick & Co, is now supplying food companies with cheaper spices and new flavour blends. In some cases, even the source of the ingredients is changed. For example, Mexican oregano instead of costlier Mediterranean oregano and garlic concentrate instead of costlier and also heavier-to-ship garlic cloves are being used. Some companies are even resorting to rationalize the product lines. General Mills reduced the number of shapes of pastas to half and, thus, trimmed manufacturing costs by 10 per cent. The meat substitute, soya bean protein, which is used as filler in many meat preparations, is now being used in larger quantities. In the recent years, the consumption of soya-protein has gone up by 10 per cent as a food ingredient. Some players even go to the extent of reducing the pack size and contents. Mars Inc., maker of M&M candies, is resorting to cutting the size of its Funsize candy pack.

Food manufacturers face not only the rising shipping costs due to increase in fuel prices but also a significant increase in the cost of sugar, wheat and other basic food ingredients. This price pressure, which is also arising out of a growing demand for meat and dairy products as living standards rise is not going to disappear soon. Food manufacturers are making these changes in recipes without sacrificing the quality and nutritional standards. General Mills has recently substituted pecans with the less expensive walnuts in its Pillsbury

Turtle Cookies and found that consumers liked walnuts as much as the costlier pecans.

The change of recipe has to be undertaken after carrying out extensive consumer research to ensure that the new revised recipe is equally acceptable to the same set of target consumers who will not be able to detect the changes made. This means that changes made should not be perceptible. Otherwise, it might impact sales. For example, Campbell Soup Company has reduced the amount of meat in its chicken noodle soup. Consumers noticed this and the sales suffered. After this episode, the new CEO made a promise not to cut corners again. Food marketers try to ensure that the most important aspect of the product—the taste—is not changed. If, however, the product recipe is tinkered with too frequently, slowly, over a period of time, the taste might change which could be dangerous for the business. Restaurants and food service companies are resorting to cheaper cut of meats in their menu.

McDonald's is testing less expensive methods of making double cheeseburgers. Some restaurants are already selling the burger with one slice of cheese instead of two. Burger King is testing smaller size hamburgers as it is trying to overcome the increasing ingredients costs.

Food marketers often change recipes to introduce new health claims like adding fibre or whole grains in the recipe or even low salt or even polyunsaturated fats in the formulation. These are done to make additional health related claims and may not be triggered by cost considerations. Studies have indicated that cocoa butter can reduce inflammation and lower blood pressure. So while substituting cocoa butter may not be harmful, it lowers the overall health benefits. These aspects have to be considered while resorting to recipe changes.

Ketchup giant H. J. Heinz has been breeding a sweeter variety of tomatoes in an effort to reduce the amount of high cost corn syrup used in the ketchup production. Heinz is also cutting back on the packaging cost. Starches and hydrocolloids can substitute very costly ingredients like milk fat solids in the ice cream, processed cheese, yoghurt, sour cream and dairy based drinks preparations.

The companies are also looking for cost cutting possibilities in the areas of transportation. Wherever possible, rail transport is being used instead of the costlier road transport.

In the health food segments, manufacturers are resorting to use by-products like rice bran, which is a by-product of the milling industry or even wheat bran, in the formulation. Rice bran and wheat bran were earlier sold as animal feed. Gradually, these are shifting to find use as health food ingredients. NutraCea Inc. sells stabilized rice bran to bread and cereal makers as a meat enhancer. The company says that its rice bran is a healthy meat enhancer because it is fat free, contains protein and can replace other meat fillers such as starch and mustard flour.

When businesses go through difficult phases, only innovation can save them. Cost cutting is a continuous process and enterprise wise efforts to exploit avenues of cost reduction in all functions and business processes are required. In this exercise, the R&D department also plays an important role. As purchased items, which go as input to food production, constitute the largest part of the cost of the finished product and, therefore, recipe modifications and or changes offer the greatest possibility of cost reduction. However, this is a difficult task and organisations have to do it with utmost care so that consumers do not feel cheated or let down by its changes.

Pricing as a Strategic Tool

Pricing is one of the most important elements of the marketing mix. But it does not generally get that much attention. Pricing, almost invariably, is decided at the end. The last thing a marketing director looks at is the price.

Two kinds of marketing directors are seen in the corporate world. The first kind is those who believe that if the product is good, it will sell at any price. This, however, is not true. No product can be sold at a price higher than its perceived value. The other kind believes that the best product should be available at the least price. Only then, they think, will the product click in the marketplace.

The latter does not appreciate the fact that one cannot get a Rolls Royce at an Ambassador's price. Ideally, however, the price of a product should reflect the product's perceived value by the target consumer.

The value perception has several components, namely the product's utility, delivery mode and, therefore, convenience, quality and, hence, the promise it fulfils, need and the brand value which again is a function of advertisement and creative communication.

Determining the perceived value of a product is not easy—it is highly subjective. One way of doing it is to research the various price options with the target consumers describing the product and its performance, preferably offering them the actual sample as proposed to be marketed for testing and obtaining their reaction after use.

But the consumers' mind is also not easy to read. They would always give indication of purchase intention at the lower end of the price option if there is no competitive product available to guide or influence the price.

Although professionally managed companies tend to do the pricing research, ultimately the product price is decided on the basis of a company's policy and affordability.

One, and the simplest, way of doing this is to apply cost plus formula. After allocating all direct and indirect costs, a fixed margin as a percentage of total cost is added to arrive at the selling price. To this, trade margins, applicable taxes, transportation and insurance charges are added to declare the maximum retail price.

The margin to be kept after meeting the cost, varies from company to company. Some companies also have a fixed policy on mark-up and trade margins. In some businesses, gross margin (gross profit) is considered to be the sacrosanct figure. Product should not be introduced if it does not deliver a certain percentage of gross profit (GP).

If the product does not have the desired GP, adequate marketing fund cannot be made available for its promotion, which is necessary for its success, and, hence, GP cannot be sacrificed because the marketing model will then become unaffordable or unviable.

For consumer products, GP should be minimum in the range of 35 to 45 per cent of net selling price; under the Indian business environment and channel structure, the higher the better. This is the requirement when marketing expenditure is expected to stabilize at 7–8 per cent of net sales. Some companies will just not introduce a high potential product if GP before marketing is less than 50 per cent. In a developed economy, the marketing expenditure is as high as 25 per cent of the net sales value and, hence, gross margin is also kept around 65 per cent while deciding on pricing.

Due to competitive pressure, in a me-too category of products, it is not always possible to decide on a price, keeping the desired margins. The solution to this problem is either to maintain parity pricing or to keep the price at desired value and use the additional margin available to fight the competition following an innovative marketing route. But if the organisation has cost advantage, fighting competition in me-too category with lower price offers a distinctive advantage to succeed.

The choice between these options will be dictated by the organisational policy, marketing skill and its ability to face the challenges of the competition. In any case, a company should resort to cost saving measures to obtain the desired GP.

Pricing can be decided from the considerations of product value, target consumers and their income profile, type of use, etc. In this process, one can price a product to skim the market.

The other method of pricing a product is psychological pricing. For example, a baby care or child-care product is normally priced higher with the assumption that mothers will be very willing to pay significantly higher prices for a quality product for their children. Quality of a product, its target segment, type of use and purpose it serves, convenience and, particularly, who takes the buying decision in the household will largely dictate the product price. For example, in the case of cosmetics and perfumes, pricing may be aimed to target the top end of the market and there is absolutely no relationship between product price and the cost of the product.

For fancy and personalized products, price can vary significantly between brands even if quality and performance is the same. For example, a Hong Kong-based company produces watches for a company based in Europe, but the same watch, when sold under the manufacturer's own brand name, does not fetch one tenth of the price at which the global brand sells.

Some companies also resort to what can be described as 'clever pricing' which is basically pricing the product a few paise less than the nearest integer. Bata is a classic example of this kind. They will put a price tag on the shoes at Rs 49.95 rather than saying Rs 50.

But as the value of small coins is nothing now-a-days and because, more often than not, retailers do not even refund such a small difference, this kind of pricing does not really serve the purpose it was originally intended to except for creating a psychological barrier in terms of price which in this case is Rs 50. As more and more brands are introduced in the market and all are talking about the same end benefits delivered through the same technology, consumers have difficulty in deciding on the right product. Pricing then becomes a very important criterion for selection. Under such competitive pressure, brand value goes down and, hence, leading brands also cannot command too much premium.

In the United States and Europe, it is reported that in a certain category of products, there are more than 200 brands to select from. Consumers, therefore, are totally confused.

Leading supermarket stores, taking advantage of this situation, are introducing store-label products, which have become the biggest threat to large corporations. If the product does not have a niche of its own, wrong pricing can even totally destroy the product prospects.

Some marketing pundits think that market share can be gained by reducing the price. If the price is reduced without deriving any cost advantage, it may trigger a suicidal price war because competitors can easily react by reducing the price further. In this game, both parties are in to lose.

It should be known that profit declines manifold with a slight reduction in price. For example, if net profit to net sales ratio of a company is 10 per cent, with one per cent drop in price, profit drops by ten per cent. If a company is known to produce quality product and is charging a premium, there is a price-value-benefit-equation established in the consumer's mind.

When the same company resorts to price reduction, customers become sensitive to price at the expense of value and benefits. It has been reported that in Europe, for some of the leading brands of tea, price-offer was given so frequently in order to gain market share that consumers now buy these brands only when they come with the offers.

These brands can never gain acceptance at their original price because of change of price-value-benefit perception in the consumers' mind. That is why Wheel was introduced to fight Nirma.

Pricing decisions and approval are normally given at the top level in the organisation. But it should not be considered only from an accountant's point of view, its strategic aspects should also be considered.

Chapter Summary

This chapter deals with the generic strategies, namely cost, differentiation and focus. All companies pursue some kind of generic strategies and the collective impact of these actions helps improve the industry category profitability. But as generic strategies can easily be imitated, they do not deliver above average performance. Organisations trying to achieve significant improvement in performance have to deal with other strategies coupled with bringing in significant improvement in costs and quality.

Organisations have to constantly upgrade in value delivery for their identified target consumers by upgrading quality at a lower cost. Delivering quality alone is no longer seen as a competitive advantage because quality is an essential part of the product delivery proposition which all organisations have to adhere to. How the product has to be priced is an important strategic consideration. Product pricing, therefore, has to be seen as a strategic tool in order to derive competitive advantage. Wrong product pricing has been seen as one of the main criteria for product failure and, therefore, pricing decisions are taken with extreme care. While reducing the price, one needs to derive a commensurate advantage in cost reduction.

IV

Creating Competitive Advantage

Offensive Strategies

THE PURPOSE of the offensive strategy is to take designed action against the identified competitor in order to exploit its weaknesses and take away the market share. One has to be careful in identifying the key strategic actions in this case. Sometimes offensive action can act as the best defence against competition. Businesses, if resources permit, must have a set of offensive strategic actions against competition. It is also possible to take offensive actions against the industry category leader if some ground rules are followed.

Offensive against industry leader

The leader in a category often enjoys enviable market share and profitability which might invite competition from the smaller players as well as from contemplating new entrants. However, it should be noted that the leader enjoys several advantages. These include:

- Reputation
- Brand image
- Brand loyalty

- Economies of scale
- Cumulative learning
- Preferred access to suppliers
- Preferred access to channel partners
- Resources for protracted retaliation against challengers
- Better knowledge of the market
- Profitable Business

The successful strategy of the challenger has to be created to nullify the key competitive advantage of the leader. For example, Nike attacked Adidas in the athletic shoes category. Pepsi attacked Coke to take away marker share from the latter.

Sometimes, the attacker gets an opportunity to go on the offensive against the leader. Sometimes change in industry structure may make the leader very vulnerable. If the follower understands the industry structure better than the leader, it may be possible for it to overtake the leader as well (Porter 1985b).

The cardinal principle in the offensive strategy is not to attack an industry leader with an imitative strategy irrespective of the challenger's staying power and access to resources (Porter 1985a). Those who have violated this principle have been seen to have failed and paid a price. For example, P&G introduced the instant coffee, Folger, which was pitted against the market leader Maxwell House of General Foods but did not succeed. Similarly, Coca Cola introduced Spectrum Wine against Seagram's which also failed (Porter 1985a). In our home ground, in India, all powder beverages including Ju-C from General Foods, which were launched and placed against Rasna, the market leader, have failed miserably. Even Tang of Kraft General Foods failed against Rasna.

Attacking the industry leader

However, it does not mean that the industry leader cannot be dislodged. There are avenues to attack an industry leader as well. Michael Porter, in his book *Competitive Advantage* (1985a), has listed a number of such possible avenues to attack a leader. These are:

- Reconfiguration: Innovating the way the business is done and reinventing through its value chain or through business process reengineering.
- Redefinition: Redefining competitive scope within the business or competing in narrow area(s) where the challenger can have incremental advantage over the leader.
- Pure spending: Selectively buying the place or position in the market through better use of superior resources or even outshouting the leader in select media or channel.

The challenger has to look at the entire value spectrum within the industry to find out appropriate avenues of attack. Based on the above broad avenues to attack, the challenger can possibly narrow down the competitive scope to improve the prospect of success. The other avenues are (Porter 1985a):

- Focus within the industry: Narrowing the basis of competing to a segment rather than across the board.
- Integration or de-integration: Widening or narrowing the range of activities performed in-house.
- Geographic redefinition: Broadening the basis of competition from a region or country to worldwide or vice versa.
- Shifting the front to attack: Suddenly change the front to attack by either focusing on weak or even strong areas of competition.
- Horizontal strategy: Broadening the basis of competition from a single industry to related industries.
- Alliance to attack the leader: Either through acquisition or through collaboration and coalition with other players.

Conditions to attack industry leader

The challenger must satisfy some basic conditions in order to make a reasonable impact on the leader in the category while attacking. These are:

- Sustainable competitive advantage—in cost or differentiation.
- Having access to a much greater amount of resources and the ability to withstand erosion in bottom line for a longer period in relation to the leader.
- Proximity to other activities to neutralize the cost advantage of the leader due to economies of scale/first mover advantage.
- Some impediments to leader's retaliation so that the leader cannot immediately retaliate against the onslaught of the challenger. For example, Cargill and Archer Daniel Midland (ADM) successfully entered against CPC International in corn milling because they satisfied all these conditions. Also, Federal Express successfully entered against Emery Air Freight (Porter 1985a).
- To succeed the challenger must capture some of the signals from the industry as well as from the leader about its vulnerability.

Signals of leader's vulnerability

INDUSTRY SIGNALS
- Discontinuous technological change: Products still being made using old technologies and not much investment being made in the R&D effort.
- Change in buyer segment: Distinct shifts in the buyer segment are being noticed.
- Changing channel: Products are now being distributed through different channels.
- Shifting input costs or quality: Significant change in the input cost and or quality specifications.
- Gentlemen's game: Players are seen to follow rules of the game and prefer peaceful coexistence rather than fighting fiercely for outperforming the competition.

LEADER'S SIGNAL
- Stuck in the middle: Not able to create any competitive advantage.
- Unhappy buyers: Not able to cater to changing buyers' needs and preferences.

- Not a pioneer of current industry technology: Still adopting old technology when there is a distinct shift in technology.
- Very high profitability: Making large profit resulting from large market share as well as low fixed cost.
- History of regulatory problems: Often seen to be getting into regulators' net such as tax authorities or competition law, etc.
- Weak performer in the parent company portfolio: Not an important player in the group companies' total performance.

Impediments to leader retaliation

A variety of factors can inhibit a leader's retaliation to a challenger. These are:

- High leader response cost: Cost of retaliation is too high.
- Different financial priorities: Leader may have other short term as well as longer term financial performance requirement constraints.
- Portfolio constraints: Highly dependent on the product for bottom-line performance.
- Regulatory pressure: Has constraints arising out of factors such as competition law or other legal constraints
- Faulty assumptions: Leader has not clearly understood the challenger's motive.
- Wrong pricing: Leader has priced the product too high which the challenger can exploit and show that the leader is charging a much higher price in comparison to what it offers.
- Longer response time: Leader takes a long time to give appropriate response to the challenger's offensive. The leader is reactive rather than proactive.
- Complacency: Leader has adopted a wait and watch policy and has not retaliated in time.

Robin Blue of Reckitt Benckiser was the undisputed market leader. When Ujala was introduced by the small timer Jyoti Laboratories,

Reckitt did not understand its motive and totally ignored it, thinking that a small company producing inferior quality fabric blue (a post wash product used normally to give extra whiteness to white clothes) cannot challenge a multinational and a leader in the category. Ujala, a dye based liquid, as against Reckitt's, Ultramarine Blue, in due course of time, emerged not only as the leader but also redefined the category. Reckitt, in the later years, introduced another dye based product to fight Ujala but did not succeed. This is a clear example of a faulty assumption on the leader's part.

Competitor selection

One cannot have a common strategy to attack everyone in the industry who are considered to be the competitors. A single strategy will not work against all competitors in the market. Therefore, before formulating any strategic initiatives, one has to identify which competitor to attack. Besides, there are good and bad competitors. The challenger will have to be careful about whom it is planning to attack. Businesses have to identify the key competitors in the market based on certain criteria. These criteria could be: whether one is competing for market share in the same space, similarity in the business portfolio, aggressively attacking the challenger's market, resorting to unethical business practices, posing long term threat to the challenger's business, trying to follow identical strategies to attack the challenger, identifying weaknesses of the competitors which can be easily exploited and finally expected retaliation and manageability. For, not being able to identify the right scope of taking offensive against an identified competitor will result in failure. But there could be many other reasons for failure in the offensive strategy.

Other reasons of failure in the offensive strategy are:

- Failure to distinguish between good and bad competitors: Attacking a good competitor is not desirable.
- Driving competitors to desperation: Taking offensive to threat its mere existence might prove unproductive.

- Having too big a share: Already enjoying a sizeable market share and trying to attack players holding small protective niches.
- Entering an industry with too many bad competitors: An industry category with too many bad competitors who do not follow regulatory guidelines.

Defensive Strategies

There are three basic approaches to formulation of defensive strategies as suggested by Michael Porter (1985a). These are:

- Raising structural barriers to dissuade competitor from entering.
- Increasing expected retaliation from the competitor.
- Lowering the inducement for attack by competition.

Many actions can be initiated under these three broad approaches to defensive strategies. These are summarized below:

Raise the structural barriers to dissuade competitor from entering

- Economies of scale.
- High marketing cost and increasing marketing spend.

Having economy of scale will reduce the cost of product, which will inhibit competitors from entering with a higher unit cost. Spending significant money on marketing will also be an inhibitory factor to enter a category. For example, Indian soft drink industry, dominated by Coke and Pepsi, has these structural barriers (high entry barriers) and others would not like to get into this category. One can, therefore, defensively increase the scale economies.

- Barriers increase if economies of scale are raised.
- Increasing the advertising spend.
- Dominating every form of media.

Fill available product or positioning gaps or options

All possible positioning options are totally exploited. For example, Cherry Blossom shoe polish has the entire range—wax polish, liquid polish, shoe shampoo, white cleaner for canvas shoes, cream, handy shine (instant shine)—a product to fill all positioning options. The purpose is to:

- Broaden product lines
- Introduce brands that match the product characteristics or brand positioning where the challenger has a continued market or is likely to introduce one which will give them an entry option
- Forecast alternative marketing themes and position products to fill in those gaps
- Defensive low pricing of the product: Pricing the product at a level which the challenger will find difficult to match
- Encourage good competitors that fill gaps without threatening the firm

Block access to channel

This will create hurdles for the competition to market and distribute their product. This can be achieved through:

- Exclusive agreement with the channel
- Increasing service frequency in the channel
- Delivering higher return on investment (ROI) for the channel partners
- Filling product line gaps
- Aggressive volume discounting
- Attractive after sales service support
- Willingness to support private label sellers
- Overstocking the trade
- Supplying products and SKUs which the channel partner want and not restricting the supply

Raise barriers and increase buyer switching costs

For certain product categories, it may be possible to raise the cost of switching to a competitive product. For example, if an existing customer of Otis Lifts wants to buy a second lift, it may work out costlier for him if he decides to buy a competitive product such as Olympus. This is achieved through:

- Free or low cost training of the buyer
- Participating in joint product development with the buyer
- Establishing ties with the buyer
- Providing free service contract for a second time purchase

Create hurdles for gaining the trial

There are several ways of doing this:

- Selective reduction of price
- High levels of couponing or sampling
- Discounting heavily
- Announcing new incentives and promotional schemes
- Blocking access to channels, etc.

Increase capital requirement

- Reduce delivery time of essential and critical inputs
- Book capital equipment in advance

Invest in developing proprietary know how

- Invest in R&D to develop proprietary technologies and processes
- Buy or collaborate for advanced level technology

Use alternative and/or superior technology

- Employ better, latest and superior technology
- Switch to low cost technology or alternative manufacturing methods

Defensively try to raise cost of inputs

- Book key suppliers' capacity in advance
- Sign preferential suppliers agreement
- Make exclusive arrangements with the better and well known suppliers

This can be achieved by:

- Avoiding suppliers that will supply to competitors
- Bidding up the price of costs or material input

Avenues of retaliation during attack

- Disruption of test market
- Litigation
- Reducing profit targets

Better understanding of competitors' motives for creating counter strategies

- Understanding competition and competitive behaviour

Defensive and offensive strategies are generally built to outperform the competition.

Evaluating defensive tactics

Which defensive strategies should be selected for implementation depends on their impact on the business. The options have to be evaluated based on the following criteria (Porter 1985a):

- Value delivered to buyers
- Relative cost structure
- Sustainability of action plan and its effects
- Clarity of actions and messages or signals given
- Credibility of the action
- Impact on competitors' goal
- Ability to match by other players

Businesses must have some defensive mechanism built in their strategic initiatives so that they can focus on key actions required for growth as well as for capturing new opportunities—both short term as well as long term. Defensive strategies and actions are to be designed keeping in mind the likely strategies and key action plan of the nearest competitor(s).

Create a Business Category You Can Own

It is always better to be the first to launch a new product rather than to become a follower. You will have a much greater chance of success (Ries and Trout 1982). If you want to occupy the leadership position in any category, you will have to innovate or create that category. IBM, in the PC industry, Microsoft in software and Xerox in photocopying are the examples of creating a business category and then dominating it for years. IBM, in the later years, lost dominance in PC industry by selling to the Chinese player, Lenovo.

There are marketing pundits who think that it is risky to venture into creating a new category and, hence, it is better that someone else does it. And when a segment is created, it is easier to enter with a better but me-too product to take away a market share from the first mover. But that is not always true. The task of the second entrant to establish a brand or category can never be easy. It is definitely going to be more difficult because, as they say, 'the early bird catches the worm'.

This principle applies to any product, brand or category. This is particularly true when the consumer's mind is always being bombarded with all kinds of information, including information on new products, through the use of multiple media. In this age of information explosion, the first person, first product or first name that enters the consumer's mind will leave the strongest impression, and will have the highest recall value. The second, even if it is better or superior, cannot even remain alongside the first one in the prospect's mind, not to speak of easily replacing the first one. Nobody, remembers the second player. Everybody remembers the topper, the first to make the history. Even the name of the close second in the race is also easily forgotten.

If the first product becomes a remarkable success, it often becomes synonymous with the category, which means it becomes generic to the category. For example, Hindustan Lever's Dalda, which is a brand name for hydrogenated vegetable oil (HVO). People might be buying any brand or even buy loose HVO but, when asked, will say that the food is cooked in Dalda. Recently, of course, the Dalda brand and business has been acquired by the Bungi group of South America. One reason why the first brand tends to maintain its leadership is that the name often becomes generic to the product category.

In India, many new categories were created by taking the first mover advantage by innovative entrepreneurs or by creative business houses. In the consumer products area, two popular examples are Pan Parag from the Kothari Group of Kanpur and Rasna from the Ahmedabad based Pioma Industries promoted by Areez Khambatta. Today, Pan Parag, generically speaking, is an over Rs 5,000 million category. Seeing its success, over a dozen national brands have later been launched but none of these brands are even close to Pan Parag in sales. It has created that category and is its leader.

Rasna, on the other hand, has a great success story. The brand was first launched in western India during the early 1970s as a cheaper substitute for squashes, cordials, juices and carbonated beverages with very limited marketing support. As the company did not have any infrastructure for distribution, the product was given to Voltas (a Tata Group Company) for distribution. Voltas distributed the product for a couple of years but sales did not pick up, partly because it was a new concept which needed time to be accepted. Around 1979–80, when sales were around Rs 15 million, Areez Khambatta decided to withdraw from the distribution arrangement with Voltas. Instead, he wanted to distribute the product through his own proprietorship company, Pioma Industries. Since then, he has not looked back. Rasna, from Areez Khambatta's Pioma Industries, is an example of how a new market can be created and can stand the test of time. Khambatta introduced Rasna in concentrate form and it now has about 80 per cent of the market share in its own segment.

The new concept that Khambatta introduced was the Rasna concentrate, and can best be described as 'one minus concept' which means that the product has all the ingredients excepting one which the consumer has to add. Most often, this ingredient which is not added in the product is a costly and bulky ingredient which increases the cost of the product significantly but consumers add that item conveniently without realizing what it costs to them. Rasna was, therefore, developed as a composite of flavour pack, acid-preservative and colour pack. Consumers are required to make the sugar syrup at home to be mixed with Rasna as per formulation to get a bulk concentrate to be kept in bottles. Now, it could be used after dilution with cold water for consumption as and when required.

The product soon became extremely popular, particularly with the middle and lower income group segments and sales started growing steadily. Today, Pioma Industries' sales are approximately Rs 3,500 million and Rasna sales have touched Rs 3,000 million where the soft drink concentrate market is itself less than Rs 4,000 million. Rasna is available in 11 flavours and contributes to 90 per cent of Pioma's turnover and about 80 per cent of the market share in that category. Like Nirma, Rasna is also a small scale industry and Areez Khambatta has done a remarkable job in managing the logistics of such high volume and yet multiple pack product manufacturing operations to maintain its small scale character to benefit from tax and other concessions. The business of this size was built following highly labour intensive manual operations, which is indeed very creditable.

His business is still growing at a rate of 15 per cent per annum and Khambatta has now ventured into other activities, introduced new products and entered into a collaboration with Campbell to market soups.

After seeing Rasna's success, many players including multinationals attempted to enter that category but none succeeded in establishing another **brand in** the 'one-minus concept' of soft drink concentrate which **Khambatta** created from nowhere. During the late 1970s and early 1980s, brands such as Trinka from Corn Products (now Best Foods International—a Unilever company), Ju-C from Kothari General Foods, Hash-Ras from Kissan and Dipy-Sip from Dipys of from UB Group have tried to enter that category but all have failed.

A couple of years ago, Khambatta attempted to extend the same concept to Rasna Spread Maker, which is basically making jams at home. The product again has everything minus sugar, which the consumer has to add. The same Khambatta who could create and own a category of business for himself is currently busy in setting up a plant to manufacture a range of confectioneries.

Pioma Industries has now extended to countries abroad and has introduced powder beverage under the same brand, Rasna and is successfully competing against Tang, a global brand from Kraft General Foods.

Whoever has attempted to introduce a new product idea or a new concept has had a much higher probability of success in creating a segment for itself. The second player in the game with a me-too product to offer has a relatively lower rate of success. The second player still has a chance provided he can differentiate and carve out a niche for itself in the consumer's mind. There is very little possibility for the third player. There are many catagories of business where even more than three players exist. But in those cases, the category would be too large. Also there will be many regional and even local players and a few will be national players. And amongst the few national or global players, the first two brands will have the majority of the market share. The third player will have a much lower share in comparison with the first two. Of course, it should be pointed out here that for the first mover in a non-existent category, it might take a long time for the consumers to accept the product but once accepted, the new category gets easily identified with the innovator.

Not all products succeed if introduced first, but then either the idea is bad or the product is well ahead of its time or even it could be too late. If the idea is well ahead of time, it only takes a longer time to get established and one should have the ability, resources and the tenacity to continue. The other reasons of product failure could be the fact that the product did not perform and there are inherent deficiencies in the product.

The second brand, of course, will not necessarily always languish forever like many other unsuccessful brands. Because in a dynamic market, there are many other factors which determine the success or failure of a new concept or a new product. Although introducing products for the first time in the marketplace has its distinctive advantages, this alone does not determine the fate of a new product. In pharmaceutical industry, a new molecule or new drug will invariably offer great advantage for the marketer if introduced in the market for the first time and rolled out in the global market quickly. Being first in the market and being first to occupy a place in the prospects' mind has significant advantages.

Time as Competitive Advantage

Time is a very peculiar resource. Everybody has the same amount of it. It cannot be inventoried or stored. Once lost, it is lost forever. Managing time more efficiently is, thus, the key to time management. Acting in time, therefore, is critical to the success of the business. It is extremely difficult to recover the lost ground arising out of delayed action in a competitive environment.

Marketing in a competitive environment means that it is imperative for the marketer to recognize customer needs, create customer values and benefits and communicate those incremental and differentiated values to the target customer quicker and better than competitors in order to obtain a competitive advantage. This is particularly true for technology products.

In order to be successful in technology marketing, one must clearly understand the correlation between market development and technology development. Markets are becoming more and more saturated and are stagnating and shrinking. Therefore, national and international competitive pressure increases for those who are trying to identify newer markets for themselves. Also the technological development cycle is becoming shorter and shorter which reduces the product life cycle. Hence, the product life cycle is also becoming shorter and shorter.

The market life cycle and product life cycle can be predicted by a careful study of the technology life cycle which lies between the two. The technology, therefore, is an important component for forecasting the product life. This means that time is a critical factor to be considered for providing competitive advantage to business.

Time as a critical success factor

According to an analysis by Arthur D. Little, if the launching time of a new product exceeds by 10 per cent in a two year development cycle, revenue loss amounts to 25–30 per cent, whereas if product cost exceeds by 10 per cent, the revenue loss is 15–20 per cent. Compared to this figure, if R&D cost exceeds by 50 per cent, the revenue loss is only 5–10 per cent. Therefore, the largest loss is due to a belated product launch (Töpfer 1995). Launching a new product at the right time is the key to success. The design, development and research activities of the organisation should, therefore, be managed to meet the target dead line of the product launch.

However, this does not mean giving R&D departments a free hand to overrun cost objectives. But, if a decision has to be taken on whether to increase the R&D effort or to postpone the product launch, it is certainly better to reduce the development time in order to meet the original planned launch date even if it costs higher to escalate the development activities. Nowadays, due to the time competition with ever shorter product life cycles, only a small share of the market volume is left for followers.

This would mean that followers have less favourable market opportunities today. As such, the first mover in the market will have a greater opportunity to recover its R&D and other development costs and make profits. The follower will be left with relatively much lower or residual opportunities (Töpfer 1995).

Recognising this fact, many world class companies have drastically reduced their new product development time to almost half or less than half in the 1990s than what it was in the 1980s as can be seen in Table 4.1. The effect of time competition can be

TABLE 4.1: DEVELOPMENT TIME ON NEW PRODUCTS

Company	Product	Development 1980 (past)	Time in Year 1990 (present)
Rank Xerox	Copiers	5 years	3
Brother	Printers	4	2
Hewlett Packard	Printers	4.5	2
Apple	Computers	3.5	1
Volvo	Trucks	7	5.3
Honda	Cars	8	3
AT&T	Telephone systems	2	1
Sony	TV sets	2*	0.75

Source: Industrimagazine, 2 (90), High Tech, 4 (90), cited in Töpfer 1995.
Note: * 1986 data.

demonstrated by the example of the falling price of microchips, computers and electronic goods and for that matter all technology products. Products are being launched in the market with better features using next generation technologies at a lower cost than the earlier models. This is possible due to drastic cost reduction using better, superior and more cost effective technologies. Global corporations are seen to be investing significantly in R&D, design and development efforts.

The classical theory of management and marketing says that a strategy is needed to occupy a chosen position in the market. And the marketing and promotional activities need to be designed and executed around the product to hold on to the chosen position for long term value and profitability.

According to Porter (1985b), there are two types of possible strategies, namely a strategy of cost and price leadership or a strategy of technology and quality leadership. However, in today's world, under the new economic order, it is no longer an option between these two strategies but a question of how to combine these two strategies to gain more competitive advantage and better opportunities for strategic manoeuvering (Töpfer 1995).

Japanese companies can be mentioned as a perfect example of combining these strategies. The competitive advantages they get from their approach, to achieve high quality and technology levels of low costs and prices are very impressive. Japanese companies located in Europe and America have also demonstrated competitive advantage over European and American manufacturers. According to an analysis carried out by McKinsey, the production cost of European and American car manufacturers are almost 30–40 per cent higher than that of their counterparts in Japan.

Japanese generally follow a parallel or simultaneous development process instead of sequential development, and therefore, they put three different development teams working simultaneously on three development briefs on the various aspects of the same product in a three track development processes. For example, one team is working on improving the features of an existing product, the second team is working on the reduction of cost of the product and yet a third team is working on technology upgradation of the product. This approach helps them take a quantum jump and leapfrog the value chain for significant competitive advantage.

It holds true for all types of technology products that the manufactured product must be as good as required by the customer and not as good as technically feasible both in terms of design features and performance and cost. In order to achieve that, technology development programme needs to come to its logical conclusion, which means that the most decisive factor for success of a technology product is 'to do the right things right'.

Customer orientation, interlinking R&D with marketing and other functions like production, quality and logistics, team work and simultaneous, concurrent and parallel engineering rather than sequential development process will arm the organisation to provide an answer to time competition.

Other reasons of failure

Although the major competitive advantage in marketing technology product has been recognized as speed or time, there cannot be any guarantee that the new product introduced in the market, well ahead of competition, will always succeed. Other reasons of product failure, as cited in R.G. Cooper's study (1994) are:

- The better mousetrap that nobody wanted (28 per cent). Too good, too few customers.
- The me-too product encountering competitive barriers (24 per cent). Customer with high brand loyalty.
- Product not competitive (13 per cent). Me-too products— cannot stand the competitive pressure of rivals.
- Product with technical deficiencies (15 per cent). Products which do not live up to promises.
- Products in the wrong environment (7 per cent). Products that nobody wanted, poor evaluation of customer requirements, of competition and of government influences.
- The steep fall in prices (13 per cent). Price cuts by competitors led to failure.

But most of these reasons can be managed by appropriate planning. The R&D department should function, as an interdisciplinary team, in close association with marketing, production, logistics and quality assurance departments. Research and Development involvement in Indian industry is one of the lowest in the world. The situation is worse in the case of technology product development areas. As a result, we have not introduced any such product worth its name using indigenous technology.

Chapter Summary

In this chapter we discussed the defensive and offensive strategies. We have outlined many scenarios where we can take offensive strategies and where we should be defensive to protect our own market share or even to attack leaders in order to take away their market share. We also discussed various strategic initiatives that we can take under defensive and offensive strategies with examples. Normally, one cannot attack an industry leader with a set of imitative strategies. However, under a given set of conditions, the industry leader also can be attacked upfront. The chapter discusses the various signals that industry leaders give to indicate that their vulnerability and businesses should be able to capture those signals to initiate any major offensive against the leader. Time is a very important element of competitive advantage. How time management can offer significant advantage to players is discussed taking cases of how businesses are significantly reducing the time of new product development. Launching a new product first and well ahead of others in the market gives significant advantage and remarkably improves the prospect of success. Products launched as me-too products have a much lower rate of success. But there are other reasons of product failures which were discussed in this chapter. Cases and examples are discussed to emphasise the point.

V

Corporate Growth Strategy

Corporate Growth Investment Strategy

ORGANISATIONS CAN grow organically exploiting current portfolio of products and current opportunities. The existing portfolio of products can be marketed in new geographic areas wherever the opportunity exists. The products can also be marketed for deeper penetration in the current market for growth. New variants can be developed to cover new opportunities in the existing markets by finding out new uses of the products and covering new positioning options and opportunities available.

Organisations can also grow inorganically through acquisitions. This helps in faster growth of the enterprise. The acquisition route for corporate growth strategy has a couple of advantages. These are:

- Faster growth
- Eliminates a potential competition in the market
- Acquires new knowledge of product and trade
- Acquires productive and running resources for the business including trained human resources
- Provides opportunity to integrate with the existing business to emerge out as a stronger player in the market
- Attain critical mass faster

- Gets more financial and marketing muscle in the market
- Become more respectable in the world of commerce.

Acquisition route for growth can be pursued if an organisation can generate enough resources either through internal accruals or through a loan. But business acquired must have the capability to generate enough surplus to service that loan. Acquisition of the right candidate in the synergistic areas normally proves to be useful. However, acquiring non-related business may become a risky proposition if the acquirer does not have the capability to add value to the business.

The other option of growth is through diversification. Businesses are known to keep diversified portfolios provided they can manage those effectively. In the days of intense competition, diversification into non-related areas sometimes proves risky. One, therefore, has to be very careful about deciding on the areas of diversification. Sometimes, having a diversified business portfolio is advantageous because it can balance the performance when some of the sectors of the business go through cyclical downturn.

One can also grow through the integration of business. Both horizontal and vertical integration and forward and backward integration are possible which can bring in additional value to the business and, therefore, improve the competitiveness of the organisation in the marketplace. Integration, therefore, is sometimes considered as a natural extension of the business to dominate the entire value chain. Which option to pursue depends upon numerous factors and there is no single answer which will be universally valid.

Acquisition and mergers

Identifying a potential target for acquisition is an important task. Organisation in pursuit of growth should have a built-in mechanism in terms of having a specific function vested with the task to look for the possible acquisition targets based on certain guidelines specific to the organisation's future growth objective, mission and the kind of business to target. These could be:

- Synergy with the existing business
- Organisation's capability in managing the acquired business
- The value it adds to the current business
- Strategic fitment with portfolio of the business
- Whether it is core to the organisation's prime activities
- Acquired candidate whether structurally attractive or can be made attractive
- Size of the business to be acquired: Whether it is feasible to raise the kind of money required to acquire it
- Financial performance of the acquisition candidate over a period of time: Whether it is a consistent performer
- Market share, position and standing of the acquisition candidate in its own category

Diversification through Acquisition

Sometimes businesses do acquire non-related business. In fact, in order to enter into a totally new category of business, it is better to go through the acquisition route for the simple reason that with acquisition one acquires the knowledge to run and manage the business and also a critical mass. But there will be a cost attached to it. Diversification through acquisition is although a preferred route for many corporations, but necessary precautions have to be applied.

To be successful in identifying the diversification of acquisition proposal, it is also necessary to understand how diversification can enhance shareholder value. These conditions can be summarised in three tests (Porter 1985a):

- Attractiveness of the industry: The industry chosen for diversification must be structurally attractive or capable of being made attractive.
- Cost of entry or acquisition cost: The cost of entry must not capitalise on all the future profit.
- Synergy with the existing operation: Acquired unit or business must derive competitive advantage from its link with the existing business or vice versa.

It is important for the business to derive the full advantages that were seen to be coming from the possible acquisition route. Therefore, integration of the business, post acquisition, is a very important task. There should be a clear strategy with respect to how the new acquired entity is to be managed. The options are as follows:

- Acquired unit to be run as an independent unit as a separate entity
- Acquired unit has to be merged with the existing business

In both the options, one has to consider the issues related to manpower resources which come along with the acquisition. If the integration of the business acquired is not accomplished properly, the benefit of acquisition will be lost significantly. Many believe that the task of merging the unit acquired with the existing business is in fact more difficult than acquiring. Sometimes it is better to allow the acquired unit to be managed by its own people who have come along with the acquisition itself.

Appropriate merger strategies will provide a significant cost advantage to the business. The profitability, knowledge capital, market presence and growth should improve as per the projected plan prepared at the time of acquisition. Therefore, the valuation of the business and the price paid for the acquisition will have to be justified.

Acquisitions or diversification: Has to be synergistic

Different corporations adopt different growth strategies. Some choose to grow organically by systematically exploiting the total potential of their main business operations. Others look for growth opportunities in diversifications or in acquisitions of existing business units.

The second option is often more attractive to many companies because it may appear to be the faster way to grow. But if the diversification and acquisition strategies are not backed by solid financial and marketing logic, such exercises can end up threatening the main business activities of the company rather than propelling its growth.

For example, when Metal Box diversified into the ball bearing business, the new business began pulling down the company's mainline activities as well. Finally, Metal Box had to hive off the ball bearing operations to the Tatas. The Tatas were more successful because they tapped the synergy that existed between the ball bearing business and their own automotive division.

There are other examples of diversification disasters. For example, when late Rajiv Gandhi set up the Ministry of Food Processing Industries and categorised the sector as an Appendix I industry, to give the sector a preferential status, several big houses including the Birlas, the Goenkas and the Modis announced plans to move into what was perceived to be a sunrise industry. Some of these industrialists later reversed their decisions after realising that it was not their cup of tea.

Those who went ahead, however, paid a heavy price. Indian Organic Chemicals Limited (IOCL) invested Rs 100 million in potato processing and introduced wafers and frozen potato products in the market. Recurring losses forced the company to withdraw its products within two years.

Similarly, some years ago, a large number of business houses started manufacturing Electronic Private Automatic Branch Exchanges (EPABX) and Key Telephone Systems (KTS). But telecommunications is a high technology field and companies entering this market have to cope with rapid technological shifts. As a result, many companies like Escorts and the UB Group—who thought they could implement their projects by merely buying a one-time technology—have later realised that it was not as simple as it had initially appeared. Many such enterprises have now turned sick and will either have to change hands or will simply close down.

When companies turn sick, they are up for grabs, but this is when another problem crops up. Unlike in the West, where profitable companies change hands overnight, in India only sick units are acquisition candidates. If a corporation acquires too many sick companies, their fund requirements restrict the growth, innovation and technology upgradation of the profitable companies within the concerned group. Thus, it is important that the newly acquired businesses or diversification projects are integrated before a corporation goes ahead with its second expansion plan.

Knowledge about a particular industry is also vital, since some industries require specialised skills. For instance, the oilseed business needs special buying and selling expertise. Those who do not have such experience often come a cropper, like Britannia did. The company diversified into soya bean processing with an Rs 250 million investment, only to disinvest after two years to S.M. DyeChem.

To be successful in identifying a diversification and acquisition proposal, it is also necessary to understand how diversification can enhance shareholder value. These conditions can be summarised in three essential tests as discussed earlier in this chapter.

For each category of industry, there will be barriers to entry and exit. Industry attractiveness can also be measured from the entry and exit barrier matrix as shown in Figure 5.1 (Porter 1980).

The best choice of industry for diversification or even for a first time entry would be that which has high entry and low exit barriers as there will be lesser competition in that space because of a high entry barrier and if the new entrant has not been able to make it good, it is easy to exit because of a low exit barrier. Industries where both entry and exit barriers are high are capable of giving high returns but are

FIGURE 5.1: ENTRY AND EXIT BARRIERS

Exit Barrier

	Low	High
Low	Low Profits Stable Returns	Low Profits Risky Returns
High	High Profits Stable Returns	High Profits Risky Returns

Entry Barrier

Source: Porter 1980.

at the same time risky. Very high capital investment is required for these kind of industries and, therefore, it is not easy to get out from these investments if the new entrant is not doing well. These are also high technology sectors. Low entry and low exit are those involving low technology such as the FMCG sector. But in these sectors, players make the entry barriers high by creating a big brand and spending a huge amount of marketing expenditure. For example, it is easy to start manufacturing carbonated soft drink beverages but big players like Coke and Pepsi have created high entry barriers because of big brands and huge marketing support they provide, which a new entrant can never match. With the entry of Coke and Pepsi, all other players, local (Parle, Campa and Duke) and multinational (Cadbury), have exited from this sector.

In the long run, the rate of returns available from competing in an industry is a function of its underlying structure. Diversification cannot create shareholder value unless new industries have favourable structures that support returns exceeding the cost of capital. If this is not possible, the company must either have the strength to restructure the industry or gain a competitive advantage where returns are well above the industry average.

Quite often companies skip the attractiveness test and take the plunge because of an untested belief that the industry fits very closely in its own business. But unless the close fit allows a substantial competitive advantage, the efforts are likely to result in poor returns.

The experience of the UB Group shows how important the attractiveness test is. During the Janata government days, the late Vittal Mallya expanded his business by buying out breweries and distilleries that had turned sick because of prohibition. The gambit made sense. Since the UB Group was a leading player in the brewing and distilling industry, it satisfied the attractiveness test and created synergies within the group. When the same group diversified later into electronics and engineering, it ignored the test and paid for it.

Many companies ignore the attractiveness test because of the low cost of entry into a particular industry. But even if the initial price is low, a one-shot gain will not offset a perpetually poor business. A large number of companies that rushed into fast-growing industries like personal computers and food processing became sick in the subsequent shakeout. The reason is that they must have mistaken early growth for long-term profit potential. Industries are profitable not because they are high-tech or have a low entry cost, they are profitable only if their structures are attractive.

Diversification cannot build shareholder value if the cost of entry into a new business eats up its expected future returns. Strong market forces, however, are at work trying to do just that. For example, a company can enter a new industry either through an acquisition or as a start up. An acquirer beats the market only if it pays a price which does not reflect the prospects of the new unit. Yet, multiple bidders are commonplace. Information flows rapidly with investment bankers and other intermediaries working overtime to make the market as efficient as possible.

These forces jack up the acquisition premiums—often disproportionately. Philips Morris paid more than four times book value for the 7Up company. Simple arithmetic shows that profits had to be more than quadrupled to sustain the pre-acquisition return on an investment. But Philip Morris was in an arena where several soft drinks giants engaged in a high pitch marketing battle. And, with its limited marketing prowess, the company could do little and was subsequently forced to disinvest its stake in 7Up (Porter 1985a).

In the excitement of finding an appealing new business, companies often forget the implications of other influencing factors that determine the success of the enterprise in the post acquisition period.

Sometimes acquirers forget to apply the cost of entry test. The more attractive an industry, the more expensive it is to get into. Coke paid a very high price to acquire Parle brands in India as the proposition was very attractive.

The most crucial test for taking decision on potential acquisition candidate is the synergy with the existing business. Either of the following scenarios must be envisaged here: The parent corporation must be able to buy some significant competitive advantage into the new unit. Or, the new unit must offer potential for significant advantage to the corporation.

Sometimes, the benefits to the new unit accrue only once at the point of entry when the parent company goes in for a major strategy overhaul or brings in a first-rate management team. Competitive advantage can also be derived if the new unit can market its product through the well developed distribution system of its sister units.

When the benefit to the new unit comes only once, it makes little sense for the parent company to hold on to the new unit over the long term. This is because once the one-time gains are obtained the diversified company no longer adds value to offset the inevitable costs imposed on the unit. It ends up being forced to sell the unit and free up corporate resources.

The most important issue in any acquisition is to understand what exactly is being acquired. For example, if it is a brand, the buying prices for manufacturing and other assets should not be disproportionate. If such assets come along with the brand, the task would be to get rid of them as soon as possible so that resources are freed up.

Sometimes, new businesses can be acquired just to kill competition to ensure faster growth of the current business, but then, profit from higher growth of the present business should be able to offset the cost of acquiring the competitor's business either in the short or medium term.

Merging to be Competitive

Of late, we have seen a lot of organisations going in for some sort of corporate restructuring in order to derive cost and operational synergies. Leading among those are the mergers of Lipton and Brooke Bond and also the merger of all breweries under one strategic business unit (SBU) and all distilleries under another SBU (United Spirits Ltd) in case of United Breweries (UB) Group. The UB Group was managing its individual breweries and distilleries earlier as separate profit centres with all functions being duplicated under each unit and reporting to its chief executive officer. Now, with the formation of SBUs, a lot of this duplication of costs and efforts has been eliminated. In fact, all large Indian companies and multinationals have completed some kind of restructuring.

Broadly, there are two kinds of corporate restructuring—external restructuring and internal restructuring. External restructuring normally arises out of strategic alliance and joint ventures, corporate sell-offs, divestment, acquisition and mergers, diversification, corporate split offs, etc.; internal restructuring arises out of the need for making faster decisions or even simply for activities undertaken for waste elimination such as business process re-engineering or activity value analysis which often leads to the formation of SBUs.

The various operational synergies that can be derived through corporate restructuring will include product line extensions, collective bargaining power, rationalisation of distribution and freight costs, sales tax benefit, gain of market share, access to export market or entry into the international market, forward and backward linkages, sharing of research and development resources and access to new products. The organisations will have either one or a combination of these benefits in mind before embarking upon restructuring. For example, Brooke Bond merged with Lipton and derived benefits of reduced distribution costs and sales tax. It will also have control of a larger market share.

Restructuring can also be necessary for gaining operational synergies, which will include saving a group company from financial bankruptcy or for initiating a turnaround. Financial synergy may also mean tax savings, increased borrowing capacity and stabilized earnings, etc.

Although the market forces and changed business environment have been the major reasons behind all corporate restructuring that we have witnessed in the recent past, studies on this subject have also revealed that environmental shocks caused by major technological shifts and deregulation are also associated with the changes in corporate strategy. Still another potential macro explanation advanced for the increase in all forms of corporate restructuring activity in the 1990s is the 'band wagon' effect.

There is no readymade solution for the restructuring process and the solution will always be species specific. That is why we have seen that on one hand, two large organisations are merged to increase market competitiveness and on the other, one large organisation has been divided into two or three smaller business units catering to specific business lines.

While Brooke Bond-Lipton is an example of the first category, dividing AT&T into three separate companies and also breaking up of consumer product business and healthcare and pharmaceutical business under two separate independent companies by SmithKline Beecham are classic examples of the second category. Similarly, the cement business of Larsen and Toubro (L&T) is de-merged into another company by the name of Ultratech India Ltd where Grasim Ltd of Aditya Birla Group has a 30 per cent holding. Although the motivation for embarking upon organisational restructuring has arisen out of the same need to be more competitive, its execution could be different.

Perils of Non-related Diversification

Multinational corporations are generally seen to have a focused approach towards their brand and business. Those MNCs which have non-related business and fragmented brands are now disposing off their profitable businesses to enable them to concentrate on their areas of core competencies. For example, Glaxo sold its profitable food business to Heinz to enable them to concentrate on their pharmaceutical business. Making profit can no longer be the sole criterion to continue in business.

It has now been accepted that one cannot run global operations on a diversified portfolio and brands because it is not possible for any corporation to have the same level of knowledge base on a wide variety of non-related portfolios. It is, therefore, essential to concentrate the resources on one's core business activity. Violating this principle can often become disastrous.

Indian business houses seem to be taking pride in claiming that they have a diversified business without realizing that, sooner or later, they will face competition in each of those diversified businesses from global masters of the game who will redefine the business they are running hitherto and will dictate new ground rules.

The decision to diversify in a new venture should always be taken with extreme care and venturing into unknown non-related areas should always be avoided. Those who think that by hiring competent people and buying one time technology (even if it is the best at that point of time), they can run any industry successfully, might learn lessons by paying a heavy price. To prove this point, more than a dozen examples can be cited in the Indian context and I chose to describe the UB Group experience.

UB Group's business is mainly alcoholic beverages (beer and liquor), food and pharmaceuticals. When Vittal Mallya died, his son Vijay Mallya took over a highly profitable, over Rs 8,000 million group with excellent marketing and distribution infrastructure. In all three categories, UB Group was the market leader and more importantly, it had an excellent manufacturing base. Vittal Mallya used to acquire new companies only in the areas of his prime business interest with the sole motive to gain control over the manufacturing base and distribution infrastructure to channelise sales of his own brands of liquor, beer or food.

When the Moraji Desai government introduced prohibition and the entire liquor industry was panicking, Vittal Mallya was acquiring one liquor company after another for a song. He realized that prohibition is unsustainable and, sooner or later, will be withdrawn. That wise decision of his has proved extremely beneficial for the group in the later years to keep the group's dominance as number one in the industry category.

But when his son took over, instead of concentrating on the core activities of the group's business, he started nurturing the ambition of getting into all kinds of non-related areas and core sector activities. He shifted the focus of the entire business to areas like telecommunications, petrochemicals, engineering, fertilizer and air services, etc., in which the group had no strength or knowledge whatsoever. Vijay Mallya thought that by hiring executives to manage these high technology oriented high investment projects, they could be made successful. The result was inevitable. What have we seen in the later years? United Telecom became a sick company and was referred to Board for Industrial and Financial Reconstruction (BIFR), UB Petro with its associated company sold to Southern Petrochemical Industries Corporation Limited (SPIC). Hindustan Polymer, a profit making company, became sick, UB Air was a non starter, Mangalore Chemicals' losses were mounting and UB Vendor Horst did not even get off the ground. Similarly, Western India Erectors and Best & Crompton too were sold.

And, to fund all these businesses, the group had to sell its core business activities such as food to Brooke Bond and withdraw its key holding from Cadburys. The group had to significantly dilute its presence in the pharmaceutical sectors. The liquidity problem was so much that the group could not fund the growth, expansion, upgradation and marketing activities of its core businesses. The profits of the core businesses such as liquor and beer, etc., were diverted to the loss-making units. As a result, the growth of the core activities suffered. During that period, competitors exploited the weaknesses of the UB Group and expanded their base and market share.

Experienced people have left the group to join the competition and helped them to create new brands. UB's arch rival in the liquor industry, Shaw Wallace, had displayed considerable growth by acquiring many regional breweries and introducing many new brands which the UB Group's trained people have helped them to establish. UB's Chairman Vijay Mallya has realised the situation in the later years and has now been focusing on his core business activities. The group is again showing signs of growth and progress in its core categories. Not only that, the group has acquired the liquor business of Shaw Wallace to become a dominant player in the category. The focus approach has helped the UB Group to acquire Whyte & Mackay, a leading Scotch whiskey manufacturer in UK. Its Bagpiper brand is going to soon overtake Johnnie Walker sales to emerge as the number one brand in terms of worldwide sales. Thus, the UB Group is now emerging as a global group in the liquor industry.

Focus and concentration on the core business is a surer way to survive in the business.

Saving through the Supply Chain Management

The function of purchasing is becoming increasingly important in corporate activities because it has now been realized that about 50–70 per cent of the value of sales accounts for material purchased depending on the type of industry. For some sectors, it is even higher. For example, in consumer electronics, this accounts for even up to 85 per cent of sales as almost everything is bought out in this industry.

Thus, great saving potential exists in efficient purchasing. Large corporations are now increasingly focusing on this function and the trend is shifting from the earlier 'world-class-manufacturing' (10–20 per cent of cost) to 'world-class-buying' (60–70 per cent of cost).

As Michael Porter (1985a) said, 'Cost is the single-most competitive advantage one can have'. And, the thumb rule says, for every rupee saved in cost, retail price will be reduced by Rs 2.50 to 3.50 depending on the company's policy and trade structure (if a product is produced at a cost of Re 1.00, it can be sold at a price varying from Rs 2.50 to 3.50, or even higher, depending on the product category and trade structure).

In most organisations, purchase activity is considered to be a factory function. The purchase executive in these organisations reports to the factory manager and is required to use only clerical skills of floating tenders, obtaining quotations, preparing comparative charts of the quotes obtained, negotiations and finally placing purchase orders and follow-up till the goods are received at the factory. The factory manager normally clears the name of the party on whom the order has to be placed. It can be assumed that his prime considerations would be current stock level, lead time of ordering and the lowest quote.

A better method of purchase activity is to manage 'lowest unit cost' at the level of the strategic business unit, which means buying division-wise rather than factory-wise. Here, emphasis is on cost analysis and it is recognised that negotiation skill is a key task to cost management.

It was then realised that there are many items and most often, bulk of the items purchased at the divisional level are common and inventory levels are built up for the same item at various units, which, if combined, can serve the requirement at a much lower level of stock. Besides, better negotiation is possible if it is done at one point for larger quantities for the entire organisation. This way one can reduce not only the number of people performing the purchase function but can also get the advantage of a bulk purchase discount. This would lead to either centralised purchasing or unit-wise coordinated purchasing. This would help the organisations in developing corporate purchase policies.

Centralised or coordinated purchasing led to the development of cross-functional purchasing which is basically centre-led with execution at the strategic business unit level. At this stage of development, there was more use of cross-functional teams to solve problems.

Activities such as vendor development, total system cost analysis, supplier certification, challenging specifications, make versus buy decisions, etc., were getting increasing focus in order to meet the challenge of ever-increasing cost of purchase in relation to sales and also increased competition, where lower cost means a competitive advantage.

Today emphasis is on world-class supply chain management. This entails cross-functional supplier development teams and co-located suppliers across the globe and regions.

The activities important to world-class supply chain management include selection of suppliers, vendor-buyer relationship design and management, upgrading supplier capabilities by collaborating on advanced technology with suppliers, identifying areas where supplier partnership makes sense and finally, continuous improvement measures of supplier performance. It is, therefore, a two-way process, which means help your supplier to improve upon his cost and quality in order to help yourself.

One might think that to have world-class supply chain management capabilities, one should be working in a multinational or transnational organisation. It is not necessarily so. Even an Indian organisation can have a world-class supply chain management team and capabilities and can derive cost advantage to compete in the global market, provided the organisation makes deliberate attempts to achieve that status.

The most important barriers in achieving world-class purchasing capabilities are information and people.

The total information regarding suppliers' database, new technology, alternative sources of material, knowledge about new specifications, new materials, capability to evaluate suppliers' cost and technology and ability to help vendors to improve upon their cost by employing new technology and other cost-saving measures, so that vendors can pass on these benefits to buyers after retaining the legitimate profit, are key to the success of such a programme. It is no longer a question of getting the best deal by employing one's negotiation skills with suppliers, rather, it is the question of helping one's supplier to get the best—a 'win–win' situation.

That, of course, does not mean that excellent negotiation skills are no longer required. Negotiation tactics can play a very important role in supply chain management. Some good negotiators are known to put off the discussion on commercial terms with the suppliers till the last minute so that suppliers become desperate to close the deal and thereby lose out on the negotiations.

Other commonly known tactics used by the negotiators include pitting one vendor against another. These traditional tactics can only yield very limited results—may be up to 1 to 5 per cent. The real advantage from the negotiation process can come through the buyer's knowledge of the vendor's activities, process and cost thereof.

The other important activities which help and provide leverage are upstream from the negotiation process where the product is designed and specified, where make versus buy decisions are made and where supplier-customer operations linkages such as the size of shipment, frequency and scheduling, etc., are defined. These up-stream activities can have even 30–50 per cent cost impact on purchases or even a material requirement can altogether be eliminated through alternative product design. This aspect is often overlooked by many organisations.

Industries should constantly benchmark their purchase efficiency as a measure of cost to sales per unit with competitive industries to enable them to improve upon this aspect further and to derive competitive advantage.

For certain categories of industries, this is critical to survival such as for retail store chains and garment and shoe manufacturing industries, etc., where the entire game is about quality and cost. Bata India Ltd has gone through turbulent times managing the supply chain. Their cost of production and procurement was higher and the competition was making inroads in the shoe industry. Just a big name is no longer sufficient—Bata was earlier the leader, today it has to struggle to survive. Through a series of supply chain related initiatives, Bata India was able to regain a lot of its lost ground. This can be witnessed from its improved performance.

In the past, many companies have overlooked the importance of supply chain management but those few who have taken steps to optimise are now enjoying strategic advantages. Best practices in supply chain management provide competitive advantage along the three critical dimensions of cost, quality and time.

Manufacturing Out-house versus In-house

In the United States, one product out of every 20 launched really succeed; which means success rate of new products is only five per cent. The situation is no better in India. Scores of consumer products are being launched every year and only a few remain in the market-place as successful brands and millions of rupees are being spent on brand building.

Because of uncertainties that prevail regarding the success of a new brand or product, marketing companies do not generally want to invest in setting up manufacturing facilities. Instead, they prefer someone else to produce the product which they can then market. Those who became ambitious and went ahead to make a significant amount of capital investment in fixed assets, often paid a heavy price. For example, Britannia Industries made investment in a soya-based product and set up a plant in Vidisha in Madhya Pradesh only to get out of it by disposing it off after a couple of years to SM Dyechem. Indications are that SM Dyechem is also in trouble. Henkel has set up a large plant in a joint venture with SPIC to produce zeolite-based environment friendly detergent and is now thriving by producing detergents for Hindustan Unilever as a contract manufacturer. Colgate Palmolive had set up a large soap manufacturing plant, with an ambitious plan to support their soap brands and also to introduce new soap brands, which it had to withdraw subsequently.

Examples are many. When no one can guarantee whether a new product—particularly a consumer product—will finally succeed or not, the question of whether to invest money for setting up a large plant is often debated. The answer definitely lies in really knowing what one's business is.

It is getting increasingly difficult to predict which new product, particularly a consumer product, will succeed. The dilemma, hence, is whether to invest in setting up a large plant or not.

An organisation is generally based on a task or mission and the more clearly this task is defined, the better focused the organisation is and, hence, has a better chance to succeed in the competitive market. For example, the Coca Cola Corporation is in the business of selling cola and Kellogg in that of selling breakfast cereal. They will not hesitate to make upfront investment in setting up a modern production facility because this is their only business and nobody knows this business better than they do and, hence, they will have to make it work for them wherever they go. If need be, they will take a very long-term view of the business and make upfront investment. Kellogg has reported profit in Mexico after 20 years of operation. In India they are already 10 years old and still making losses.

Once the task of the organisation is extended over a broader category, the investment might become risky. For example, if a company's strategic business area is defined as household goods, chances are that out of the many products that the company has in its basket, some will fail and if the investment is locked up in creating production facilities for those items, it would not only amount to a waste but would also create a trauma in the organisation. Once you invest in the production facilities, you also employ the labour force to run the plant, and if a project fails to take off, withdrawing from the business becomes very difficult—which is much easier to manage if you have made no capital investment.

There are many other advantages associated with the decision to get the product made out-house. Generally, large companies subcontract manufacturing jobs to small-scale industries who enjoy many benefits in taxes and their overhead costs are also much less in comparison to large-scale industries. Besides, they are more flexible in the sense that they can upgrade or downgrade production, or if need be, can switch over to producing something else without much of a trauma. If the product is excisable, the excise duty, which is paid at the manufacturer's transfer price, would be much lower. If, on the other hand, the marketer becomes the manufacturer, excise is payable at the marketer's selling price, which would be much higher. The end result is that if a product is subcontracted outhouse, it would be available to the marketer at a much lower cost than if the marketer were to decide to manufacture the product himself. This facility, of course, in later years was with-drawn and excise duty was correlated with the maximum retail price (MRP) of the product for branded consumer goods but still, sourcing from a third party is often less costly. Of course, the manufacturer will retain its profit margin before transferring the rights of the product to the marketing company. But that would be too small a price to pay in comparison to the investment and the associated risk that the marketing company has to take. Besides, even after paying manufacturing profit to the sub-contractor, the product still works out to be cheaper.

There are two kinds of sub-contract manufacturing agreements that are in practice, namely Conversion Contract and Principal-to-Principal Contract. In the former arrangement, all material inputs are supplied by the principal and contract manufacturer only does the job work and charges on a per unit basis to cover his cost and profit. The goods in this case will be said to have been manufactured by the principal.

In the latter arrangement, all inputs are procured by the contract manufacturers and one party exclusively manufactures the product for the other party to sell. Which kind of arrangement is preferable depend on the tax structure of the product to be manufactured and also on the company's policy.

Large companies, including the multinational corporation which have recently set up their operations in India, are all following this approach by getting their product made outside in their own brand name, as per their own formulations and methods of manufacturing under their own quality control checks and supervision. By drafting the agreement suitably, one can keep the formula and its method of manufacturing a secret but subcontract manufacturers automatically acquire this knowledge. This does not bother the brand marketer as brand is much more valuable a property than the product formulation.

All capital investments are viable at a minimum economic capacity, which means that if the plant is operated below the break-even capacity, there will be cash loss. In a new product launch, getting the market share either from the existing player or from the expanded market does not happen overnight. Because of the dynamic market conditions, frequent fluctuations of demand also cannot be ruled out which can alter the financial feasibility of an investment in a fixed asset. By contracting the manufacturing operations out-house, all these uncertainties and risks can also be avoided. Some of the very successful products and brands that one sees in the market and uses regularly are not really manufactured by the company that markets and owns those brands. Examples are many—Dettol Soap and Harpic of Reckitt and Coleman (now known as Reckitt Benckiser India Ltd) and many other products. These products are manufactured through subcontract units. The Dettol soap is a very successful and profitable brand in the premium segment. But the soap is manufactured by Godrej Soaps Ltd and VVF. Of late, of course, Dettol buys the noodles from VVF and converts them to soap in their own plant set up in Uttaranchal which enjoys a tax holiday.

There are, of course, some problems faced by the companies while organizing out-house manufacturing of their products. The subcontractor might give an attractive price to start with to market the product but once the product is a success, might try to create pressure to increase the price unreasonably. To overcome such a situation one can consider, if volume justifies, more than one subcontractor for each product.

Other problems associated with the subcontracting operation include disruption of production due to strike or lockout which can jeopardize the marketer's operation. But, these things can also happen in one's own plant. If there are any improvements or cost-economy derived by the sub-contractor in these manufacturing operations, it is unlikely that he would pass on such benefits to the marketer. For these reasons, one should work very closely with the sub-contractors considering them not as outsiders but as partners in one's own value chain so that problems and also benefits can be jointly shared and resolved.

Finally, there is a social and economic purpose that this kind of relationship of subcontractors and marketers serve and that is: If large corporations do not subcontract either partly or wholly, their manufacturing requirement to small-scale sectors, the very survival of the latter will be difficult, if not impossible. This association, therefore, is for mutual benefit. Besides, small and medium sectors are a source of large employment avenues, and are, therefore, a part of the mainstream of the economy and harnessing that will only help improve the overall economy of the country and, hence, the sustainability.

Chapter Summary

In this chapter we discussed major acquisition, diversification, mergers and other forms of growth strategies. Companies deliver growth and shareholders' expectations either organically or through acquisitions and mergers. Post liberalisation, we have seen a series of mega mergers and acquisitions. We have discussed the basic rules for acquisitions in order to make those decisions really meaningful. If the prospective acquisition candidate does not provide any synergy it will not serve the growth objective. Rarely have non related diversification or acquisition worked.

Other key growth strategies include the critical decisions related to managing supply chain and getting efficiency in the system and the manufacturing strategy to decide whether to focus on key strengths and functions or do it better at a much lower cost. Now a large part of the companies' manufacturing operations are outsourced to capture incremental value for the customers. Procurement functions have become increasingly important. Organisations are required to design appropriate procurement strategies to reduce the cost of the product. Many cases have been suggested for the growth strategies that companies can pursue highlighting pitfalls and the measures to overcome those.

VI

Portfolio Management

Portfolio Analysis

IN ORDER to decide the allocation of resources to various business portfolios that an organisation can have, we normally do an analysis using the Boston Consulting Group's (BCG 1976) Portfolio Analysis Matrix (Figure 6.1).

Cash Cows will generate resources to support the stars of the business. The resources should be withdrawn from the businesses which are classified as Dog (low market share and low growth category). Businesses have limited resources and, therefore, have to channelise the resource which can go to deliver better performance and help build the future stars for the business in order to create a dominant position in the industry. For this purpose, the BCG Portfolio Matrix is quite helpful in understanding the performance and future of the various businesses that the organisation has.

If required, some of the businesses even need to be even divested. McKinsey–GE Investment Priority Screen also helps in taking these decisions. If a business division is not adding significant value to the business or is less attractive, it is better to sell those businesses to free up the resources which can support well performing and more attractive businesses that the organisation has. It is also to be noted that businesses have to be sold when the residual value of the business

FIGURE 6.1: BCG MATRIX

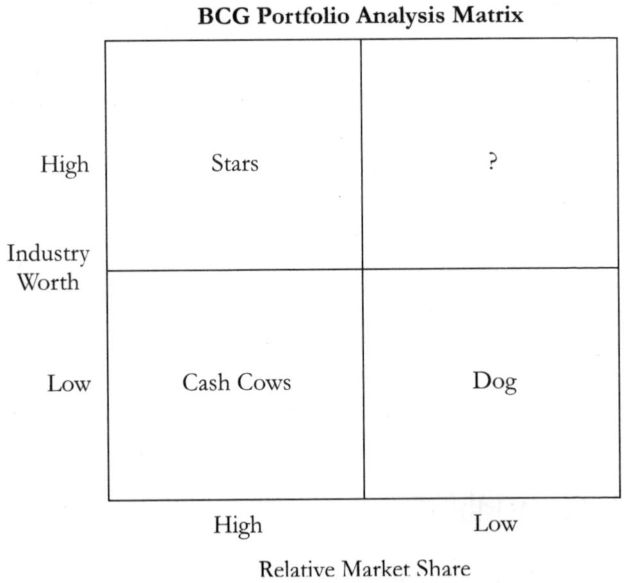

BCG Portfolio Analysis Matrix

	High Relative Market Share	Low Relative Market Share
High Industry Worth	Stars	?
Low	Cash Cows	Dog

High   Low

Relative Market Share

Source: BCG 1976.

is still high. One should not wait for the time when the value that a business delivers is totally eroded because there is no buyer for those businesses. When residual value is still good, but cannot be held at that level for long, is the right time to dispose of the business. McKinsey–GE Screen provides a good framework for this analysis (Figure 6.2).

Joint Ventures

Joint ventures (JVs) are normally pursued when an organisation needs a partner to supplement its own capabilities to perform in a given market environment. Sometimes it becomes even essential to pursue the joint venture option, particularly when businesses need either technical or business knowledge in an area. JVs also help in reducing the risk of the business because it has to be shared. There are other occasions when one needs to go for the joint venture route.

**FIGURE 6.2: McKINSEY–GE INVESTMENT
DIVESTMENT MATRIX**

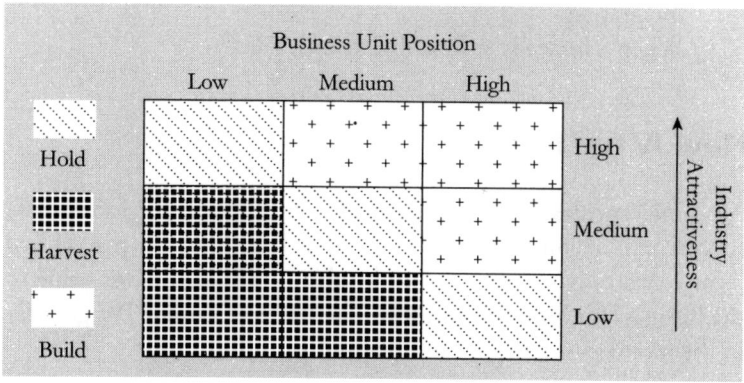

Source: http://www.mbaknol.com/strategic-management/gemckinsey-matrix.

When is a JV worthwhile

- Company needs to review its dedicated internal resources.
- When a company needs infusion of new resources and capabilities.
- If the required skills and experience are not available in-house and cannot be developed on a short notice, an external vehicle may be a good option.
- New business opportunity is not the company's core competency.
- When the objective is to enter a new region, product area or customer segment or develop entirely new capabilities.
- Alliances have a lower success rate when control is important.
- A joint venture typically involves no premium unlike M&A where a buyer will normally have to buy a control premium of 20–50 per cent over the current stock price.
- A JV or a contractual alliance is a safer alternative in terms of integrating an acquired company.
- JV with equity participation is a better option when there is gain by integrating assets or liabilities or when the size of the acquisition is large requiring setting up a new company.

- Contractual alliance is required when value creation is driven by improved coordination and learning, not resource integration.
- When risk needs to be reduced and shared.

How JV has fared

All joint ventures have not delivered results. But still, globally, the success rate of joint ventures is not that bad. Over 50 per cent of joint ventures have been seen to be able to add significant value to the business for both the partners. The status of various JVs globally in the recent past has been summarised as:

- More than 5,000 joint ventures and more contractual alliances have been launched worldwide in the past five years.
- The largest 100 JVs represent more than $350 bn in combined annual revenues.
- Both equity and contractual alliances can be ideal for

  - Managing risk in uncertain markets.
  - Sharing the cost of large scale capital investments.
  - Injecting new found entrepreneurial spirit into mature business.

- In 1991, McKinsey assessed the performance of 49 joint ventures and alliances and found that 51 per cent were successful.
- In 2001, McKinsey again assessed the outcome of more than 2,000 alliance announcement and the success rate was 53 per cent.

Many JVs have failed and the reasons could be numerous starting from mismatches in their respective cultures and value systems in managing the business, desire to dominate over the other partner, taking divergent view on the business and its future and resource constraint in terms of one of the partners. It has been seen that JVs fail both when businesses are doing well as well as when businesses are not delivering the expected outcome. One has to learn managing a joint venture and derive synergy in operation for the benefit of both the partners in the game. Other reasons for the failure of JVs are:

- Badly planned and executed launch
- Lack of attention
- Strategic conflict between allied companies
- Governance gridlock
- No operational synergies

Key challenges of JVs

- Building and maintaining strategic alignment
- Creating a governance system that promotes shared decision making
- Managing the economic interdependencies between the corporate parents and JV:
  - Starbucks: Coffee purchasing and roasting, creation of beverage concentrate and quality assurance
  - PepsiCo: Distribution of JV products to grocery, convenience and mass market stores
  - Starbucks/Pepsi jointly: Marketing and Product development
- Building the organisation

Managing JVs for success in a cross-cultural and diverse socio-economic set up will have many challenges, which have been summarised in Table 6.1. It is of paramount importance that interests of all parties involved in JVs be kept in mind and a transparent process is put in place at the beginning itself to avoid any conflict later. It has been seen that JVs start breaking up both when they are not doing well and also when they are doing very well.

Managing strategic conflict

It is important to give sufficient attention to managing the potential conflict if a joint venture has to succeed. All strategic differences

TABLE 6.1: KEY CHALLENGES FOR MANAGING JVs

	Strategic Issues	Governance Issues	Economic and Organisational Issues
Key JV challenges	Partners in the JV may have different strategic interests that may affect the nature and degree of integration.	Relative share of control of the JV, which can complicate decision making process. Parent company has separate reporting systems, processes and metrics.	Transfer price can become an issue. Parent office offers many resources to JV, which affects the economics. Performance of JV is less transparent when compared with that of partners wholly owned businesses. Managing cultural differences as well as conflicting incentives and career paths.
Key to successful JV operation	Align the JV partners interests around JVs objective upfront. Set clear goals and realistic objective acceptable to partners in JV.	Set clear governance criteria and processes. Set clear protocols for decision making.	Establish fair and transparent pricing policy and systems. Establish good risk and performance management system for JV. Create a compelling value proposition for JV employee and secure commitment from key staff and managers in the parent company.

Source: Developed by the author.

between parents are unlikely to get resolved during the deal making phase. It is essential to develop a comprehensive business plan incorporating:

- How and where the JV will compete
- Project how the JV might expand beyond its initial scope
- Set financial targets
- Plan capital expenditures

- Create a blueprint for the organisation
- Need to draw up performance contracts that make key JV managers accountable

It is also important to manage the inevitable setbacks by acting quickly and by paying adequate attention to communication.

Managing interdependencies

Some of the key considerations for managing interdependencies are:

- Start addressing economic interdependencies as soon as agreement begins to look likely.
- Dedicate resources to resolve interdependencies up front:
  - Which services and resources each parent would provide.
  - Construct service level agreement that specify transfer pricing and access rights, etc.
- Challenge and limit interdependencies.
- Joint teams must develop transparent and honest methodologies for calculating transfer pricing.

It is necessary to create the right organisation model for successful JVs:

- Choose the organisational model carefully. This could be:
  - Independent
  - Dependent
  - Interdependent
- Select people carefully who want to join the team
- Obtain commitments from parent company staff

Forging Alliances with Foreign Collaborators

During the 1970s and 1980s, there was a boom in acquisitions and mergers in the international business scenario. The same was observed in India as well. But in the 1990s, particularly after liberalisation, there has been a significant rise in international joint ventures. We have not heard of any big acquisition after Dunlop and Shaw Wallace which were acquired by Manu Chhabria during the late 1980s. The merger of Ponds, Lipton and Brooke Bond with Hindustan Lever is the result of international acquisitions which had taken place during the late 1980s.

Many a times, joint ventures fail because of various problems and issues which are often either overlooked while selecting the partners or are a result of mismanagement of those issues. In the Indian context, two examples are Kothari-General Foods and Mody-S. C. Johnson (SCJ). In both these cases, their foreign collaborators walked out after a couple of years of the association. And, interestingly enough, both General Foods and SCJ are keen to re-enter India but the pre-condition of their re-entry is to get permission for a 100 per cent owned entity; and, never a joint venture again. They got permission to start a wholly owned entity in due course of time and, in this way, started their operations subsequently.

Often cultural differences are cited as the reason for the failure of joint ventures but that cannot be the sole reason. Joint ventures can be of many types such as know-how and patent licensing or technical collaboration, franchising or even co-promoting a business with equity participation. Whatever might be the type of joint venture, the most important aspect one should consider is the matching of objectives and goals of two or more prospective partners. Often conflict arises because of non-matched business philosophy that the partners have, which starts surfacing once they start working together. If business houses are getting into a different line of business for which a joint venture partner is being sought, so that all technical marketing and managerial expertise are brought into the business by the prospective partner, it is imperative that the first party undergoes cultural changes to get adjusted to the new culture required to run the new business.

The general perception is that broad mutual understanding and reaching an agreement on key issues are enough to initiate a joint venture partnership. But in international joint venture contracts, it is absolutely essential that extra care is taken in framing the type of joint venture agreement contemplated and some ground rules are observed in writing such a contract. More importantly, nothing should be left to the imagination or to an attitude that problems and issues can be resolved mutually as and when, and if, they arise. The contract should provide an equitable net gain, which is roughly in proportion to the resources they have put in. But, it should ensure that both sides feel happy with what they take out of the joint venture. Some form of a reward structure should be in place so that the joint venture does not get reduced to a 'minimal engagement' partnership.

Management control is another area that often leads to disputes, although, it is relatively simple to address and is largely based on the shareholding pattern of the partners in the joint venture. But control should reflect the quality and cost of inputs and the company with the greater control bears the lion's share of the managerial costs. Management controls directly linked with shareholding pattern do not always solve all issues because minority shareholders also need to have a say. Because there is no partnership, ultimately all decisions are forced through by the majority shareholders. It is, therefore, important that minority shareholding is reflected in the equitable control.

Sometimes joint ventures are created from the thinking that the new venture could be a source of selling one of the partner's product or services, which means an income without any marketing and selling efforts. Such an arrangement is an expression of lack of confidence in the partnership and there are a number of instances to indicate that such collaboration ventures do not last.

There are many such joint ventures in India where the foreign partner has supplied the plant and equipment and process technology to the joint venture at the market price (or may be at a higher than market price) and have taken 10–20 per cent equity in the new venture. In such an arrangement, foreign partners are also seen to provide buy-back guarantees subject to acceptable prices and quality so that the Indian partners find them more attractive. But after selling the plant and equipment and setting up the project at a fee, these foreign partners are not to be seen anywhere because they have already recovered their equity holding and would be looking around for yet another joint venture partner, leaving everything to their Indian partner to manage. Buy-back guarantees have no meaning because price and quality will be the very excuses that the foreign partner will give for not taking or buying back the product. Getting into the trap of such exploitation should be avoided. In India many businesses have suffered falling into this trap of forming joint ventures.

Prospective foreign partners, most often, are not familiar with the local rules and regulations and; therefore, it is necessary for their Indian partner to make them clearly understand the business rules, regulations, laws and ethics that are practiced and considered important in India so that nobody in the partnership leaves anything to assumptions.

Joint ventures also tend to fail when Indian partners resort to making substandard products and take an attitude of profiteering to the discomfort of their foreign partner. For example, Indian Compressors Ltd (ICL), a small firm in Okhla, has a technical collaboration with Cryo Pumps A.G. Switzerland, to manufacture cryogenic pumps in India. Indian Compressors Ltd has no technical capabilities and, therefore, produces substandard quality pumps and sells them at an exorbitantly high price. Their client would obviously be the public sector from where orders can be obtained through the tendering process and that too for a product category which is imported and ICL is the only local party manufacturing cryogenic pump with foreign collaboration in India.

People tend to resort to sign joint ventures with good foreign companies which have a name and standing in the international market only to increase the prospects of their current business. They, in fact, have little or no interest in the new venture for which the agreement has been signed.

The most important thing about the success of a joint venture is to build a relationship based on minimum outcome scenario and by creating realistic expectations. Over expectations about the prospects of the joint venture often lead to discomfort when the actual outcome is not in line with the expectations. It is, therefore, very important that total ground work, including a detailed market research, is done before making any business projections in a joint venture.

Although it is true that many issues can be sorted out through negotiations and discussions in an open culture even if they arise after the joint venture has been formed, adequate care and some basic precautions need to be followed. Also, selection of the partner is as important as managing the process of forming the collaboration, and managing the joint venture successfully thereafter. After all who wants to have a Coke-Parle type of a joint venture where disputes started from the day the partnership was signed.

Re-examining the Brand Premium

How much premium can a consumer pay for the brand name and image associated with that brand? That is the question that many multinational corporations and corporate analysts are now seriously addressing. There is no doubt that a good brand can demand a premium over smaller brands and store-label brands. But the question is how much? In the international market, smaller brands and store-label brands are exploiting the gap in price against established big brands and introducing me-too category products at lower prices.

In the Western countries, companies are seen to lose brand share and leadership position in a very short time—a trend not seen in the Indian market because market here is highly segmented and competition is much less. Brand loyalty in India is also high. With liberalisation, the situation here is also becoming very much similar. The value perception between two brands changes with education, exposure to media and product awareness. And, consumer societies and activists are trying to do exactly the same—helping to increase consumer awareness. When consumers become increasingly aware of the product constituents, performance, benefits and, hence, the value, the difference between the two brands reduces as long as quality is comparable. The premium of a brand is, thus, the value that consumers attach to unknown benefits and quality attributes. When this unknown becomes known, the premium reduces.

The global premium brands were created by large corporations through strategic marketing and after spending huge advertisement and promotional funds. They are now being challenged by smaller companies which can deliver an identical product through identical technology at a much competitive price.

Today consumers are very discerning and are not willing to pay for organisational inefficiencies. Organisations are, therefore, busy understanding the value of the brand and how much premium it can fetch to decide about the future course.

In 1993, the Unilever group had announced a huge restructuring programme to reduce costs and to re-examine the power of brands. John Campbell, European food analyst, at that time had said, 'Because Unilever is probably one of the most efficient producers, it suggests that other people will also have to look into their cost structure.'

Some marketing pundits think that brand building by advertisements will create loyal customers who would be willing to pay higher prices. They view decline in sales of a particular brand as a temporary phenomenon during inflation and believe that consumers abandon cheaper labels to return to familiar brands when recession ends and when they can afford the extra cost. Unilever's action obviously has cast doubts on this theory. Consumers are value-conscious and brands have to convince them that it is worth paying a premium. One can obviously not take a very simplistic view and proclaim the death of brands but the brands have to re-look at themselves.

Philip Morris cut the price of Marlboro cigarettes in the US in 1995, followed by Procter & Gamble, which reduced the price of its Pampers diapers. Large corporations are realizing that promotional money only helps to push the trade stock but not consumer off take. Under the circumstances, it is always better to reduce the price and pass on the benefit to consumers to establish new price-value-benefit-equation.

Restructuring might mean reducing the hierarchy and the number of people, disposal of non strategic business and resources reallocations, etc., to derive cost economy. In restructuring, sometimes very profitable businesses are also hived off if the organisation, in its own assessment does not consider itself as the 'natural owner' of the business. Corporations can be considered as a 'natural owner' provided they are a significant player in that category, have key core competencies in the business over competition, and set the consumer trend by providing leadership in the category. It was clearly established by various studies that profit is not the sole criterion for running a business unit if the business is not naturally one's own because in the long run such profit cannot be sustained in a highly competitive environment. Better growth is obtained if such resources are diverted to support the business which is naturally and strategically one's own.

Fighting for Brand Share

In the United States and in other developed economics, it is often seen that a corporation loses market share to its nearest competitor in a short span of time. This phenomenon is not generally witnessed in India where industry leaders seem to maintain their dominant position over years.

We have seen cases like 'Nirma' dominating the detergent segment and giving Hindustan Lever a run for its money. But 'Nirma' is in a different segment; its consumer profile is not the same as that of 'Surf'. Nirma's dominance in the cheaper price detergent segment forced Hindustan Lever to launch 'Wheel'.

After the exit of Coke, in 1977, Parle was able to gain market leadership, controlling about 60 per cent of the country's carbonated beverage industry from about 20 per cent when Coke was in India. But when a powerful multinational like Pepsi came and opened shop in India, Parle was initially seen to be quite scared about losing market share and offered a lot of resistance to Pepsi's entry. But, it could withstand the onslaught of Pepsi and maintain its leadership position till it 'gave in' to Coke.

In India, brand loyalty is quite high and it takes a long time for consumers to switch brands. But with increased levels of awareness and more media pressure, this trend may be reversed. So far we have seen competition in different price and consumer segments with various players trying to carve out a niche for themselves in the marketplace. With increased competition and more and more MNCs coming in, we will see a real fight for brand share. The mere fear of that fight has prompted many Indian business houses, particularly in the consumer products segment, to either go in for strategic alliances or sell out.

Whenever there is competition, it is the leader who is very vulnerable because smaller players have their own local pockets of strength and often go unnoticed. In order to fight a leader, it is essential to study its market behaviour and its strengths and weaknesses. It is the weaknesses of the leader that a competitor should exploit.

Most common weaknesses of a market leader could be (*a*) high cost structure, (*b*) age-old technology, (*c*) inefficient and outdated production facility, (*d*) built-in bureaucracy and complacency resulting in slow reaction time, etc. If these are coupled with other problems like pressure of shareholders to produce desired financial performance, which restricts the market leader's ability to spend and do innovations to fight competition, then the task of the competitor to gain market share from the leader becomes much simpler.

One of the easiest route to attack the leader is by offering quality at a lower price. It is generally seen that a leader can never fight on the price front because of its higher cost structure.

It should be remembered that quality should not be perceived as lower in relation to lower price. The quality should be as good or perceived to be even better than the leader and fight should be on price-quality equation. If the competitor can manage this communication exercise very efficiently, the possibility of success is very high.

Initially, this exercise may not be sustainable, as the bottom-line will come under serious pressure. But, if the competitor can maintain a low cost structure through innovation, thereby ensuring a good margin even at lower price, it will increase its ability to fight the leader. This task is easier if the leader depends heavily on the performance of the brand for its bottom line. In that case, the leader cannot afford to continue such a price war indefinitely—for, every rupee spent by the competitor, the leader has to spend many more. But, the MNCs have enormous financial muscle and staying power and can outlast the local leaders in a brand fight.

Another way to fight a leader is to launch a tactical war by launching schemes and activities in a localised geographical market, forcing the leaders to spend and react for protecting their share in the whole country and thereby spending many times more.

In both these exercises, the competitor must clearly understand the market structure, behaviour of the leader in that structure and how the leader was able to maintain its position in relation to its financial performance. One more important factor is that without having a real advantage in cost leadership, it would be counter productive to launch a price war with the leader. Look at Pepsi, the company has so far not made any profit and possibly if all its accumulated loss is taken into account, it is unlikely to make profit soon. Realising this, their partners, Punjab Agro, and Voltas have already dissociated from Pepsi. In spite of having multinational advantages, Pepsi could not create any significant dent in Parle's position because structurally, Pepsi was an unviable proposition. It has realised this and, therefore, later on tried to get out of those unviable investments. Besides, Pepsi did not have any cost leadership over Parle. In fact, Parle had the cost advantage.

The other way of gaining market share is to get into product variants or into such a segment which the market leader is not satisfying. There is always a first mover advantage. When all attempts of Parle, to establish a cola brand against Coke, in India, failed it launched Limca—a lemon-lime drink, in the early 1970s, which was able to keep the entire organisation going. When Nestle decided to get into the tomato ketchup market and when Kissan was the market leader, it expanded the market by introducing variants like sweet-n-sour ketchup. Once the competitor is seen to be innovative in a particular market segment, the leader will obviously be seen in poor light. This makes the competitor's task easier.

In the liberalized market environment, local leaders will have to prepare themselves for the transition not only by making the organisation lean and mean and by incorporating cost effective technology and superior marketing skill but also by realigning themselves with the changed market structure. Otherwise, they are likely to lose out to global brands.

Chapter Summary

Resources are not only limited but they are also scarce. Hence, putting resources to productive use is a key imperative of the business. Systematic decision making process for corporate resource allocation needs a careful study and analysis of the current business portfolio. This chapter deals with the various methods of portfolio analysis such as BCG matrix and GE-McKinsey Screen, etc. There are various modes of entry into a new geographical territory. One such option is formation and management of joint ventures and strategic alliances. It has been seen that about 50 per cent of joint ventures fail.

Unless adequate attention is given from the start of the formation of JVs, the experience in the subsequent years will not be rewarding and will often lead to failure. The chapter deals with such issues and how to manage the joint venture conflicts in order to ensure success of these joint ventures and alliances.

Consumers are becoming more educated and knowledgeable about what they buy. Consumer activist groups help consumers to learn about what goes into the products as well as educate them about their rights and privileges. Brands, therefore, can no longer command the kind of premium they used to and, thus, we can see that local brands are taking away the market share from well known national and international brands. Corporations are fighting for brand share in a fiercely competitive market. In this chapter, we also discussed the issues of managing the brand premium and how we can effectively fight to retain the brand share.

VII

Globalisation and New Order Organisation

Globalisation

Factors accelerating process of globalisation

THERE ARE various factors responsible for accelerating the process of globalisation. These are:

- The growing scale, mobility and integration of capital market
- Liberalisation leading to reduction in economic and trade barriers
- Advances in Information and Communication Technologies (ICT)
- Other key drivers of globalisation include:
  - Cost drivers: Marketers shifting production to least cost countries
  - Market drivers: Businesses constantly in search of new growing markets
  - Government policy drivers: Liberalisation of policies in stages further facilitate the process of globalisation
  - Competition drivers: Intense competitive activities open up new markets and improve product quality and service at reduced cost

Impact of globalisation on business

The significant impact of globalisation can be summarised as:

- Creation of global markets across sectors
- Changing nature of competition
- Emergence of global customer segment
- New economies and the value of intangibles
- Need for alliance partners
- Localised impact in terms of realigning the competitive forces and technology upgradation

Opportunities created by globalisation

Globalisation has created many opportunities. These are:

- Inflow of goods, services and capital
- New investment and employment opportunities
- Expanding market through integration of various economies around the world
- Faster growth in economy
- Improvement in technology and quality of products and services
- Reduction in price with improved quality
- Opening up of many new businesses
- Increased consumerism

Globalisation has created great opportunities for India, which it is embracing only in part. The key imperatives are:

- The central challenge in reaping greater benefits from globalisation lies in improving the investment climate important for:
  - Large and formal sectors
  - SMEs
  - Informal sectors

- Agricultural productivity
- Off-Farm employment
- The investment climate is itself a key issue to poverty eradication
- There are large variations across the Indian states in the quality of the investment climate and strength of reforms

Imperatives of doing business on a global scale

Doing business on a global scale has thrown up many new challenges. The key imperatives of doing business on a global scale are:

1. The situation is highly competitive
2. Customers expect highest global/world class products and services
3. Failure to meet a contractual obligation, even once, is not tolerated
4. Trade terms are most often difficult to meet
5. Highly price competitive
6. Very high cost of distribution, hence trade margins are higher
7. Elements of import/other country specific levies
8. Higher cost of marketing/advertising
9. Market intelligence needs to be of the highest standard and up to date
10. High product liability cost
11. Need to adhere to cross country/international trade regulations and practices
12. Countries' prestige/political fall out if goods fail to meet specifications
13. Difficulty in settling trade disputes, if any, as per the Geneva convention
14. High standards of safety and environment related regulations
15. Need to be very aware of the country-specific import/export regulations
16. It takes a long time to establish an assured business relationship with the overseas buyer
17. Businesses are difficult to project and plan to win

18. Frequently changing customer requirements/expectations. For specific product lines, one needs to constantly upgrade/ change the product design
19. Need for frequent bulk supplies on a short notice
20. Constantly changing trade environment
21. Import price fluctuates because of competition from other countries whereas the cost normally increases
22. There is no control over the marketing operations in the importing country
23. Large value addition takes place overseas in the importing country, whereas the exporter needs to move on a shoe-string budget
24. Good knowledge of local market conditions, language, culture, etiquette, business customs and systems are a must
25. Important to have thorough knowledge of the competition and its product and prices
26. Familiarity is a must in banking and international finance
27. Presence of many Non Tariff Barriers (NTBs) to trade and commerce introduced by the importing countries

Liberalisation

Essential conditions for liberalisation

Countries are evolving through the process of liberalisation. Therefore, all countries are not at the same stage of evolution. They are, in fact, in different stages of liberalisation which are influenced by country-specific situations including economic, social and the political environment. The essential conditions of liberalisation are:

- Liberalising the rules, regulations and climate
- Removal of quotas and tariff
- Providing freedom to the business and industry
- Providing infrastructure facilities
- Removal of bureaucratic hurdles
- Encouraging research and developments

- Encouraging competitiveness based on quality, price, delivery, and customer service, etc.
- PSUs to be made private. Alternatively, provide autonomy to the public sector to compete with private sector companies
- Providing administrative and governmental support
- Developing money market and capital market

Investment Climate

The stage of liberalisation and socio-political environment will dictate the investment climate of a country. These are:

- Investment climate is determined by the existence of sound regulation of the industry including:
  - Promotion of competition
  - Overcoming bureaucratic delay and inefficiency
  - Fighting corruption
  - Improving the quality of infrastructure
- Investment climate should include both rural as well as urban productivity and investment
- Promote rural entrepreneurship to create employment opportunities
- Programme to fight against poverty and bring them into the mainstream development process
- Empower poor people and invest in them to ensure that they are fully involved in both the process of growth and the rewards from growth

Investment climate and poverty eradication

Eradication of poverty reduction has some relationship with the investment climate. Investment in social and development projects creates new employment opportunities for productive purposes where unemployed and poor people can be preferentially engaged to help them come out of the poverty line. Investment climate, therefore:

- Plays a crucial role
- Off-farm employment opportunity is critical to poverty reduction. Rural investment can make that happen
- In China, it is growing at the rate of 12 per cent for the last 20 years as against the rate of 2 per cent in India
- Sustaining infrastructure investment will help improve non-farm employment opportunities
- Non-farm employment will boost agriculture further and will, thus, kick off further linkages

Variation in the investment climate among Indian states

India offers a big opportunity of middle class buyers who aspire for better quality of life and MNCs and large Indian Businesses are constantly trying to woo this class by introducing new products and services. India is one of the countries where the savings rate is of a high order. Although consumption expenditure in India is one of the lowest, the huge size of the buyer population makes India an attractive destination for foreign investment. National Council of Applied Economic Research (NCAER) had carried out the survey to provide estimate of household and consumption expenditure as shown in the Table 7.1.

TABLE 7.1: ESTIMATES OF EARNINGS AND SAVINGS

	NSHIE* 2004–05 (24 states)	CSO** 2004–05 (All India)
Estimated population (million)	1,027	1,090
Estimated household (million)	205.4	230.1
Personal disposable income (Rs billion)	13,390	25,330
Private Final Consumption Expenditure (Rs billion)	10,044	18,900
Household Saving (Rs billion)	3,346	6,870
Savings Rate (%)	25.00	27.10

Source: *National Survey of Household Income and Expenditure.
**Central Statistical Organisation.

A survey conducted by CII amongst 1,000 firms in 10 states shows a significant difference. Productivity, thus, also varies in these states as will be revealed in Figures 7.1 and 7.2.

**FIGURE: 7.1: COST ADVANTAGE
OF DELHI AND OTHER STATES**

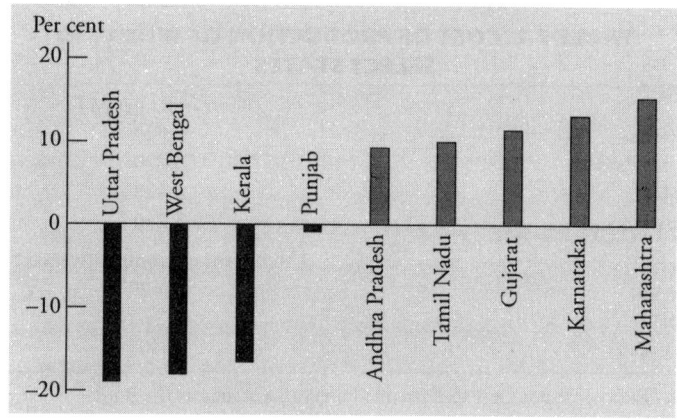

Source: CII and World Bank 2001.

**FIGURE 7.2: PRODUCTIVITY GAPS BETWEEN STATES WITH
GOOD AND POOR INVESTMENT CLIMATES**

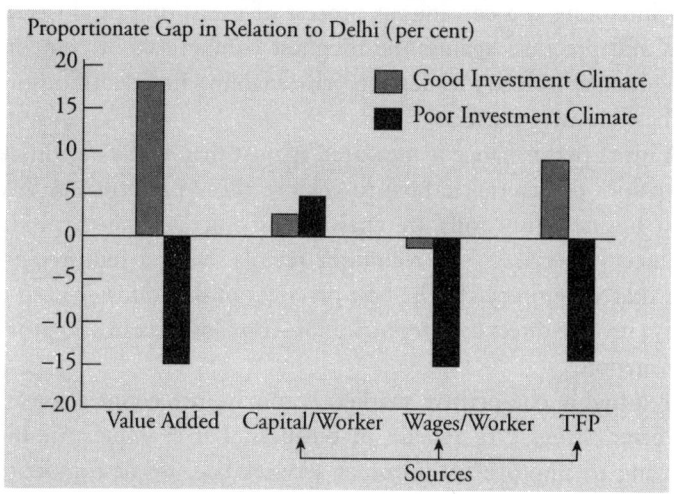

Source: CII and World Bank 2001.
Note: TFP = Total Factor Productivity.

In India, we have a significant difference between the investment climate amongst the various states resulting in gap in productivity as can be revealed from Figure 7.2.

The productivity gaps influenced the cost of production of a major crop like wheat as shown in Table 7.2.

TABLE 7.2: COST OF PRODUCTION OF WHEAT IN SELECT STATES

	Cost in Rs per MT
Haryana	2,923
Madya Pradesh	3,770
Punjab	3,428
Uttar Pradesh	3,280
	Coefficient of Competitiveness*
Haryana	0.7609
Punjab	0.7362
Rajasthan	0.8405

Note: *Ratio of Input Cost to Earnable Foreign Exchange at the Border.

Benchmarking Competition

Benchmarking is a continuous process of measuring products, services and practices against the toughest competitors or companies recognised as industry leaders, thereby enabling the identification of the best industry practices.

A firm's performance is measured against that of the best-in-class companies to determine how to achieve those performance levels. Most business functions are analyzed as processes which produce products or services. The technique reveals the best industry practices that are employed. The best practices of the industry need not always involve direct competitors. Non-competitors can also provide information.

In a highly competitive market, corporate behaviour changes in the firms' struggle to remain in business. For example, Air India is trying to improve its customer services because of competition from private airlines. But this is reactive behaviour. In a competitive environment, however, one has to become proactive.

Benchmarking does not mean simple emulation. Besides, emulations may only help a company meet the competitor's performance, but it is unlikely to come up with practices to beat them. If business has to derive competitive advantage, we need to constantly analyse the competitors' position, strength, weakness, product, resources, organisation, new product development and strategy. There are three basic types of benchmarking, as enumerated below:

- Strategic benchmarking involves the comparison of different business strategies to identify key elements in a successful strategy.
- Operational benchmarking generally involves competitive costs and competitive differentiation in functional areas like engineering, manufacturing, distribution and sales.
- Management benchmarking involves analysis of support functions like HRD, MIS, planning and logistics management.

It has been reported that globally top performing companies are actually benchmarking the competition on cost, quality, time and sales.

Benchmarking comprises of five basic steps:

1. Identification of functions

Functions that can be benchmarked include unit cost, inventory norms, customer satisfaction, etc. In general, the activities which are important in providing a competitive advantage should be selected. For example, a company interested in measuring the production cost should benchmark a significant or growing proportion of that cost.

2. Selection of performers

The competitor or the industry leaders are normally considered for benchmarking; although, the exercise can also be conducted against any organisation or industry which has demonstrated excellence in a particular function.

3. Data collection

There are many ways to collect data on competitors. Identifying sources of information about rival firms or industry leaders can be a formidable task. Company employees, customers, suppliers, and distributors are a useful source for obtaining competitive information. Newspapers, trade journals, magazines, government publications, corporate annual reports, company publications, consultants and presentations at professional meetings can also provide valuable information.

4. Set performance goals

Establishing operational goals for improvement involves careful planning of incorporating new processes and practices in business. Performance goals and selection of best practices must be incorporated into functional and operating plans of businesses. Performance goals should be designed to surpass the best-in-class.

5. Implementation

Benchmarking is a means to improve performance to gain superiority. Implementation should involve periodic assessment of attempts to reach stated goals. This helps an organisation to take corrective action if performance does not meet goals.

Intense international competition and declining profitability are encouraging many firms to improve their competitive performance. One of the long-term initiatives that are being employed to improve performance is competitive benchmarking. It helps managers compare the performance function by function and to determine why performance differs and to establish performance goals to become the best or at least to improve.

By forcing companies to measure their performance against that of the best companies to identify strategies to improve performance further, benchmarking shows considerable potential for improving competitive performance.

Measuring Organisational Performance

It is said that short-term results can only ensure long-term survival because if a company does not survive the short term then there is no long term for it. Although security analysts give maximum weight in their analysis to a company's short-term earnings, this could be quite unreliable and often quite misleading as a measurement of the company's performance, particularly for over the longer term. In other words, short term result is no guarantee for long term performance if the intrinsic factors and fundamentals are not strong enough.

The first important test is to know the company's current market standing in the relevant market. If a company is producing a product for consumption by all age groups but if in the marketplace it is only consumed by the older age group then the future of the product is suspect. Similarly, 'if a specific medicine or drug is only being prescribed by old loyal doctors and not by younger doctors, there is no future for the medicine. Who is buying your product is therefore, very important to know,' observes Peter Drucker (1964).

It is also important to know how the short-term results are obtained. If a non-seasonal product reflects a seasonal pattern of sales, there is something wrong. If sales at the end of the year are abnormally high, the reason could be transferring of stock from factory warehouse to distributor's warehouse in order to achieve short-term results. And many companies, including the well known and reputed ones, are seen to resort to these kinds of practices to achieve short-term results to retain the shareholders' confidence in the management and also to hold on to the market capitalisation. But smart investors can filter through those financial figures.

Some products are sold only by offering high trade loads when traders stock high quantities and sell later. This is what can be referred to as buying future sales. Instead of giving frequent trade loads, it may be better to reduce the price of the product and give the consumer this benefit. Companies are also known to produce short-term results by manipulation. This can be seen, particularly, when they plan to go for a new public issue.

The number of innovations that a company has produced during the year under review is another important question. Successful companies will demonstrate increase of innovative power in their relevant market segment. For example, in India, Hindustan Uni-Lever can claim to be an innovative company in the soap, detergent and personal care category. Smaller companies have also occasionally shown innovation. Innovations are taking place in the financial and banking industry in India as well.

Another important criterion of performance is productivity which is a measure of improvement. It is important to know, in measurable terms, whether productivity for different categories is improving and not only in overall terms but also in various business functions. It is also important to know why productivity parameters have changed. For example, labour productivity, if improved by mechanizing the production process, is only going to give wrong indications. Here, labour productivity has not increased but capital expenditure, in terms of modernisation, has changed that index and, hence, is not enough when compared to another successful company which has improved both (Drucker 1964).

The financial health of a company can be gauged from its liquidity position. It is said that a liquidity crunch is worse than a profit crunch because if a company suffers from the latter, it can resort to disposing of unprofitable operations. But, if faced with a liquidity crunch, profitable operations are normally offered for sale (Drucker 1964). If a company would like to retain profitable operations under a liquidity crisis, the units which are offered for sale are unlikely to fetch the right price. Moreover, during a period of liquidity crisis, the company cannot even fund or support a bright marketing idea. It can even be forced to postpone it and, hence, will lose an opportunity.

Finally, the profitability of an organisation is the ultimate test of its performance. It is important to know how resources are deployed and what results have been produced over a period of at least three years. If the resources are inflation adjusted, so should be the profit. Also, while calculating the profit, non-recurring income should be deleted. Financial statement of the organisation should give true reflection of its performance. For example , if the profit target is delivered either through sale of an asset or by adjusting the overheads or even by postponing booking of some costs incurred in that financial year then these factors should be taken into account to understand the real term performance of the company. Some companies are even known to club the profit of their trading operations of non-related products or services (normally reported as other income) in their manufacturing company in order to keep market prices of the stock at the desired level and also to keep the investors' confidence in the company but wise investors can easily see through these figures and can very well understand how their investment is being utilized.

Signals of Organisational Decay

We have seen several organisations going downhill or being completely wiped out, as they are unable to perform in the face of competition and the changed business environment. The difference between the rate of change within the organisation and outside the organisation will determine how fast the organisation is going to die. But there are many early signals, which if diagnosed, and if corrective action is taken then organisations can turn around or can even become winners.

The first danger signal is that if the company's product lines, formulations and label, etc., remain unchanged for a long time, then there must be something wrong. A product can have a very long economically useful life but with the change of time, the product formulations, its primary and secondary packaging, its label, its delivery mode and overall presentation will definitely change. On the contrary, if this remains the same for decades, there must be something wrong and, therefore, should be taken as an early danger signal. In a rapidly changing business environment, companies which do not change will sink.

The second signal of organisational decay is the cost. If an organisation is costlier with respect to its nearest competitor in terms of delivering the same value for its products and services, sooner or later the organisation is going to lose market share to its competitor. Even with an escalated cost, if an organisation keeps its product price the same in the marketplace as that of its competitor, the bottom-line profit will decline, which will reduce the organisation's ability to do product development and innovations and, therefore, the future of the organisation will be in danger. Also, lower margin will force the organisation to cut its marketing budget which will have its effect on the organisational performance. Two organisations with different cost structures, in the same category of industry, cannot survive for long. The company having the higher cost will eventually disappear.

The third danger signal for an organisation is not adjusting to the change in technology or to the technological shift. Technology is changing very fast, which very often makes today's product obsolete tomorrow and organisations should constantly adjust themselves to the new realities instead of clinging on to its age-old systems of production and value delivery. Otherwise, it is going to lose out to competitors who will switch over to harnessing the new technology, new systems, and new opportunities to deliver superior value and, therefore, will have an edge over the organisations that are not willing to change.

The technological change can redefine and/or reposition a product or an industry. And, if such signals are ignored, it could mean a disaster or a starting point of the decline. At any point of time, no organisation should think that it is all mighty and, therefore, invincible. If the organisation is complacent then it should be perceived as a danger signal. The Swiss watchmakers became too complacent about their competency. When an inventor pointed out that the quartz movement would replace the main-spring technology, the Swiss overlooked the former's potential. Although the quartz technology was discovered in Switzerland, the Japanese recognized its potential first and captured on this powerful signal for change, and companies like Seiko captured the market. Having enjoyed 65 per cent share of the world market for all types of timepieces in 1968, all Swiss watchmakers apparently thought that their watches, which were based on the mainspring technology, were too good to be affected by such a change in technology. The end result was that the Swiss lost 25 per cent of their market in a matter of one year. And in 1980, the Swiss' share of the world watch market had dipped to 10 per cent.

And finally, organisations should see the danger signal when they are no longer innovative. In this age of competition only innovative companies will survive. Organisations will have to create a culture for innovation and will also have to put material and human resources for innovations to take place. If this is not happening then organisations must take note of it and take remedial actions as the innovations and their quality will determine not only the future growth but also the organisations' very existence. Innovations do not happen automatically, they have to be cultivated.

As has been discussed earlier, there are organisations which change for the better and there are others that change for the worse and eventually perish. And there are still others that refuse to change and should, therefore, see the writing on the wall. Dinosaurs were giant creatures that became extinct because they could not adapt to the environment. If organisations remain static or become immune to the changes outside or even lose their customer focus, they are bound to disappear one day. In fact, of the 43 excellent companies identified by Tom Peters and Robert Waterman (1994) in their best-seller book, 'In Search Of Excellence', two thirds of them had deteriorated in performance in just five years and some of them, including Atari and Avon, went into serious difficulties. Performance can never be guaranteed, it can only be ensured by constantly striving to meet and exceed the customers' expectations. Metal Box was a very well respected company in India during the 1970s. But it did not capture the signals of change in the packaging technology and continued producing only OTS (open top sanitary) cans and that too at a higher cost. In the subsequent years, they disappeared altogether.

Organisation Structure for Facing Future Challenges

If the business realities are changing, organisations cannot afford to remain static. Majority of the Indian business houses had started as small family-owned businesses, which have grown today to become big multi-product, multi-unit corporations as well as multi-location enterprises. Multinational Corporations (MNCs) initially started their operations in India through trading activities. Then followed the legislations that foreign companies will not be allowed to run only trading businesses; as a result, MNCs were forced to start manufacturing activities in a small way and gradually grew to their present sizes. As the businesses grew, the employee numbers, management layers and the grades also gradually increased.

Successful Indian companies diversified into many non-related areas whereas multinationals remained in their own core business activities. A careful study would reveal that Indian companies have grown much faster than MNCs in spite of the fact that MNCs are believed to have better managerial skills, systems and technological advantage. Relatively much slower growth of MNCs was possibly due to their inflexibility because they are large global businesses and also because of their lack of knowledge of the local market conditions. Because of competitive pressure, both MNCs and Indian companies are required to respond quickly to the fast changing technology and complex business environment. The task ahead, therefore, is to create a new organisational structure to face the future challenges.

The traditional organisational structure for both Indian companies and MNCs is divisionalized profit centres. Some of the MNCs (Reckitt Benckiser India Ltd) have even tried the regionalized organisational structure in order to exploit local regional potential in a culturally diversified country like India. This concept is believed to be more flexible, quick to address local issues and, hence, more functional. But legal systems and other organisational issues have made this experiment unsuccessful and the company had to roll back again to its traditional structure. Some companies, including large public sector companies run business divisions as Strategic Business Units (SBU).

Organisational structure has a direct relationship with its cost and effectiveness. Competitors in the same business cannot have different cost structures for an indefinite period. Sooner or later, the higher cost company will be forced out of competition. One of the significant cost elements in any organisation is its manpower cost which varies from 10 to 15 per cent of net sales in a typical manufacturing organisation and due to competitive pressure, it is imperative for large organisations to design, at optimum cost, an effective organisation in line with the realities of the present business environment.

Secondly, organisational effectiveness also has a direct bearing on its functional and cross-functional structure. If the number of layers increases, response time cannot be quick. If an organisation has more people than required then it tends to increase the layers and grades in order to keep the people motivated and interested in the company's business. At one point of time, United Breweries (UB), the largest liquor and alcoholic beverages company in the country had positions like vice president, senior vice president, group vice president and executive vice president. Even in the later years, there were half a dozen presidents in each function. The Escorts Group, which is now facing difficult times, had ten levels of executive layers up to the position of vice president. There were assistant vice president, vice president and senior vice president positions. But post 1990s, in the face of both escalating cost and need to become effective and quick to respond, organisations will be required to reduce the number of layers.

It has been observed that a typical manufacturing organisation has up to as many as 14 levels between the boardroom and the shop floor. In the 1970s and 1980s, many staff functions such as marketing coordinator, manager-special projects, executive assistants and so on were created to accommodate people, who would now be called 'plateaued performers'. Adding layers or creating non-functional posts has happened despite our knowledge of the fundamental N + 1 attributes of bureaucracies, namely that, if an organisation of 100 people adds one extra person, it adds 100 extra possible liaison and communication links (Drucker 1992).

The earlier concept of profit centres for multi-product and multi-unit organisations will now have to be reorganized into self-managing SBUs in order to clip the corporate staff down to minimal numbers and limited functions. 'New order' organisations, it has been suggested, may in future, have as few as four hierarchical levels namely, customer facing staff, supervisors, managers and directors. Organisations are required to reduce layers and create a lean and mean structure not only from cost but also from the functional point of view.

Then, how can the de-layering of the organisations be attempted? Often, de-layering a large integrated organisation may denude it of the very competence that it seeks. When the adverse effects of this emerge, organisations have been known to panic and build up new posts and not necessarily in the best way. If the de-layering is not attempted on a scientific basis, it may not reduce the numbers to make the organisations flat or slim and at the same time very functional and effective. The number at each level has to be determined by ascertaining the quantum of job and a decision has to be taken regarding how much of that is to be done in-house and how much part can be done out-house or even contracted out in order to stay slim. Otherwise, employee strength may still remain the same or even increase even if the number of layers is reduced.

Peter Drucker (1992) has said that organisations of the future will run more like symphony orchestras and hospitals with self managing autonomous professionals in charge and no more than half the levels of managers and no more than one-third the number of managers.

Future organisations will have to be slim but the danger of adding layers to again make the flat organisations fat always exits. Attempts to solve this problem were the real driving force behind the movement to 'empower' employees, in the hope that this will reduce the need for supervision and permit some natural de-layering. Empowerment of employees by delegating authority with responsibility will drastically reduce the need for supervision. But such a stage can come only through total quality management programmes by taking a systems approach. Organisations of the new economic order will have to undergo this process of change and gradually become slim, cost effective and optimum corporations. This task is not going to be easy and is possible to implement only with the involvement of everybody working as a team. The first task in that direction is to build up the confidence and trust among the members of the organisation—particularly between workmen and management.

Again, in Peter Drucker's (1992) words,

Administrative structure will, like flower beds, tend to become overgrown with both flowers and weeds and only the most strenuous efforts, commitment, and expense will keep proliferation at bay. There are good reasons for encouraging the flowers; it is only the weeds of empty jobs, feeble functions and unconstructive additions which should be excised.

Chapter Summary

The forces of globalisation and liberalisation have made the organisations think differently. The manifestation of a new economic regime has forced the organisations to restructure, de-layer and make them lean and mean. Organisations have become more performance focused. They have started comparing performance with the best in class and constantly benchmarking themselves to remain focused and performance oriented. This chapter discussed the various imperatives of globalisation and performance measurement systems in organisations and how benchmarking is done to understand the areas of improvement. In addition to this, signals of organisational decay and failure were also discussed. Organisations have to constantly evolve and the chapter deals with the futuristic organisations to cope with the constantly changing business environment triggered by the new era of competition and technological advancement.

VIII

Competitiveness

International Competitiveness

ORGANISATIONS WILL have to be globally competitive to compete in the international market. Businesses, therefore, are required to upgrade in terms of the cost and quality dimension to appeal to global customers from diverse cultures. The product features and performance standards also need to be optimized to meet the customers' requirement and statutory regulations across countries. Of course, some factors are not within the control of the management at the firm level. Competitiveness, therefore, depends on numerous factors. But businesses have to be competitive to succeed in the marketplace.

Governance Factors Impact Competitiveness

Every country needs to regulate firms in some way. For example, safety, pollution, public health and fair trade practices, etc., are required to be regulated. This is true for all countries. The institution of economic governance is important for creating an investment climate. The issue is to what extent this should be done and also the nature of regulation. According to World Business Environment Survey managers' report, executives spend 5 per cent of their time in Latin America, 10 per cent in East European countries and 16 per cent in India in dealing with the bureaucracy. The exit clause and bankruptcy and labour redundancy laws are very cumbersome in India—about 60 per cent of the cases are in the High Court for over 10 years now. In SME sectors this has been recognised and the ceiling has been raised from 100 to 1,000 employees for the exit clause.

Productivity growth comes from the movement of capital and labour from less productive to more productive activities. And if regulations make it difficult, much of the benefit of the open market economy is lost.

A CII report indicates that a typical power project needs to obtain 43 clearances at central government level and 57 at the state level. To set up a retail chain in India, there are over 30 licenses required. And, for every new store, these licenses have to be obtained again.

To have a vibrant SME sector, a functional public power grid is essential. Other infrastructural needs are seaports, airports, road, railways and communication. Custom clearance time in India is twice of what one needs in other South East Asian countries. For example, sending an identical textile shipment to US from India costs, on an average, 20 per cent more than it does from Thailand and 35 per cent more than that from China.

Competitiveness

World Competitiveness Yearbook 2000 (International Institute for Management Development) ranks 47 countries including, Organisation for Economic Co-operation and Development (OECD), plus emerging market economies on a range of factors. India's rank is 43rd and China's is 31st. Even now, the things have not changed much. In 2007, India's rank in the competitiveness index was 47.

Competitiveness is a useful indicator of overall health of the organisation. This is measured at the country level, industry level as well as at firm level. In the new economic policy regime and emerging era competitiveness index, the trend serves as a reliable measure of success and failure of strategy and policy. If an organisation is not competitive, it is likely to perish.

Definition

At the country level, it indicates the extent to which a national environment is conducive to business. And at the industry level, it indicates the extent to which an industry/segment offers potential for growth and returns. The collective ability of an industry on performance factors such as productivity, cost, market share and technology will determine its ability to compete globally. If a firm is competitive it will have the ability to conceive, design, engineer, manufacture, distribute and service a battery of product(s) better than its competitor on a sustained basis. And, at the same time, will be able to deliver growth, profits and take care of the larger social responsibility.

Table 8.1 provides the competitive index of various countries.

Comparison of India and China on certain parameters has been given in Table 8.2.

Indicators of competitiveness

The indicators of firm-level competitiveness include the firm's own position in international benchmarking, size of the firm and growth

TABLE 8.1: COMPETITIVENESS INDEX OF VARIOUS COUNTRIES

Country	Ranks		
	2002	2000	1999
USA	1	1	1
Singapore	5	2	2
Canada	8	8	10
Australia	14	10	11
Japan	30	24	24
Korea	27	28	41
Malaysia	26	27	28
China	31	30	29
India	**42**	**39**	**42**

Source: IMD 2002.

TABLE 8.2: TRADITIONAL AND EMERGING INDICATORS OF COMPETITIVENESS

Traditional	Emerging
• ROI	• Intangible Assets
• Physical Assets	• Human Capital
• Patents	• Structural Capital
• Expenses	• Social Capital
• Long-term debt	• Balance Scorecard
• Short-term borrowings	• Green Biz
• Inventories	• Intellectual Capital

FIGURE 8.1: COMPARISON OF INDIA AND CHINA ON VARIOUS PARAMETERS

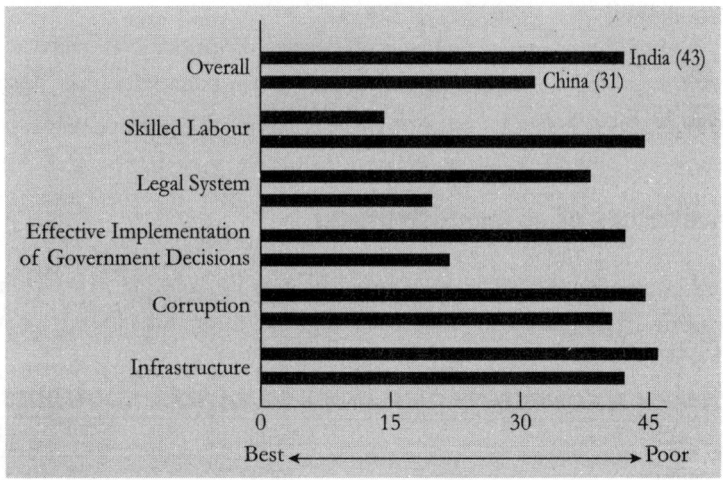

Source: IMD 2000.

rate, productivity, returns, Economic Value Added (EVA), and international performance in terms of global trade, etc. (Table 8.2).

Indian national competitiveness is a reflection of a macroeconomic phenomenon, cheap and abundant labour forces, bountiful natural resources and government policies. The competitive advantage that India has is that some of the industry category is competitive arising out of cheap labour costs, favourable exchange rate and stable BOP (Balance of Payment). The only meaningful concept

TABLE 8.3: WORLD DEVELOPMENT REPORT 2005

Country	GNI (PPP) in $ Billion
US	10,914
China	6,435
Japan	3,641
India	3,068
Germany	2,267
France	1,640
UK	1,639
Italy	1,543
Brazil	1,322
Russia	1,279

Source: World Bank 2005.

Notes: GNI = Gross National Income; PPP = Purchasing Power Parity; NRI's contribution for India is 9 per cent and for China it is 70 per cent.

of competitiveness at the national level is productivity which is low in India in international comparison (Table 8.3). In terms of overall GDP per person employed and manufacturing value added per worker India will be way below Singapore, Hong Kong, Taiwan and South Korea.

In terms of global competitiveness, India has a long way to go. While India is emerging as a leading global and emerging economy, in comparison to China, it is far behind. China has benefited much from early liberalisation policies, as well as, from a regimented political system that it has as opposed to the democracy in India. At the firm level, many actions are being initiated but country level competitiveness has a significant influence on the firm level performance in the global market.

Expand Geographic Boundaries for Growth

Business grows when products and services are sold in newer territories and it is much easier to achieve faster growth of the business by resorting to geographic expansion rather than trying to either expand the market or increase market share in the existing territory through deeper penetration. But there is no guarantee that the experience in the new geographic area will always be good or even as per the expectation. Marks & Spencer has been a consistently profitable and successful company despite the ups and downs of the UK retail spending. When M&S decided to expand its operations to France, it ran into problems. As a fallout of the economic liberalisation, some of our large Indian corporate houses have already ventured into the international market and have opened up their offices and establishments in new geographical markets. Definitely, if India wants to become a global player, it is necessary that Indian business houses expand their activities to international market, failing which India will get reduced to becoming a playground of global players. But the experience of all those who have already ventured into the international market may not be equally good.

The first issue that needs to be addressed before deciding any geographic expansion is whether the organisation has the necessary resources and knowledge required to expand operations into the new territory. New territory requires new resources and if the existing resources are spread onto a larger geographical area, it may become inadequate to produce any impact. Good companies are often seen to be able to defend their market share against the ups and downs of the domestic economy by devoting all their energies and focusing the total resources to guard the business against any competitive onslaught. But the same organisation may not be good enough to face the ground realities in an alien country. And the end result will be that the company wil not be able to deliver anything or will achieve very little for the shareholders by resorting to geographical expansion.

International expansion should be perceived as a major growth opportunity and, therefore, should be thought of as a way of beating global competitors and not escaping from the vagaries of the domestic market.

It should not be pursued simply for the reasons of portfolio balance or entry into a new growth market without a proper strategy because it can precipitate a major managerial problem. A careful study, therefore, needs to be undertaken to identify high growth market areas with a strong rationale for entering into that market with a well chalked-out strategy for providing competitive advantage.

In the absence of a strong rationale, international expansion efforts are unlikely to be successful. The added costs of investment abroad are substantial and will simply eat into the returns.

The entry strategy into the international market could be joining hands with a local company having interest in a similar business, thereby bringing in not only the synergy but also the local expertise; acquiring an ongoing company in the new geographic area which will provide a ready access to the market for exploitation; acquiring a distribution set up for a similar product line of the company, intending to introduce into the prospects territory or even setting up the project from the grass root level. The multinationals coming to India are seen to follow either of these methods. Coca Cola acquired Parle, Heinz acquired Glaxo, whereas Kimberly Clark and S.C. Johnson joined hands with Hindustan Unilever and Sara Lee tied up with Godrej. But Pepsi started from the grass root level and so has Kellogg. Each entry strategy has its own merits and demerits and a particular strategy that will suit a corporation may not suit the other.

The geographic expansion of any organisation takes place through five identified strategies from domestic, international, multinational, global, to transnational corporations. Although this nomenclature is often used interchangeably, in reality these are different stages, models and processes through which an organisation gradually evolves from being a domestic company to a transnational.

At stage one, the company focuses on domestic markets, domestic suppliers, and domestic competitors. At stage two, it extends marketing, manufacturing and other activities to other countries and the underlying strategy at this stage is expansion which means products, advertising and promotion, etc. developed for the home country are extended to other markets around the world. At this stage, the company discovers that the markets in each country are really different and, therefore, tries to adjust to local conditions and evolves to stage three and pursues a multi-domestic strategy to become a multinational corporation.

Organisations at this stage will develop products to suit each market and we, thus, see Pepsi launching 'Leher' *namkeens* and *bhujias* (Indian snacks). From stage three, the organisation makes a major strategic departure to become a truly global company by following either a local or global marketing strategy, but not both. In stage five, the company is geocentric in its approach and orientation. Transnational corporations, therefore, recognise similarities and differences of various markets and adopt a global view.

There always needs to be a good rationale for international expansion, such as identification of attractive market opportunities which genuinely lend themselves to exploitation by companies with exceptional skills and capabilities. India and China are two markets which offer opportunity for expansion to many multinational corporations. There could also be other rationales for expansion. For example, in the pharmaceutical industry, the cost of development of any new drug has become so high that only through international exploitation of the market can such a research initiative become profitable. The same is true in the area of high technology products such as computers and information technology products where, because of fast technological change, the product life cycle has become very short and, therefore, the organisation has to very quickly recover the investments before the product becomes obsolete and this is possible by resorting to geographical expansion.

To become successful in the new geographic market, organisations must have knowledge of the new market, the marketing environment and the product, which should be integrated with the knowledge of the marketing function and discipline together with a strong rationale and the necessary resources. If these elements are missing, the decisions regarding international expansion could turn out to be disasters and then impossible to manage.

Chapter Summary

The chapter deals with the factors responsible for the competitiveness of the firm and the industry. It also compares the competitiveness index of various countries and how competitiveness is managed at the firm level and industry level. To become globally competitive is a key imperative for expanding the geographical boundaries. If the organisation is not competitive, it cannot realize its ambition of eventually becoming a global enterprise. The key dimensions which can be managed within the organisation to improve the firm's competitiveness index were also discussed. This chapter deals with these issues with respect to international competitiveness.

Not all organisations can become global and a part of the reason is the organisation itself. The other reasons are its products and services. The chapter deals with the issues of geographic expansion and what it takes to create a global enterprise.

IX

Managing Innovation and Creativity

Managing Innovation

IN THE present day context of a competitive business environment, only those will survive who can be more innovative to outperform the competition in terms of product performance and services. Good and talented managers will, therefore, be in demand. But having good human resources and talented people does not mean that innovation will automatically happen in the organisation. Although human talent is the first requirement, getting innovative output and winning products needs efficient innovation management. In retrospect, success always appears to be simple but making an innovation work is not that simple, particularly when nine out of every ten products launched in the market have failed. The innovation can be a result of hard, organised and purposeful work if the need for it is identified. But innovation could also be either the result of an accident or 'the wild imagination of the genius mind' which, of course, cannot be taught (de Bono 1992).

The latter type, described as an extraordinary incident, is definitely a rare affair and is the first type which contributes to over 90 per cent of all innovations that have ever taken place in this world. The innovation that is a result of organised and purposeful work can be practiced and businesses have to learn how to utilise organisational resources to make it happen routinely to create competitive advantage.

Apparently, it seems that those people who take or have the natural ability to take risks can be better innovators. But, in reality, it is not so and, thus, successful innovators are conservative and, therefore, 'opportunity focused' rather than 'risk focused'. As it is generally said, 'necessity is the mother of invention', the need gets the innovative mind working. Many breakthrough innovations were made under pressure. Thus, when survival itself is threatened, organisations look for great innovations to happen which can sail them through the difficult days.

One of the essential conditions for innovations to take place is, therefore, identifying the need for it. The second most important aspect of innovation management is to identify the person or group of people who will be capable of finding a solution to the problem. That person may or may not be within the organisation but once the team or the individual is identified, the task is to provide resources, support and encouragement for the result. The team can be constituted with identified talented people within the organisation along with the recognised consultants drawn from outside with a defined brief and tasks.

While organisations will be on the lookout for good and efficient managers for encouraging innovations, talented people will also be looking around for an organisation where they can utilize their skill and knowledge better. Therefore, wherever this marriage takes place, these organisations are likely to be more innovative. Organisations will be required to look for talents and induct them into the business for facilitating innovations. It is said that a good managing director is the one who can hire people who are smarter than him, to work for him. This would mean that organisations will have to undergo a change to enable them to attract talent. 3M is said to have a practice of hiring talented scientists and technologists with entrepreneurial skills to work in their R&D laboratory, giving them total freedom to pursue their own interests. The result is the commercialsation and patenting of so many successful products from apparently mundane ideas like 'Post-it' and such. There are various successful approaches to innovations practice which can become the basic guidelines for managers and direct their innovative pursuit. An innovative product is the result of a bright idea that comes from the assessment of a particular need.

Sony's development of the Walkman is a brilliant example of how existing technological capabilities can be utilised to create an entirely new product to meet the need. In the recent times, someone from South America has claimed that it is he who has first developed the concept of entertainment while on the move and Sony has copied the same. But whoever is the inventor of the product, the innovation itself has made a remarkable commercial success story. In the recent times Apple's iPod and iPhone or even Intel's chips can be cited as good examples of such innovation

The other sources of innovation which an organisation needs are to identify the gap between the process time and cycle time to understand the wasteful process steps. The change in the market structure of a particular industry offers significant opportunity for innovation. For example, as fallout of liberalisation, Indian car manufacturers suddenly faced the global competition and to keep their own product(s) acceptable in the marketplace, local models have undergone changes in design, performance, quality, fuel economy, cost, aesthetics and finally safety aspects including environmental safety. The change of the demographic profile and its perception of a product and services offer a significant opportunity for innovation. Demographics are defined as changes in population, its size, age structure, composition, employment, educational status and income. These external changes have most predictable consequences. Service industry, health care industry and consumer goods industry can make a realistic prediction about the future needs from these external changes and direct their innovative practices to exploit the opportunity these changes will offer.

Finally, the most important source of innovation is new knowledge derived from technological breakthrough. Knowledge based innovation differs from all other forms of innovation in its basic characteristics such as the time span, predictability, failure rate and the management challenges. This is particularly true for the kind of innovation that we are currently seeing taking place in the areas of information and communication technology and in biotechnology including medical biotechnology and genetic engineering. When technology is fast changing, the product life cycle becomes shorter and, hence, the question of making innovations faster than the competition, for exploitation of the opportunity. Otherwise, the entire effort can become non-remunerative for followers with a much lesser and residual market opportunity. Exploitation of knowledge based opportunity can not only provide a new market opportunity but can also be a source of fame and reputation for an organisation. But the risk associated with it is also high either on account of technological failure or technological redundancy. A good example in the Indian context in this connection is the failure of the three dimensional television sets that were introduced by Nicky Tasha—a company which has now become virtually nonexistent—in mid eighties. After a decade long inactivity the company is now being revived to produce auto components.

The uncertainty associated with innovation justifies the high failure rate of the innovative firms. It is only part of the story that the vast majority of attempts at innovation fail. The real reasons lie in the apparent inability to anticipate the future impact of successful innovation even after establishing its technical feasibility. Often, there is no recognized way of knowing which new discoveries may turn out to be relevant or to what realm of human activity they eventually apply. But private organisations will naturally allocate their R&D resources to projects that they hope will turn out to be relevant and the organisations are expected to be capable of making their own assessment and judgment which will differentiate successful and innovative companies from the rest. After all if one out of 10 innovative products and discoveries that the companies make become successful in the marketplace, the financial success of the company is assured. Hence, it is worth taking the risk of uncertainty in the uncertain terrain of innovation.

Managing Information and Creativity

It is generally said that information is knowledge and knowledge is power. Today, information and communication technology has almost reached its zenith. Computation technology and capability is today opening up the unthinkable power of innovation.

The general feeling is that if complete information is available and is properly and competently analysed, the human factor in the decision-making process gets considerably reduced. This means that the need for thinking and creativity will get diminished. But in reality it will go on increasing because we have to make sense of the information that we receive and create. It becomes a matter of interpretation. It is like the example that a glass half filled can also be interpreted as half empty, whereby the former interpretation will mean no opportunity but the latter interpretation will mean an opportunity to fill the glass.

Similarly, if a particular community is not in the habit of wearing shoes, it can be interpreted either as no opportunity to market shoes in that segment or a big opportunity to get the community into the habit of wearing shoes.

As Edward de Bono, the first author to suggest and innovate the concept of lateral thinking, observed:

> Many people believe that if data is analyzed, new ideas can emerge. This is totally wrong as our mind is generally conditioned to see what it wants to see. But the reverse is almost true. Which means that if you have an idea, data can be obtained and analyzed to confirm whether that idea is worth pursuing or not. (de Bono 1991)

Hence, information can never substitute the creativity of the human mind. Therefore, organisations which are heavily dependent on data-based management are unlikely to succeed in the domain of creativity.

The question, therefore, still is about how information can be managed effectively. One way of tackling it is to formulate a hypothesis. The hypothesis provides us with a framework through which we can look at the information. Hypothesis also gives us something to work towards either for proving it or for disproving it.

But, creativity is very much involved in formulating hypotheses. Also, there is always a danger of postulating anything at the early stage.

When we do not have any hypothesis, we flounder, but when we do have one, it poses the danger of closing our mind towards other possibilities and we are likely to start looking at the information which only has relevance to this hypothesis. Hence, it is better to have many hypotheses for a particular problem, which will eventually help to open up many possibilities (de Bono 1992).

These days, the cost of failure is so high that, almost invariably, all organisations resort to carrying out an extensive market research before launching any new product. Even then, the chances of success of any new product are not more than 10 or 20 per cent. This is an indication that there is a high need for creativity in interpreting data and looking at the various possibilities.

It might just be possible to have complete data about the past and also reasonably accurate data for the present, but it is certainly not possible to get complete information about the future. So how do we predict our future and that too how accurately? All we can do is extrapolate the present trend or continue the present cycle or even foresee certain convergences that might produce new effects. But what happens if this hypothesis is not true. All the future planning of the organisation will go wrong. Hence, we need to use creativity in order to put forward certain future possibilities. Organisations today, therefore, need lateral thinkers. But, it will be unreasonable to expect that all organisations will have lateral thinkers.

In that case, managers will have to be trained on lateral thinking tools and techniques. This training, to a set of managers who will be responsible to steer the company into the future, will help in building capability in creativity and innovative activities.

The term 'lateral thinking' was first introduced by Edward de Bono in 1967 and refers to the thinking that is linear, sequential or logical. In the *Concise Oxford Dictionary* it is defined as 'seeking to solve problems by unorthodox or apparently illogical methods'. With lateral thinking, we move sideways to try different concepts and different perceptions.

Using mathematical tools and computer programmes, it become much easier, but the perceived value of that information can differ from person to person and a creative person can have multiple perceptions of an information or situation. But, at the end of our creative thinking, we will have to come back to solid logic to present ideas that are sound, workable and of testable values. But to get to those concrete and solid creative ideas, we need to think laterally.

Analysis of information is very important in order to find solutions to any problem, particularly for a problem which has a direct cause and effect relationship.

But there are problems for which we can find a cause but those causes cannot be removed. Such problems cannot be solved by analysis. Only information and analysis of information are not enough to find answers to those issues. In complex business organisations, problems are aplenty. How to tackle these problems will largely determine the success or failure of an organisation in a highly competitive market. The only route to addressing these issues is through innovation and creativity. Information, therefore, can never substitute creativity.

Chapter Summary

Innovation is the key to success. It should not happen by accident or by chance. It needs to be managed so that it happens as a routine. This chapter deals with innovation management within the enterprise. It is important to manage the volume of information that businesses generate in order to take meaningful and purposeful decisions. No organisation can survive for long if it fails to innovate the way in which the business will be done in future in order to create incremental value for customers. But still, some firms are seen to be more innovative in their business processes and product offering than others and, therefore, their chances of survival are much higher. The chapter deals with the issues within the organisation which are required to be managed to become more innovative. Management issues regarding information and creativity have also been also discussed in this chapter.

CHAPTER SUMMARY

X

Corporate Excellence

Managing Risk for Corporate Excellence

DOING BUSINESS involves taking decisions and concluding deals and every deal is a calculated risk. No decisions are possible without exposing oneself to a certain element of risk. If we do not take risks, the possibility of accomplishing something big is considerably reduced. Business decisions are taken to win at the end of the game and not on the basis of 'win some and lose some'.

All business decisions and deals are normally made after doing considerable home work and the risk then becomes directly proportional to the unknown and the validity or accuracy of the knowledge that was acquired before taking decisions.

In gambling, however, decisions are taken without any valid knowledge and information and that is how risk taking is quite different from gambling.

Anyone who takes an initiative or pursues an opportunity is taking some sort of risk. But successful people do not see risk as simple risk. They always look at the potential risks as the opportunity for innovation, potential gain and for bettering their performance or even for achieving something remarkable in life which they aspire to. Brilliant people or achievers of extraordinary performance are seen to be pursuing some objective or pursuing some plan or even following a path which others may consider to be sheer madness.

Some knowledge cannot be obtained at the time of taking decisions but many a times, after decisions are taken and actions emanate from them, new knowledge surfaces and corrective actions or a change in the course of earlier decisions becomes possible and the ill-effects of the original decisions are, thus, minimised or counter balanced in a significant way. Some of the potential risks associated with any kind of decision on a futuristic basis may not really arise at all and, if some ground rules are followed, the risk can be managed with a much higher degree of confidence for achieving the end objective (de Bono 1992).

The basic question that needs to be addressed is why the decision is necessary to be taken or sought in the first place. If the valid reason(s) is identified, an in-depth analysis has to be done on the current state of affairs. At this stage, one has to collect all available and valid data which will provide either possible solutions or at least will give a sufficient clue which will help in taking a decision.

The most important lesson that need to be learnt in risk management is to take decisions based on valid data and not on opinion. Even if there is an expert opinion or advice, the same must be established using valid data.

The same set of data can be interpreted differently by two different managers. It is, therefore, necessary to investigate further in order to take a decision if the initial set of information is insufficient for taking valid decisions.

Data analysis should be done very carefully in order to arrive at correct decisions and to minimise the risk. There are standard data analysis tools and methods available which should be used for data processing. One can even do a programme of a decision model or even draw a decision tree and feed all valid data to find the solution for a problem.

It is generally believed that risk is proportional to the reward. Higher the risk, the bigger is the reward. The General who prides himself on taking risks may be a heroic figure but we should not forget that he also wastes a lot of lives and opportunities (de Bono 1992).

Risk reduction or risk mitigation or even risk dodging is not exactly risk aversion. The best way to averse risk is not to do anything at all. Deciding to take the risk of action and then setting out to reduce or mitigate that risk, as much as possible, is definitely a better way of managing the risk. Risk normally arises from uncertainty and, hence, in a broader sense risk is synonymous with uncertainty.

All business decisions are taken based on the knowledge universe which can be classified as certain, probable and uncertain. It is generally believed that an acceptable level of business risk depends upon one's personal values, cultural factors and the ability to manipulate situations and abstract concepts and finally the individual's risk appetite. But one needs to have a more structured approach to the analysis of risk, particularly when alternatives are available for investment decisions.

Although risk analysis is normally undertaken for investment decisions, it is not limited to the same. It is applied in other cases as well. For example, for the acquisition of another existing firm, closing down of a manufacturing plant, starting a new venture requiring significant investment, decisions in competitive bidding situations, decisions with respect to short term and long term horizon in a business taking crucial business decisions in life, etc.

Just as investment is by definition a risk, so is innovation. They are undertaken after doing considerable home work and the risk then becomes directly proportional to the unknown. Sometimes not taking any decision is also a risk. There are situations where a decision cannot be avoided whatever might be the associated risks.

As we have seen, there is risk involved in ascertaining as to whether something will work, whether it will have a significant value, whether the market will accept it, the whether production process will be feasible, whether goods can be produced at the projected cost, whether it can be sold at an acceptable price, whether customers exist as was visualized at the time of making investment decisions in business, etc. Every decision in business, thus, involves a risk. In addition to this, there is a risk that a competitor may catch up quickly or leapfrog whatever has been done so far. With all these risks, it is a wonder that innovation occurs at all and that businesses still carry on.

Some inventors take decisions which, to many outsiders, appear to involve lunatic risk. Herman Kalin has said, 'Risk-taking is the essence of innovation'. Market awareness and market research are usually reckoned to be absolutely essential when developing a business which will help in minimising risks.

Sometimes, risk lies in direct proportion to how hard one is prepared to make a decision work. Working hard to make a decision work is possibly even more important than making the decision in the first place. Working hard will also reduce the perceived initial risk.

Sometimes one company's risk might be an opportunity for another and vice versa and if both companies combine, risk can be reduced drastically. This can be regarded as risk sharing in a joint venture. Corning was a glass manufacturing company and it had done a lot of research in fibre optics. When it decided to introduce this new optical fibre material in the market, a lot of risk was perceived, although the internal assessment was that the new material will be a significant breakthrough for the cable television industry. They contacted BICC, the biggest cable manufacturers in Britain, and got together to manufacture telecommunication cables to reduce risk which helped them to make the proposition work (de Bono 1992).

To sum up, there are four way of minimising risk. First, there is assessment of the situation and a choice between taking and not taking a risk. Second, there is the balancing of one risk against another as in currency hedging. Third, there are actions to reduce risk, such as taking a parachute when flying. Fourth, there are actions to modify the decisions and make them work after the decisions have been taken (de Bono 1992).

There is always the risk that relates to the outside world and the risk that relates to the effectiveness of the risk taker. Finally, it may not be always possible to correctly predict the changes in the outside world; no matter how wise people may be in hindsight. 'So things can change in an unexpected manner and upset the best plans of an entrepreneur. The measure of a person's worth then becomes the way he extricates himself from the crisis' (de Bono 1992).

Managing an Entrepreneurial Venture

It is not very difficult to make an ongoing organisation grow. Only the degree of growth might depend on the organisation, its people and most importantly the quality of leadership. It is relatively difficult to turn around a sick company. But to give a shape to an idea, and build a successful venture around it, is one of the most difficult tasks.

There is no doubt that an element of uncertainty always exists about the success of a new venture but adherence to certain ground rules will definitely improve the chances of a positive outcome.

Although, generating a very good idea is the first step to starting a new venture, it must be remembered that just having a brilliant idea is not enough. If sufficient resources and managerial capabilities cannot be committed, as required, for the idea to make it a success, the idea by itself will not be of much use.

One should, therefore, utilize the available organisational resources to develop and evaluate many alternative proposals for investment and allow the process to take the time needed to develop good alternatives.

The basic task of business development is not about finding brilliant ideas for investment, but about developing a sound business proposition around an idea.

It is generally believed that entrepreneurial skill is the key to success of any new venture. But the reality is that, although, entrepreneurship is a precondition for the success of a new venture, there must be a balance exercised by suitable control mechanisms so that the firm does not get involved in too many unrelated and demanding ventures than it cannot realistically handle. A control mechanism, therefore, has to be there in any organisation to evaluate and screening of alternative investment proposals and then go ahead with deciding on the prospective new venture.

An entrepreneur is normally in a hurry to act fast and, therefore, likely to make investment in his project in which he has faith. But controllers of funds do not want to commit themselves to any investment before all possible consequences have been considered and carefully evaluated.

To run any new business, some core competencies are required. Many people confuse acquiring knowledge with competency. The reality is that there is a vast difference between knowing and being able to transform that knowledge into purposeful action.

Generally, most of the competencies required to implement the new venture are acquired from external sources. These competencies can be developed by organising in-house training programmes, recruiting people with experience in the business, hiring consultants, and cooperating with future customers or companies, etc.

But one should remember that developing and acquiring competencies is actually a process of learning and it is not possible to predict, in advance, exactly what kind of competencies will be required. Although one can learn and act during the project life cycle in a continuous manner, the success of the new venture will depend on how quickly and accurately these competencies are acquired and transformed into purposeful action.

The venture task should always be kept manageable and should never be greater in scope and volume than the managerial and financial resources of a company. As starting a new venture from the scratch involves uncertainty at every stage, one has to restrict the number of alternatives to make the task manageable.

Besides, fragmenting of resources will greatly reduce the chances of success in a new venture. Those who have violated this fundamental principle have paid a price. Some people think that if it is possible to fund multiple projects, it should not be difficult to start one more new venture. But they do not realise that it is not possible to acquire the key competencies required to successfully run all the new ventures, in diverse fields, at the same time. The result is failure. A good example in this context is the UB Group's decision to diversify into telecommunications, engineering, fertilizers, petrochemicals, airlines and air-taxi service, hospitals, etc., all at the same time since none of these new businesses were working well for it. Not only that, these unsuccessful new businesses were a constant threat to the existing businesses and the focus was getting lost as to 'what was their real business'.

Organisations that entered into new ventures, where new marketing techniques or production processes were required, sooner or later also had to develop new accounting systems and administrative controls. For example, moving from batch to continuous process or from selling to bulk customers to direct end users necessitates new measures of control and administration. The organisations, therefore, need to change or create different structures and competencies to face the new realities to make a new venture a success.

Getting into new areas of business can often lead to a relatively long pay back period. One reason is the price that the new entrant has to pay to learn the business. Besides, many a times, initial investment soon has to be followed by additional large investment simply because if the initial investment has managed to establish a bridgehead, it has also to create a strong position in the new market through additional investment (Drucker 1992). This is exactly what we are seeing in case of multinationals such as Coke, Pepsi, Heinz and Kellogg. All of them are making contingent investments to make their basic investments profitable and also all of them are prepared for a long pay back. As they are planning well in advance, a 10–15 years payback period does not seem unusual to them.

The basic issue is to continue and to maintain the support if the vision does not coincide with the reality as is frequently the case. One of the reasons of failure is that studies conducted within the organisation often underestimated the true capital requirement and lacked the resources to make the ventures a success. Their visions were evidently too grandiose for the resources available.

New ventures, sooner or later, have to become an integral part of the company's and the group's business strategy. But this integration does not seem to be easy. Many organisations are, therefore, seen to run new entities as separate organisations as long as it is profitable, although, everyone agrees that integration is necessary. But there are forces to change their view because sometimes vision of the venture has changed and at other times, the business strategy of the company has changed or both have changed.

It should be appreciated that the new venture and the business strategy can develop in different directions during the long time to plan and implement any major new venture. Hence, after running a successful venture for a long time, corporations are seen to realise that some of their businesses are not a strategic fit with their current organisational vision; although, these businesses are very profitable. They then decide to divest these businesses which should not be seen as a sign of failure.

Selection of project, selection of process and technology, project site and availability of resources and finally, timely implementation of the project are some of the fundamental requirements for the success of any venture, but these issues have a fair degree of certainties and are, therefore, relatively easier to manage.

The real issue is with respect to managing uncertainty which any new venture will face once the physical part of the project is implemented and the venture goes on stream. Therefore, if an organisation wants to venture into new areas, the first requirement is to create a positive influence for such ventures, for effectively managing processes for success.

Organisation to Discharge Corporate Social Responsibility

A natural fallout of liberalisation and new economic reforms would be what we call the survival of the fittest. On the one hand, there will be pressure on organisations to reduce cost and on the other hand, stakeholders will be making demands and the organisations have to be managed to deliver those expectations. The issues that need to be addressed are how one can manage the business to be more profitable and at the same time discharge corporate social responsibility. The organisation, as we all know, is owned by its shareholders and they are, therefore, its legal controllers. But there are many stakeholders of the organisation. And, there is a constant debate as to whether the organisation needs to be managed only to increase the shareholders' value by maximising the profit of the organisation and by a judicious investment of the surpluses or does it have a responsibility towards its stakeholders at large? No one questions the basic objective of business to increase the shareholders' wealth. But while doing so, we also need to keep the larger interest of the society and environment in mind. Otherwise, businesses will not be sustainable.

As we all know, a company that is delivering high shareholder value today may be on the brink of a collapse tomorrow. Moreover, companies that have not made any profit for many years can still have a high stock market value. For example, the Tata Group did not deliver good performance during the 1990s but its stock market value did not sharply decline, indicating that the investors still had a great deal of confidence in the Tata Group's ability to perform better

in course of time. Any attempt to measure organisational performance must, therefore, take into account multiple indicators. This
aspect needs to be carefully assessed before we take a decision on either to hive off or to close down our public sector undertakings. The
stakeholders in an organisation will typically fall under five identified
categories namely, investors, employees, customers, suppliers and the
relevant community.

Some theorists believe that all stakeholders are deemed to have
equal status. Employees, for example, are no less important than, say
the shareholders. Moreover, it is the employees who generate shareholders' value. One can, therefore, ask a question that if shareholders
get 20 per cent return on their investment in a particular year, should
the employees also get 20 per cent rise in their emoluments in that
year? Under normal conditions, this is not necessarily a given. Moreover, all employees do not get same increase.

Thus, the stakeholders' theory runs directly counter to modern
capitalism which would claim that a company should be run solely
to earn a good return on its shareholders' capital, provided it behaves
towards those other groups of people in a socially acceptable manner.
In one scenario, companies exist to benefit all concerned and in the
other, just the shareholders.

There is nothing wrong in this theory as its basic essence is the
creation of value for the organisation. The question is how this value
or trade surplus is to be distributed. Should it be given as a reward
to only shareholders or to other stakeholders too, such as employees,
customers, suppliers and the community at large as their share of
contribution for the exceptional performance of the organisation?
It is normally seen that organisations do selectively reward their employees and some organisations even engage themselves in some form
or the other in community development and other types of charity
work. But not necessarily without any motive for further gain. This
is done in some way as a trade-off. The question, is it acceptable
behaviour? Possibly not.

Can any organisation perform better without the involvement,
support and cooperation of all stakeholders? The answer is a straight
no. High profit can be generated for the shareholder by producing
goods and services at the least cost and selling those at high price,

thus exploiting the opportunity available. 'The buy low and sell high' theory can also be interpreted as a concept which encourages squeezing the suppliers and exploiting the customers. Albeit, this is only possible when there is no competition and when organisations enjoy a monopoly situation. Although such a situation does not exist in this competitive marketplace any longer. But even in such a situation, organisations should not lose sight of the fact that they have a responsibility towards other stakeholders and not only towards the shareholders who are the legal owners of the organisation.

By virtue of the fact that shareholders have legal power to direct the policy and strategy of the organisation, can they shut their eyes to discharging other responsibilities for their stakeholders? Possibly, the answer again is a straight no. But unfortunately, the existing controls and systems cannot stop organisations from working solely for their shareholders if they are only to be governed by the dictums of the market forces.

The ownership and management of the organisation can change, depending on the needs and performance of the current owners. But can we afford to remove employees only because the organisation is not delivering either the profit or the shareholders' expectation? Organisations have the liberty to sack people in the name of restructuring just to maximise the shareholders' return on their investment, although, reduction in employee cost will not necessarily result in increased value? But their responsibility towards them cannot be ignored. It is high time that organisations recognize that they cannot survive unless they deliver value to their chosen stakeholders. Defining the purpose of an organisation or a company is an important responsibility of the board or the governing body. Without a clear purpose an organisation will drift and be buffeted by the shareholders in the markets it competes in.

Chapter Summary

This chapter covers the corporate governance issue. It starts with the issue of risk management. Doing business itself means taking some element of calculated risk. But organisations must have a risk mitigation mechanism in place to overcome and control the eventual risks. The first section discusses the risk management mechanism for growth and survival. The entrepreneurial ventures require special skills and abilities to manage and create success stories. The success rate of new ventures is very low. Creating a success story, thus, requires different skills, abilities and approach. This chapter deals with the issues involved in managing new ventures. Finally, corporate social responsibility (CSR) is an important governance issue to which organisations must give adequate attention. Remaining insulated from the society's needs and environment protection issues will ruin the business. This chapter deals with some issues related to CSR. Businesses have to be concerned with all issues involving the stakeholders as well as the environment to be able to create a sustainable business unit over a longer run.

XI

Case Studies

Introduction

IN THE new economy, the service sector has shown a significant growth in India. Over 50 per cent of the country's GDP is contributed by service sector. This, of course, is an indication of the country's economic development. But the question is whether India will be able to keep dominance, particularly in the IT sector in future. Performance in IT sector in India is still limited to large low cost workforce replacing high cost labour of western countries. Any significant breakthrough like Google, Facebook or Twitter has not been developed in India. Only having low cost labour and English speaking advantage will possibly not be able to get a larger part of the IT contract from Europe and America. The players in India will require new strategies for survival and growth. These will include better cost management, more aggressive marketing, having development and marketing offices abroad and even in countries which offer better cost advantage, looking at markets other than Europe and America, focusing also in domestic market opportunities, forging alliances with other competing countries like China and South East Asian countries.

In this section we will be discussing some Indian cases. These cases have been selected based on their performance over the years to identify what are the key strategic elements that helped them to be globally competitive. The case studies have been carefully selected to drive the key survival and, more importantly, winning strategies that we discussed in the earlier chapters. All five cases have started their journey with a humble beginning and have gradually emerged as globally competitive enterprises. These companies are, therefore, the face of what India Inc. can do in the global market. I have made an attempt to summarise the key strategies at the end of each case that helped the company to perform in a highly competitive global economic scenario.

In the IT sector, we have cited the Infosys success story; although, it is not the number one player in India. The biggest player is Tata Consultancy Services Ltd followed by Infosys Technologies Ltd. The ranking of the IT companies in India are given next.

Industry rankings

Genpact, WNS Global Services and IBM-Daksh lead the NASSCOM Top 15 BPO rankings.

Tata Consultancy Services Ltd, Infosys Technologies Ltd. and Wipro Technologies Ltd are the top three players in the NASSCOM top 20 IT software and services exporters rankings (Table 11.1) and NASSCOM's Top 20 IT-BPO employers.

Case I: Infosys Technologies Limited

Infosys Technologies Ltd is a multinational information technology service company headquartered in Bangalore, India. Infosys was founded on 2 July 1981, in Pune by N.R. Narayana Murthy and six others: Nandan Nilekani, N.S. Raghavan, Kris Gopalakrishnan, S.D. Shibulal, K. Dinesh and Ashok Arora, with Raghavan officially being the first employee of the company. N.R. Narayana Murthy started the company by borrowing Rs 10,000 from his wife, Sudha Murthy. The company was incorporated as 'Infosys Consultants Pvt. Ltd.', with Raghavan's house in Model Colony, north-central Pune as the registered office.

Today, it is one of India's largest IT companies with over 100,000 professionals (including subsidiaries) as of 30 September 2008. It has nine development centres in India and over 50 offices worldwide.

Case Studies   **167**

TABLE 11.1: NASSCOM TOP-20 IT SOFTWARE AND SERVICE EXPORTERS, FY 2007–08

Rank	Company
1.	Tata Consultancy Services Ltd
2.	Infosys Technologies Ltd
3.	Wipro Technologies Ltd
4.	Satyam Computer Services Ltd
5.	HCL Technologies Ltd
6.	Tech Mahindra Ltd
7.	Patni Computer Systems Ltd
8.	I-flex Solutions Ltd
9.	Mphasis an (EDS company)
10.	Larsen & Toubro Infotech Ltd
11.	CSC in India
12.	Aricent
13.	Syntel Inc
14.	Prithvi Information Solutions Ltd
15.	Hexaware Technologies Ltd
16.	Polaris Software Lab Ltd
17.	NIIT Technologies Ltd
18.	Sonata Software Ltd
19.	Mastek Ltd
20.	Genpact India

Source: NASSCOM.

Its annual revenues for the fiscal year 2007–08 exceeded $4 billion with a market capitalisation of over $14 billion.

Infosys defines designs and delivers technology-enabled business solutions that help Global 2000 companies win in a flat world. Infosys also provides a complete range of services by leveraging their domain and business expertise and strategic alliances with leading technology providers.

Table 11.2 lists the key milestones and accolades that have defined the journey of Infosys so far.

The Offerings:

• Business and technology consulting
• Application services, systems integration
• Product engineering
• Custom software development, maintenance, re-engineering

- Independent testing and validation services
- IT infrastructure services
- Business process outsourcing

Infosys pioneered the Global Delivery Model (GDM), which emerged as a disruptive force in the industry, leading to the rise of offshore outsourcing. The GDM is based on the principle of taking work to the location where the best talent is available and where it makes the best economic sense with the least amount of acceptable risk. Infosys takes pride in building strategic long-term client relationships. Over 97 per cent of their revenues come from existing customers.

TABLE 11.2: KEY MILESTONES AND ACCOLADES

Year	Key Milestone
2008	Infosys crosses revenues of $4.18 billion. Employees grow to over 90,000. Reports Q4 revenue of $1,142 million.
2007	Infosys crosses revenues of $3 billion. Employees grow to over 70,000. Kris Gopalakrishnan, COO, takes over as CEO. Nandan M. Nilekani is appointed Co-Chairman of the Board of Directors. Opens new subsidiary in Latin America. Reports Q2 revenue of over $1 billion.
2006	Infosys celebrates 25 years. Revenues cross $2 billion. Employees grow to 50,000. N. R. Narayana Murthy retires from the services of the company on turning 60. The Board of Directors appoints him as an Additional Director. He continues as Chairman and Chief Mentor of Infosys.
2005	Records the largest international equity offering of $1 billion from India. Selected to the Global MAKE Hall of Fame.
2004	Revenues reach $1 billion. Infosys Consulting Inc. is launched.
2003	Establishes subsidiaries in China and Australia. Expands operations in Pune and China, and sets up a Development Center in Thiruvananthapuram.
2002	Touches revenues of $500 million. Nandan M. Nilekani takes over as CEO from N.R. Narayana Murthy, who is appointed Chairman and Chief Mentor. Opens offices in The Netherlands, Singapore and Switzerland. Sponsors secondary ADS offering. Infosys and the Wharton School of the University of Pennsylvania set up The Wharton Infosys Business Transformation Awards (WIBTA). Launches Progeon, offering business process outsourcing services.

(Continued)

Year	Key Milestone
2001	Touches revenues of $400 million. Opens offices in UAE and Argentina and a Development Center in Japan. N.R. Narayana Murthy is rated among Time Magazine/CNN's 25 most influential businessmen of the world. Infosys is rated as the Best Employer by Business World/Hewitt.
2000	Touches revenues of $200 million. Opens offices in France and Hong Kong, a global development centre in Canada and UK, and three development centres in the US. Re-launches Banks 2000, the universal banking solution from Infosys, as Finacle™.
1999	Touches revenues of $100 million. Listed on NASDAQ. Infosys becomes the 21st company in the world to achieve a CMM Level 5 certification. Opens offices in Germany, Sweden, Belgium, Australia, and two development centres in the US. Infosys Business Consulting Services is launched.
1998	Starts enterprise solutions (packaged applications) practice.
1997	Opens an office in Toronto, Canada. Infosys is assessed at CMM Level 4.
1996	The Infosys Foundation is established.
1995	Opens first European office in the UK and Global Development Centers at Toronto and Mangalore. Sets up e-Business practice.
1994	Moves corporate headquarters to Electronics City, Bangalore. Opens a Development Centre at Fremont.
1993	Introduces Employee Stock Options (ESOP) programme. Acquires ISO 9001/Tick IT certification. Goes public.
1987	Opens first international office in Boston, US.
1983	Relocates corporate headquarters to Bangalore.
1981	Infosys is established by N.R. Narayana Murthy and six engineers in Pune, India, with an initial capital of $250. Signs up its first client, Data Basics Corporation in New York.

Source: http://www.infosys.com/about/who-we-are/pages/history.aspx.

Think flat—the new mantra @ infosys

The world is getting flattened by forces of globalisation, changing demographics, ubiquity of technology and regulatory compliance. The Pulitzer Prize winning author and columnist, Thomas Friedman, in his unique way of putting things, says 'The World is Flat'.

At Infosys, there is the privilege of looking at these changes from a different perspective—from the other side of the world. Infosys embraced this concept by declaring, 'we call our perspective "Think Flat", because we believe this change is as much about changing the business mindset as it is about changing our strategies and operations' (Infosys website). Companies must grasp the impact of the evolving business environment, respond to challenges and harness opportunities to succeed. To win, companies must address the shifts of the Flat World:

- Optimize cost to fuel growth
- Think faster innovation
- Think money from information
- Think winning in the turns

Delivering innovation—the Infosys way

Software Engineering & Technology Labs (SETLabs) is the research arm of Infosys which is at the forefront of anticipating and shaping the evolution of technology and its impact on business. Innovation delivery is through targeted research, centres of excellence, global internship and engagements (Figure 11.1).

Reflection of transparency in business operations

Infosys took a significant step in fostering sustainable growth by publishing its Sustainability Report 2007–08. The Report discloses information on activities in economic, social and environmental areas. It will be published annually, in accordance with the guidelines of the Global Reporting Initiative (GRI).

Narayana Murthy, Chairman and Chief Mentor of Infosys said, 'Our core corporate assets walk out every evening. It is our duty to make sure that these assets return the next morning, mentally and physically enthusiastic and energetic' (Infosys 2008a: 1)

And Nandan M. Nilekani, Co-Chairman, Infosys says, 'At Infosys, we believe that our future growth will only be viable and prosperous if we look at sustainability in all its dimensions—environmental, social, political and economic' (Infosys 2008b: 4).

FIGURE 11.1: DELIVERING INNOVATION

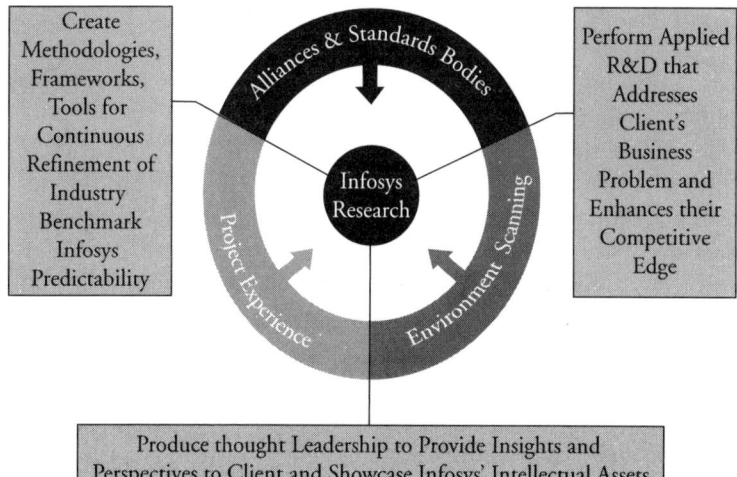

Software Engineering & Technology Labs

Create Methodologies, Frameworks, Tools for Continuous Refinement of Industry Benchmark Infosys Predictability

Alliances & Standards Bodies

Infosys Research

Project Experience

Environment Scanning

Perform Applied R&D that Addresses Client's Business Problem and Enhances their Competitive Edge

Produce thought Leadership to Provide Insights and Perspectives to Client and Showcase Infosys' Intellectual Assets

Source: http://www.infosys.com/research/pages/index.aspx (accessed on 10 June 2010).

The Infosys Sustainability Report 2007–08 covers GRI parameters that impact business risks, opportunities as well as stakeholders: Economic performance, innovation in offerings, people engagement, and corporate social responsibility initiatives.

The Infosys Sustainability Report is aligned with the GRI sustainability reporting guidelines and meets the requirements of Application Level A+. The Report conforms to the principles of the United Nations Global Compact (UNGC), the world's largest global corporate citizenship initiative.

Initiatives beyond business

In 1996, Infosys created the Infosys Foundation in the state of Karnataka, operating in the areas of health care, social rehabilitation and rural uplift, education, arts and culture. Since then this foundation has spread to the Indian states of Tamil Nadu, Andhra Pradesh, Maharashtra, Orissa and Punjab. The Infosys Foundation is headed by Sudha Murthy, wife of Chairman N.R. Narayana Murthy.

In 1997, Infosys started the 'Catch them Young Programme', to expose the urban youth to the world of Information Technology by conducting a summer vacation programme. The programme is aimed at developing an interest and understanding of computer science and information technology. This programme is targeted at students in Grade IX level.

In 2002, the Wharton Business School of the University of Pennsylvania and Infosys started the Wharton Infosys Business Transformation Award. This technology award recognizes enterprises and individuals who have transformed their businesses and the society, leveraging information technology. Past winners include Samsung, Amazon.com, Capital One, RBS and ING Direct.

Since 2004, Infosys has embarked on a series of initiatives to consolidate and formalize its academic relationships worldwide under the umbrella of a programme called AcE—Academic Entente. Through case study writing, participation in academic conferences and university events, research collaborations, hosting study trips to Infosys Development Centres and running the InStep Global Internship Program, the company communicates with important stakeholders in the academia.

Infosys' Global Internship Program, known as InStep, is one of the key components of the Academic Entente initiative. It offers live projects to interns from the universities around the world. InStep recruits undergraduate, graduate and PhD students from business, technology, and liberal arts universities to take part in an 8 to 24-week internship at one of Infosys' global offices. InStep interns are also provided career opportunities with Infosys.

In 2008, Infosys along with National Institute of Advanced Studies (NIAS) created 'Infosys Mathematics Prize' for excellence in Mathematics research.

Infosys also has the largest training centre for a private sector organisation in Asia. The training centre is located in Mysore, Karnataka. It currently accommodates 4,500 trainees each year. In 2009, a new training centre has been opened which accommodates 10,000 trainee software professionals. This new centre is also located in Mysore.

Tables 11.3 and 11.4 and Figures 11.2 and 11.3 detail the historical statistics related to the performance of Infosys between the years 1998 and 2008.

TABLE 11.3: PAST PERFORMANCE (1998–2008): A GLIMPSE

	1982	1999	2000	2001	2002	2003	2004	2005	2006	2007	2008
Financial performance											
Income	0.12	509	882	1,901	2,604	3,623	4,761	6,860	9,028	13,149	15,648
Operating profit (PBIDTA)	0.04	202	347	765	1,038	1,272	1,584	2,325	2,989	4,225	4,963
Interest	—	—	—	—	—	—	—	—	—	—	—
Depreciation	—	36	53	113	161	189	231	268	409	469	546
Provision for taxation	—	23	40	73	135	201	227	325	303	352	630
Profit after tax**	0.04	133	286	623	808	958	1,243	1,859	2,421	3,777	4,470
Dividend	—	12	30	66	132	179	196	310	412	649	758
One-time/Special dividend	—	—	—	—	—	—	668	—	830	—	1,144
Margins (%)											
Operating profit margin	33.3	39.7	39.3	40.2	39.9	35.1	33.3	33.9	33.1	32.1	31.7
Net profit margin**	33.3	26.1	32.4	32.8	31.0	26.4	26.1	27.1	26.8	28.7	28.6
Return on average net worth**	96.9	54.2	40.6	56.1	46.6	38.8	40.7	43.8	39.9	41.9	41.4
Return on average capital employed	96.9	63.5	46.3	62.6	54.4	46.9	48.1	51.4	44.9	45.7	—
Per share data (Rs)*											
Basic EPS**	—	2.59	5.41	11.78	15.27	18.09	23.43	34.63	44.34	67.82	78.24
Dividend	—	0.47	0.56	1.25	2.50	3.38	3.69	5.75	7.50	11.50	13.25
On-time/Special dividend	—	—	—	—	—	—	12.50	—	15.00	—	20.00
Book value	—	10.86	15.75	26.26	39.29	53.98	61.03	96.87	125.15	195.41	235.84
Financial position											
Share capital	—	33	33	33	33	33	33	135	138	286	286
Reserves and surplus	0.04	541	800	1,357	2,047	2,828	3,220	5,107	6,759	10,876	13,204
Net worth	0.04	574	833	1,390	2,080	2,861	3,253	5,242	6,897	11,162	13,490

(Table 11.3 continued)

(*Table 11.3 continued*)

	1982	1999	2000	2001	2002	2003	2004	2005	2006	2007	2008
Debt	–	–	–	–	–	–	–	–	–	–	–
Gross block	–	169	284	631	961	1,273	1,570	2,183	2,837	3,889	4,508
Capital expenditure	–	72	160	463	323	219	430	794	1,048	1,443	1,370
Cash and cash equivalents	0.02	417	508	578	1,027	1,639	1,839	1,683	3,779	5,610	7,689
Investment in liquid mutual funds	–	–	–	–	–	–	930	1,168	684	–	–
Net current assets	0.06	473	612	798	1,293	2,018	1,220	2,384	3,832	7,137	8,496
Total assets	0.04	574	833	1,390	2,080	2,861	3,253	5,242	6,897	11,162	13,490
Shareholding related											
Number of shareholders	7	9,527	46,314	89,643	88,650	77,010	66,945	1,58,725	1,95,956	4,88,869	5,55,562
Market capitalisation – period end	NA	9,673	59,338	26,926	24,654	26,847	32,909	61,073	82,154	1,15,307	82,362
Public shareholding (%)***	–	67.18	67.55	67.69	68.08	68.32	65.56	70.20	66.55	64.35	64.31
Credit rating											
Standard & Poor's								BBB	BBB	BBB	BBB+
Dun & Bradstreet							5A1	5A1	5A1	5A1	5A1
Corporate governance rating											
CRISIL - (GVC)							Level 1	Level 1	Level 1	Level 1	Level 1
ICRA							CGR 1	CGR 1	CGR 1	CGR 1	CGR 1

Source: Infosys 2008a.

Notes: The above figures are based on Indian GAAP (stand-alone).

*Calculated on a per share basis, adjusted for bonus issues in previous years.

**Excluding extraordinary activities/exceptional items. Fiscal 2007 and 2008 include a tax reversal of Rs 125 crore and Rs 121 crore, respectively.

***Total public shareholding as defined under Clause 40A of the Listing Agreement (excludes shares held by founders and American Depository Receipt holders).

FIGURE 11.2: SELECT HISTORICAL DATA

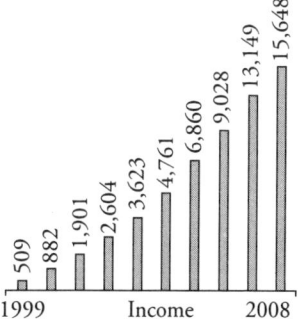

1999   Income   2008

509 882 1,901 2,604 3,623 4,761 6,860 9,028 13,149 15,648

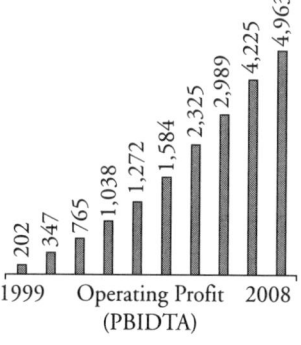

1999   Operating Profit   2008
(PBIDTA)

202 347 765 1,038 1,272 1,584 2,325 2,989 4,225 4,963

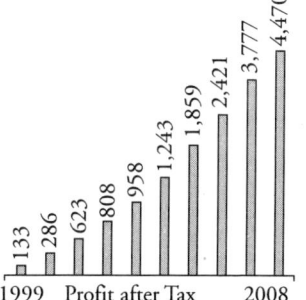

1999   Profit after Tax   2008

133 286 623 808 958 1,243 1,859 2,421 3,777 4,470

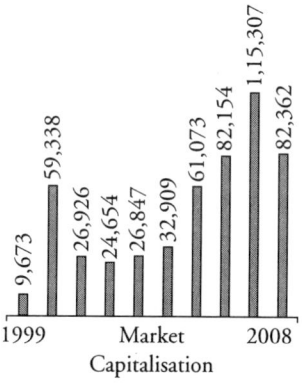

1999   Market   2008
Capitalisation

9,673 59,338 26,926 24,654 26,847 32,909 61,073 82,154 1,15,307 82,362

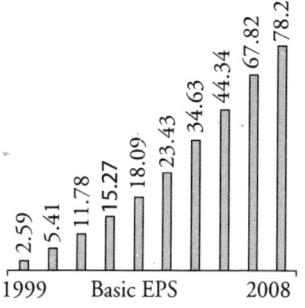

1999   Basic EPS   2008

2.59 5.41 11.78 15.27 18.09 23.43 34.63 44.34 67.82 78.24

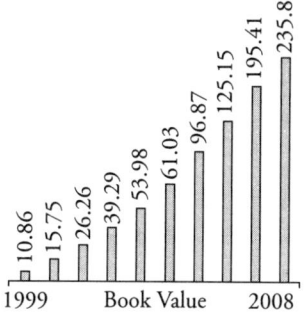

1999   Book Value   2008

10.86 15.75 26.26 39.29 53.98 61.03 96.87 125.15 195.41 235.84

Source: Infosys 2008a.

TABLE 11.4: THE YEAR AT A GLANCE—FY2007–08

(in US $ million, except per share data)

	2008	2007	Growth (%)
Indian GAAP - Stand-alone			
Financial performance			
Income	15,648	13,149	19.0
Gross profit	6,772	5,871	15.3
Operating profit (PBIDTA)	4,963	4,225	17.5
Profit after tax:* Before exceptional items	4,470	3,777	18.3
After exceptional items	4,470	3,783	18.2
EPS (par value of Rs 5/- each)			
before exceptional item:* Basic	78.24	67.82	15.4
Diluted	77.98	66.33	17.6
Dividend			
Per share	13.25	11.50	15.2
Special dividend	20.00	–	–
Financial position			
Capital expenditure	1,370	1,443	(5.1)
Fixed assets	3,931	3,107	26.5
Cash and cash equivalents	7,689	5,610	37.1
Net current assets	8,496	7,137	19.0
Total assets	13,490	11,162	20.9
Debt	–	–	–
Net worth	13,490	11,162	20.9
Cash and cash equivalents/total assets (%)	57.0	50.3	–
Market capitalisation	82,362	1,15,307	(28.6)
Indian GAAP - Consolidated			
Income	16,692	13,893	20.1
Gross profit	7,485	6,435	16.3
Operating profit (PBIDTA)	5,238	4,391	19.3
Profit after tax:* Before exceptional items	4,659	3,861	20.7
After exceptional items	4,659	3,867	20.5
EPS (par value of Rs 5/- each)			
before exceptional item:* Basic	81.53	69.11	18.0
Diluted	81.26	67.59	20.2

(Table 11.4 continued)

(Table 11.4 continued)

	2008	2007	Growth (%)
US GAAP			
Revenues	4,176	3,090	35.1
Gross profit	1,723	1,313	31.2
Operating income	1,151	852	35.1
Net income*	1,155	850	35.9
Earnings per equity share: Basic	2.03	1.53	32.7
Diluted	2.02	1.50	34.7

Source: Infosys 2008a.
Note: 1 crore equals 10 million.
*Net profit for 2008 and 2007 includes a reversal of tax provision of Rs 121 crore ($29 million) and Rs 125 crore ($30 million), respectively.

FIGURE 11.3: GAAP DATA—FY2007–08

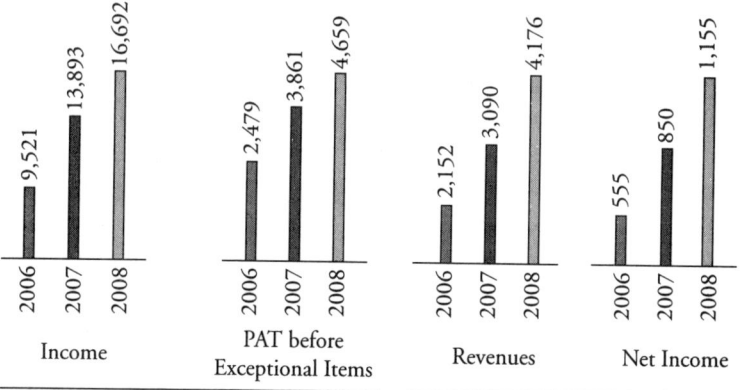

Indian GAAP Consolidated (Rs crore)   US GAAP ($ million)
Source: Infosys 2008a.

Key Strategic Drivers for Growth:

- The business model of Infosys was a judicious mix of entre-preneurial zeal and flexibility. In the foundation of Infosys, the seed to become an ethical business firm was sown, based on a highly competent and skilled workforce in the area of software development technology.

In the first phase of the evolution of Infosys, the entire process of software development was carried out at the client site. Infosys earned its profits from the price differential between the cost of software developers in the US versus that of the cost of software developers in India.

- Then as other players entered the market to take advantage of the low wage environment, Infosys differentiated itself from others by improving the technical excellence and customer responsiveness.

- As the business grew, Infosys created an offshore software development centre (OSDC) in Bangalore. Thereby, allowing it to increase the productivity through 24-hours operations. This enhancement in productivity was possible because OSDC enabled both economies of scale and skill by bringing the work back from the client site, which in turn led to increase in the internal learning of individual software engineers. During this time, the company was focused on building infrastructure and developing its skill base.

- By setting up marketing offices in the US, London, and around Europe, it ascertained that the overseas market could be effectively tapped. Thereby, being effectively able to realize the call by Narayana Murthy for 'growth, growth, growth'. To achieve growth on a constant basis, Infosys achieved two very demanding benchmarks in the arena of software quality standards: by achieving ISO 9001 certification and by achieving the Carnegie Melon University Software Engineering Institute Capability Maturity Model (SEI CMM), Level 4.

- Infosys not only had the American process discipline but also had 'Indian middle class heart'. Thereby enabling the people to innovate within the architecture of certain fixed processes. The atmosphere was very collegial and except for scheduled meetings there were no fixed timings for anything. The employees could work according to the hours that suited them. The work culture encouraged debate and challenges but not impoliteness or unpleasantness. 'You can be critical, but not discourteous', said Narayana Murthy.

- Infosys had a very conservative financial structure. Infosys abhorred debts and deployed cash reserves in completely secure but low return deposits. Infosys pioneered Employee Stock Option Plan (ESOP). While in many organisations ESOP did not deliver expected results, Infosys was able to distribute the wealth amongst those employees who even helped to create more wealth for the company. This also enabled it to realize the founding premises of creating wealth and to distribute it among those who helped create it. This also became the major weapon for the company to attract and retain the best local talent, despite the constant threat from various quarters.

- With the fierce pace of competition, propelled by globalisation, Infosys was confronted by three key challenges: commoditisation, cost and competition. To protect and enhance its margin, Infosys decided to go global, this enabled it to move up in the value curve.

- This moving up in the value curve could be achieved by focusing on two key tasks:

  - By creating an international brand equity
  - By localisation at the customer interface

- To create brand equity was the key to move to a value-based model. Infosys did this successfully by listing on NASDAQ. Then it decided to develop domain-specific knowledge. For this it selected financial services, health care, telecommunications and engineering as focal industries.

- One of the key challenges for the global IT services company was location-wise domain knowledge within the home countries of the important customers and also to develop better customer relationship. To sort out this problem, Infosys opened Proximity Development Centres (PDC), which were staffed with local people, who had a high awareness of the local culture and could build relationships very easily.

- Meanwhile Infosys was also envisioning the development of new back end centres in the cost effective regions of the world, thereby becoming truly global.

Case II: Anand Milk Union Ltd (AMUL)

The origin

Over five decades ago, the life of an average farmer in Kheda District was very much like that of his/her counterpart anywhere else in India. His/her income was derived almost entirely from seasonal crops. The income from milk was undependable. Milk producers had to travel long distances to deliver milk to the only dairy, the Polson Dairy, in Anand. There, the milk often went sour, especially in the summer season, as producers had to physically carry milk in individual containers. Private traders and middlemen controlled the marketing and distribution system. These middlemen decided the prices and the off-take from the farmers by the season. As milk is perishable, farmers were compelled to sell it for whatever they were offered. Often, they had to sell cream and ghee at throw-away prices. In this situation, the private trader made a killing. Moreover, the government at that time had given monopoly rights to Polson Dairy, which was run by a person of Parsi descent (around that time Polson was the most well known butter brand in the country) to collect milk from Anand and in turn supply it to the Mumbai city (about 400 kilometres away). Another problem faced by the farmers was that in winter, the milk output of buffaloes doubled, which caused prices to fall down even further. India ranked nowhere amongst the milk producing countries of the world in 1946. Gradually, the realisation dawned on the farmers with inspiration from the then nationalist leaders Sardar Vallabhbhai Patel (who later became the first Home Minister of free India) and Morarji Desai (who later become the Prime Minister of India) and local farmers, freedom fighter and social worker, Tribhovandas Patel, that the exploitation by the traders could be checked only if they marketed their milk themselves. AMUL was the result of the realisation that the farmers could pool in their milk and work as a cooperative.

AMUL (Anand Milk Union Limited) was thus formed in 1946 as a dairy cooperative movement in India. It is a brand managed by an apex cooperative organisation called GCMMF (Gujarat Cooperative

Milk Marketing Federation) which was set up as a marketing arm and is jointly owned by around 2.7 million milk producers in the state of Gujarat.

AMUL means 'priceless' in Sanskrit. The brand name 'Amul', from the Sanskrit '*Amoolya*', was suggested by a quality control expert in Anand. Variants, all meaning 'priceless', are found in several Indian languages. Amul products have been in use in millions of homes since 1946.

Amul, is based in the town of Anand, in Gujarat, and has been a classic example of a successful co-operative in India. It is one of the best examples of co-operative achievement in a developing world. The Amul pattern of business model has established a unique and appropriate model for rural development. The White Revolution, in India, was spurred by Amul, thereby making India the largest producer of milk and milk products in the world.

Amul is the largest food brand in India and the world's largest pouched milk brand with sales registering a quantum growth of 22.9 per cent to reach Rs 52.55 billion during 2007–08. Currently, Amul has 2.7 million producer members with a milk collection average of 7.4 million litres per day.

SETTING UP OF KAIRA DISTRICT CO-OPERATIVE MILK PRODUCERS' UNION (KDCMPUL)

The Kaira District Co-operative Milk Producers' Union Limited (KDCMPUL) commenced pasteurizing milk for the Bombay Milk Scheme in June 1948. By the end of 1948 more than 400 farmers joined this village cooperative society and the quantity of milk to be handled by one union increased from 250 to 5,000 litres a day. Meanwhile, Dr Verghese Kurien, fed up being at the government creamery in Anand, Gujarat, which held no challenge, volunteered to help Tribhovandas Patel, the chairman of KDCMPUL, in setting up a processing plant. The success of Amul was instrumental in launching the White Revolution that resulted in increased milk production in India. It is officially termed as Operation Flood by Amul. The breakthrough technology of spray-drying and processing buffalo milk, developed by H.M. Dalaya, was one of the key factors that contributed to the Revolution.

CREATION OF GUJARAT COOPERATIVE MILK MARKETING FEDERATION (GCMMF)

In 1954, Kaira District Co-operative Milk Producers' Union built a plant to convert surplus milk produced in the winter season into milk powder and butter. In 1958, a plant to manufacture cheese and one to produce baby food was added. Subsequent years saw the addition of more plants to produce different products. In 1973, the milk societies/district level unions decided to set up a marketing agency to market their products. This agency was the Gujarat Cooperative Milk Marketing Federation (GCMMF). It was registered as a co-operative society on 9 July 1973.

GCMMF today: An overview

Established in 1973, GCMMF is India's largest dairy products marketing organisation. It procures milk from 2.7 million farmers who are its members and aims to provide remunerative returns to the farmers and also serve the interests of consumers by providing quality products, which are good value for money. GCMMF markets and manages the Amul brand.

It is the apex marketing federation for 13 district cooperative milk unions. The federation includes 12,792 village dairy cooperative societies of Gujarat. The products of its member unions are marketed and distributed under the brand name 'Amul'. GCMMF is the largest exporter of dairy products. It has a significant presence in the Gulf, South Asian Association for Regional Cooperation (SAARC) region, USA, Singapore, Hong Kong, Philippines, Cambodia, Japan, Vietnam, China, Australia and Africa. As on 31 March 2008, GCMMF had an absolute net worth of Rs 1,200 million. The federation reported a profit after tax (PAT) of Rs 150 million on revenues of Rs 52.64 billion for 2007–08. Table 11.5 give a snapshot of the key statistics related to GCMMF's operations.

From mid-1990s Amul has entered areas not related directly to its core business. Its entry into the ice cream segment was regarded as successful due to the large market share it was able to capture within a short period of time—primarily due to the price differential and

TABLE 11.5 : GCMMF: A SNAPSHOT 2008

Members	13 district cooperative milk producers' unions
No. of Producer Members	2.7 million
No. of Village Societies	13,141
Total Milk handling capacity	10.21 million litres per day
Milk collection (Total, 2007–08)	2.69 billion litres
Milk collection (Daily Average 2007–08)	7.4 million litres
Milk Drying Capacity	626 Mts Per day
Cattle feed manufacturing Capacity	3,090 Mts per day

Source: http://www.amul.com/organisation.html (accessed on 4 June 2010).

the brand name. It also entered the pizza business, where the base and the recipes were made available to restaurant owners who could price it as low as Rs 30 per pizza when the other players were charging upwards of Rs 100.

In September 2007, Amul emerged as the leading Indian brand according to a survey by Synovate to find out Asia's top 1,000 brands.

Products marketed by GCMMF

BREADSPREADS
- Amul Butter
- Amul Lite Low Fat Breadspread
- Amul Cooking Butter

CHEESE RANGE
- Amul Pasteurized Processed Cheddar Cheese
- Amul Processed Cheese Spread
- Amul Pizza (Mozarella) Cheese
- Amul Shredded Pizza Cheese
- Amul Emmental Cheese
- Amul Gouda Cheese
- Amul Malai Paneer (cottage cheese)
- Utterly Delicious Pizza

MITHAEE RANGE (ETHNIC SWEETS)
- Amul Shrikhand (Mango, Saffron, Almond Pistachio, Cardamom)
- Amul Amrakhand
- Amul Mithaee Gulabjamuns
- Amul Mithaee Gulabjamun Mix
- Amul Mithaee Kulfi Mix
- Avsar Ladoos

UHT MILK RANGE
- Amul Shakti 3 per cent fat Milk
- Amul Taaza 1.5 per cent fat Milk
- Amul Gold 4.5 per cent fat Milk
- Amul Lite Slim-n-Trim Milk 0 per cent fat milk
- Amul Shakti Toned Milk
- Amul Fresh Cream
- Amul Snowcap Softy Mix

PURE GHEE
- Amul Pure Ghee
- Sagar Pure Ghee
- Amul Cow Ghee

INFANT MILK RANGE
- Amul Infant Milk Formula 1 (0-6 months)
- Amul Infant Milk Formula 2 (6 months above)
- Amulspray Infant Milk Food

MILK POWDERS
- Amul Full Cream Milk Powder
- Amulya Dairy Whitener
- Sagar Skimmed Milk Powder
- Sagar Tea and Coffee Whitener

SWEETENED CONDENSED MILK
- Amul Mithaimate Sweetened Condensed Milk

FRESH MILK
- Amul Taaza Toned Milk 3 per cent fat
- Amul Gold Full Cream Milk 6 per cent fat

- Amul Shakti Standardised Milk 4.5 per cent fat
- Amul Slim & Trim Double Toned Milk 1.5 per cent fat
- Amul Saathi Skimmed Milk 0 per cent fat
- Amul Cow Milk

CURD PRODUCTS
- Yogi Sweetened Flavoured Dahi (Dessert)
- Amul Masti Dahi (fresh curd)
- Amul Masti Spiced Butter Milk
- Amul Lassee

AMUL ICE CREAMS
- Royal Treat Range (Butterscotch, Rajbhog, Malai Kulfi)
- Nut-o-Mania Range (Kaju Draksh, Kesar Pista Royale, Fruit Bonanza, Roasted Almond)
- Nature's Treat (Alphanso Mango, Fresh Litchi, Shahi Anjir, Fresh Strawberry, Black Currant, Santra Mantra, Fresh Pineapple)
- Sundae Range (Mango, Black Currant, Sundae Magic, Double Sundae)
- Assorted Treat (Chocobar, Dollies, Frostik, Ice Candies, Tricone, Chococrunch, Megabite, Cassatta)
- Utterly Delicious (Vanilla, Strawberry, Chocolate, Chocochips, Cake Magic)

CHOCOLATE AND CONFECTIONERY
- Amul Milk Chocolate
- Amul Fruit & Nut Chocolate

BROWN BEVERAGE
- Nutramul Malted Milk Food

MILK DRINK
- Amul Kool Flavoured Milk (Mango, Strawberry, Saffron, Cardamom, Rose, Chocolate)
- Amul Kool Cafe
- Amul Kool Koko
- Amul Kool Millk Shaake (Mango, Strawberry, Badam, Banana)

HEALTH BEVERAGE
- Amul Shakti White Milk Food

(*Source:* http://www.amul.com/organisation.html [accessed on 4 June 2010])

Exports

Despite the ban on export of milk powder during the initial six months of 2008, because of which the export of bulk milk powder were adversely affected, it is indeed surprising that the export turnover has more than doubled during the year, registering a recorded turnover of Rs 1,250 million in 2008 against the previous year's turnover of Rs 600 million.

Key competitors

The success story of Amul inspired many Indian State Governments to replicate the Amul business model in their respective states. The other brands which were introduced by designing their business models on the lines of Amul could not make it that big. But in their respective states, these brands have a significant presence. For example, Vijaya in Andhra Pradesh, Nandini in Karnataka, Milma in Kerala, Omfed in Orissa, Aavin in Tamilnadu and Sudha in Bihar.

The success story: Key drivers

The success story of Amul can be attributed to a host of factors which are detailed below. However, the most prominent among them is 'people', i.e., the milk producers per se. It is the willingness of the milk producers and their integrity and solidarity to come together with a sole mission to help themselves and empower so as to protect, grow and contribute to rural development.

BUSINESS MODEL

The Amul business model is a three tier organisation structure which is popularly known as 'Anand Pattern' cooperative system. The three tiers include:

- **Village Cooperative:** This constitutes the primary link, with around 250 member milk producers. It has membership of milk producers of the village and is governed by an elected management committee consisting of nine to 12 elected representatives of the milk producers. The main function of this body is to collect surplus milk from the milk producers of the village and make payment based on the quality and quantity.

*   **District Level Milk Union:** This constitutes membership of village societies of the district and is governed by a board of directors consisting of nine to 18 elected representatives of the village societies. The main function of this agency is to process milk into various milk and milk products as per the market requirements. Besides, it also provides input services to the producers and other support to village level societies. The union procures milk from the village societies of the district and arranges transportation of raw milk from the villages to the milk union.
*   **The State Level Federation:** This forms the apex tier of the business model governed by a board of directors consisting of one elected representative of each milk union and has the membership of the milk union of the state. It provides support services, to the milk unions and members, such as technical inputs, management support and advisory services. The main function of the federation is to market the milk and milk products manufactured by the milk unions.

The model innovatively combines the productive genius of farmers with professional management and modern technology. The facilities at all the three levels are farmer-owned. The works of co-operatives are able to build markets, supply inputs and create value-added processing and offer remunerative payment for good quality produce and timely supplies.

MARKETING MIX: THE RIGHT BLEND

The Value Added Product: Product development at Amul was driven by the inherent nature of the basic raw material, i.e., the milk which is a highly perishable commodity and has to be processed on the same day to avoid any kind of wastage, thus, leading to innovation by developing value added products of milk such as buttermilk, milk powder and ice cream, etc., thus, diversifying into different product categories by utilizing the surplus milk.

The Low Cost Value for Money Pricing: At the time when Amul was formed, consumers had limited purchasing power and modest consumption levels of milk and other dairy products. Thus, Amul has adopted a low-cost price strategy to make its products affordable and attractive to consumers by guaranteeing them value for money.

The Consistent Advertising and Promotion Strategy: With a Tagline like 'Utterly Butterly Delicious', advertising played a key and prominent role in the success of the Amul brand. It all started in the year 1967 with the introduction of Amul baby (a chubby butter girl usually dressed in polka dotted dress) showing up on hoardings and product wrappers and is the mascot for the Amul brand. The advertisements were very simple, innovative and fresh in their content and approach. They depicted both national and international current affairs, issues and controversies pertaining to politics and sports, etc. All of these were well packed and represented in the form of advertisements and were related to Amul. They were very catchy with the viewers and received a good response and recall contributing to a good brand image for Amul.

Amul advertisements are one of the longest running ads based on a theme, now vying for the Guinness record for being the longest running ad campaign ever.

A Highly Efficient Distribution Network with Deep Penetration: Over the recent years, the federation has successfully introduced new product lines. In order to leverage the distribution network strengths, to optimize market supervision expenditures, to achieve increasing efficiency while keeping the distribution infrastructure lean, focused and productive, the Federation amalgamated its different distribution networks. Today, it operates an efficient distribution infrastructure consisting of 46 sales offices, catering to 3,000 distributors and over 500,000 retailers.

THE UMBRELLA BRAND BENEFIT
The network follows an umbrella branding strategy. Amul is the common brand for most product categories produced by various unions: liquid milk, milk powders, butter, ghee, cheese, cocoa

products, sweets, ice-cream and condensed milk. Umbrella branding has helped GCMMF reduce advertisement cost and also to build a big power brand in processed food. No other brand will be comparable to Amul in the dairy products category.

Amul's sub-brands include variants such as Amulspray, Amulspree, Amulya and Nutramul. The edible oil products are grouped around Dhara and Lokdhara, mineral water is sold under the Jal Dhara brand while fruit drinks bear the Safal name.

By insisting on an umbrella brand, GCMMF not only skillfully avoided inter-union conflicts but also created an opportunity for the union members to cooperate in developing products.

MANAGING THIRD PARTY SERVICE PROVIDERS

Since the beginning, it was recognised that the unions' core activity lay in milk processing and the production of dairy products. Accordingly, marketing efforts (including brand development) were assumed by GCMMF. All other activities were entrusted to third parties. These include logistics of milk collection, distribution of dairy products, sale of products through dealers and retail stores, provision of animal feed, and veterinary services.

ESTABLISHING AND IMPLEMENTING BEST PRACTICES

A key source of competitive advantage has been the enterprise's ability to continuously implement best practices across all elements of the network: the federation, the unions, the village societies and the distribution channel.

In developing these practices, the federation and the unions have adapted successful models from around the world. It could be the implementation of small group activities or quality circles at the federation, or a TQM programme at the unions or housekeeping and good accounting practices at the village society level.

More important, the network has been able to regularly roll out improvement programmes across to a large number of members and the implementation rate is consistently high.

For example, every Friday, without fail, between 10 a.m. and 11.00 a.m., all employees of GCMMF meet at the closest office, be it a department or a branch or a depot to discuss their various quality concerns.

Each meeting has its pre-set format in terms of Purpose, Agenda and Limit (PAL) with a process check at the end to record how the meeting was conducted. Similar processes are in place at the village societies, the unions and even at the wholesaler and C&F agent levels as well.

Examples of benefits from recent initiatives include reduction in transportation time from the depots to the wholesale dealers, improvement in ROI of wholesale dealers, implementation of Zero Stock Out through improved availability of products at depots and also the implementation of Just-in-Time in finance to reduce the float.

Kaizens at the unions have helped improve the quality of milk in terms of acidity and sour milk. For example, Sabar Union's records show a reduction from 2.0 per cent to 0.5 per cent in the amount of sour milk/curd received at the union. The most impressive aspect of this large-scale roll out of small and continuous improvement (kaizen) is that improvement processes are turning the village societies into individual improvement centers.

TECHNOLOGY AND E-INITIATIVES

GCMMF's technology strategy is characterized by four distinct components: new products, process technology, complementary assets to enhance milk production and e-commerce.

Few dairies of the world have the wide variety of products produced by the GCMMF network. Village societies are encouraged to install chilling units by giving subsidies. Automation in processing and packaging get priority as does HACCP certification. Amul actively pursues developments in embryo transfer and cattle breeding in order to improve cattle quality to increase milk yields.

GCMMF was one of the first FMCG (fast-moving consumer goods) firms in India to employ Internet technologies to implement B2C commerce.

Today customers can order a variety of products through the Internet and be assured of timely delivery with cash payment upon receipt.

Another e-initiative underway is to provide farmers access to information relating to markets, technology and best practices in the dairy industry through net enabled kiosks in the villages.

GCMMF has also implemented a Geographical Information System (GIS) at both ends of the supply chain, i.e., milk collection as well as the marketing process.

Farmers now have better access to information on the output as well as support services while providing a better planning tool to marketing personnel.

RETAILING

The strategic thrust placed on opening Amul Parlors since 2002 has started yielding desired results. In anticipation of the paradigm shift in the macro economic scenario and the burgeoning threat of organized retailers, Amul Parlors are then the answer to counter the potential threat from competitors. Increasing the visibility of the Amul brand in the retail market, these company-owned outlets helped enable direct interface with consumers and provided an ideal platform to showcase their entire range of products.

Through a concerted team effort, Amul has managed to create 2,300 Amul Parlors in 2007–08, which generated a sales turnover of Rs 1,070 million. The outlets have not only helped brand Amul to become ubiquitous but have also managed to provide a very rewarding employment opportunity to hundreds of entrepreneurs across India.

During the new financial year, it has been decided to set up 10,000 outlets by 2009. To achieve this challenging goal, certain potential locations such as railways, airports, universities and shopping malls have been identified

The success of Amul can be traced to the following:

- High-quality products sold at reasonable prices
- The genesis of a vast co-operative network.
- The triumph of indigenous technology
- The marketing savvy of farmers' organisation
- A proven model for dairy development

CASE III: Reliance Industries Limited

Dhirubhai's success journey starts from nowhere to the top of the Indian industry. Dhirajlal Hirachand Ambani commonly known as

Dhirubhai, initially set up Reliance Commercial Corporation (the name was subsequently changed to Reliance Textile Industries in the late 1960s and further to Reliance Industries in the mid 1980s) with a mere Rs 15,000 at Bombay in 1958. From there to a synthetic yarn, textiles and petrochemicals empire in 1994 with a market capitalisation in excess of Rs 80 billion, thus, becoming India's number 1 private sector company. This phenomenal growth by Reliance Industries Limited (RIL) has kept up with the words of Dhirubhai that 'Growth has no limit in Reliance'.

The growth journey of RIL exemplifies the fact as to how a company can take advantage of government policies to its advantage and how by keeping the public (i.e., the shareholders) on their side, can fight any odd situation of financial crunch.

Initially starting from a trading house in 1958, RIL's phenomenal growth has been due to continuous consolidation by adapting to the market demand. RIL kept on gearing itself with the latest market demand, thereby, steadily switching over from rayon fabric to nylon and then to polyester. Side by side, they started setting up their own manufacturing plants and always ensuring that the plant adopted the latest state-of-the-art technology. The number 1 position of RIL could be sustained because they altered the very structure of the market. Traditionally, there was a three tier textile market consisting of the manufacturer, the wholesaler and the retailer. Reliance opted to bypass the wholesaler, thereby, enhancing its profit, increasing the speed to market and increasing their customer base, as they owned their own showrooms and franchised across the country.

Strategies adopted by RIL that led to this spectacular growth envied by rivals were threefold. The first strategy was to become a manufacturing powerhouse by going for 'world class' capacity that could compete in cost and quality on a global scale. The second strategy that it followed was to purchase technology from the best foreign source rather than to enter joint ventures. This let them work at their own pace and become self-reliant. The third strategy was that of time management. By adopting quicker ways of working, they squeezed time from both their projects as well as from operations. These strategies led to the lowest cost, best quality, enhanced customer service which eventually contributed to its phenomenal growth. RIL has continuously upgraded technology and capacity, keeping an eye on the growth in the market.

The RIL financial success story is a departure from the prevailing practice among the Indian businesses. They mobilized funds directly from the public. One of the foremost points that favoured RIL through the various turmoils that it faced was the confidence shown by the public in its ability to conduct business for their benefit. RIL has been known as the zero-tax company because of its excellent tax planning ability. As a result, though the profit continued to grow, yet the company has not paid a single rupee to the exchequer as corporate income tax.

In Reliance, like other family managed businesses of the world, families have the last word in decision-making. Verbal decisions work because of the trust, which depends upon the individuals' capacity to deliver.

So far Reliance has managed the break-neck speed of growth by bringing the talent from outside India. But now they have gone for a radical change whereby they have to come up with an organized process for nurturing and developing the human resources of the company. Meanwhile, they have to tap the vast resource pool of talent present in the country.

Reliance: Emerging as the largest private company in India

The Reliance Group is India's largest private sector enterprise with total revenue in excess of Rs 990 billion ($22.6 billion) with profits of Rs 62 billion ($1.4 billion). This group was founded by Late Dhirubhai Ambani (1932–2002) initially as a textile manufacturing company which subsequently evolved as a global giant featuring in the Forbes Global list of world's 400 best big companies and in the Fortune 500 list of world's largest companies.

Incorporated in 1958, Reliance has successfully completed a backward integration strategy that has transformed it into India's largest private-sector company, and number two in overall (behind state-owned Indian Oil Co. Ltd). Reliance's petrochemicals division is fully integrated and includes exploration and production; refining (the company has built one of the world's largest and most modern complexes in Gujarat); and marketing through a chain of more than 1,000 service stations; and the production of petrochemicals, including polymers, polyester intermediates and others. These chemicals are used to support Reliance's continued textile operations, which focus particularly on the production of polyester fabrics. Following the 2004 acquisition of Trevira, the company has become the world's leading polyester manufacturer, with production levels topping 25 million meters per year. The company's textile range includes polyesters, acrylics and finished garments. Dhirubhai epitomized the spirit of 'dare to dream and learn to excel'. Figure 11.4 depicts the growth trajectory of RIL from 1992 onwards and projected into 2011.

FIGURE 11.4: GROWTH CHART OF RELIANCE INDUSTRIES LTD

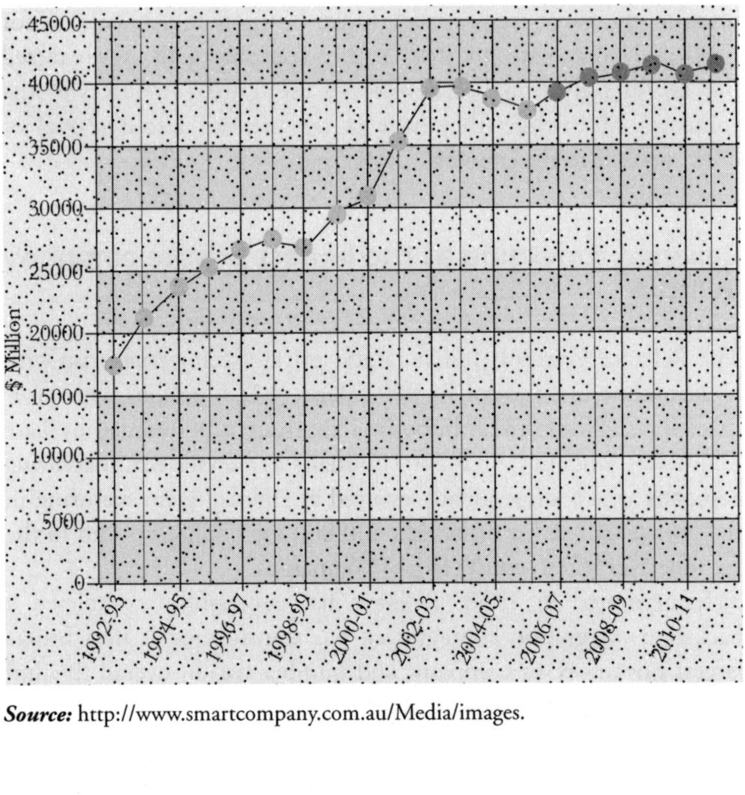

Source: http://www.smartcompany.com.au/Media/images.

The flagship company, Reliance Industries Ltd (RIL) alone accounts for:

- Seventeen per cent of the total profits of the private sector in India
- Seven per cent of the profits of the entire corporate sector in India
- Six per cent of the total market capitalisation in India
- Weightage of 13 per cent in the BSE Sensex
- Weightage of 10 per cent in the Nifty Index

One out of every four investors in India is a Reliance shareholder. Reliance is today not only a fully integrated petrochemical business but also diversified into many other core business categories. These include:

- Energy production and distribution
- Telecommunications
- Capital finance
- Petrochemicals
- Polyesters fibre intermediates
- Petroleum refining
- Insurance

Table 11.6 gives the financial highlights of Reliance for the decade of 1998 to 2008.

How it all began

Dhirajlal Hirachand Ambani travelled to the port city of Aden at the age of 16. There, Ambani began working as a clerk pumping gas at a service station. Ambani remained in Aden for nearly 10 years, rising to become Burmah Shell's marketing manager.

Ambani quit Burmah Shell and, for a time, worked in the insurance field. In 1958, Ambani decided to return to India and start up a new business as an exporter of Indian goods to Aden. Finding housing for his young family in a Mumbai slum, Ambani at first rented office space, or rather a desk, for two hours per day. Initially, Ambani's exports included spices as well as fabrics.

Initially Ambani was selling yarns to textile manufacturers. The first textile mill in Naroda was opened after receiving clearances to manufacture cloth from polyester fibre.

TABLE 11.6: FINANCIAL HIGHLIGHTS OF RELIANCE

(Rs in 10 million)

	2007–08	$ mn	06–07	05–06	04–05	03–04	02–03	01–02	00–01	99–00	98–99
Turnover	34,713	139,269	1,18,354	89,124	73,164	56,247	50,096	45,404	23,024	15,847	10,624
Total Income	36,116	1,44,898	1,18,832	89,807	74,614	57,385	51,097	46,186	23,407	16,534	11,232
Earnings Before Depreciation, Interest and Tax (EBDIT)	7,212	28,935	20,525	14,982	14,261	10,983	9,366	8,658	5,562	4,746	3,318
Depreciation	1,208	4,847	4,815	3,401	3,724	3,247	2,837	2,816	1,565	1,278	855
Profit After Tax	4,850	19,458	11,943	9,069	7,572	5,160	4,104	3,243	2,646	2,403	1,704
Equity Dividend (%)	–	130	110	100	75	52.5	50	47.5	42.5	40	37.5
Dividend Payout	407	1,631	1,440	1,393	1,045	733	698	663	448	385	350
Equity Share Capital	362	1,454	1,393	1,393	1,393	1,396	1,396	1,054	1,053	1,053	933
Equity Share Suspense	–	–	60	–	–	–	–	342	–	–	–

Equity Share Warrants	419	1,682	—	—	—	—	—	—	—	—	—
Reserves and Surplus	19,520	78,313	62,514	48,411	39,010	33,057	28,931	26,416	13,712	12,636	11,183
Net Worth	20,301	81,449	63,967	49,804	40,403	34,453	30,327	27,812	14,765	13,983	12,369
Gross Fixed Assets	31,714	1,27,235	1,07,061	91,928	59,955	56,860	52,547	48,261	25,868	24,662	22,088
Net Fixed Assets	21,159	84,889	71,189	62,675	35,082	35,146	34,086	33,184	14,027	15,448	15,396
Total Assets	37,336	1,49,792	1,17,353	93,095	80,586	71,157	63,737	56,485	29,875	29,369	28,156
Market Capitalisation	82,049	3,29,179	1,98,905	1,10,958	76,079	75,132	38,603	41,989	41,191	33,346	12,176
Number of Employees		25,487	24,696	12,540	12,113	11,358	12,915	12,864	15,083	15,912	16,640
Contribution to National Exchequer	3,414	13,696	15,344	15,950	13,972	12,903	13,210	10,470	4,277	3,719	2,893

(Table 11.6 continued)

(Table 11.6 continued)

	2007–08	$ mn	06–07	05–06	04–05	03–04	02–03	01–02	00–01	99–00	98–99
Earnings Per Share – Rs	3.34#	133.9 #	82.2	65.1	54.2	36.8	29.3	23.4	25.1	22.4	18.0
Turnover Per Share – Rs	23.88	958.1	814.2	639.6	525.0	402.8	358.8	325.2	218.5	150.4	113.8
Book Value Per Share – Rs	13.97	560.3	440.0	357.4	289.9	246.7	217.2	199.2	140.1	129.9	129.8
Debt:Equity Ratio	0.45:1	0.45:1	0.44:1	0.44:1	0.46:1	0.56:1	0.60:1	0.64:1	0.72:1	0.82:1	0.86:1
EBDIT / Gross Turnover (%)	20.8	20.8	17.3	16.8	19.5	19.5	18.7	19.1	26.8	30.6	31.2
Net Profit Margin (%)	14.0	14.0	10.1	10.2	10.3	9.2	8.2	7.1	12.8	15.5	16.0
RONW (%)	28.8	28.8	23.5	22.7	21.9	17.0	14.8	16.1	20.0	21.8	19.0
ROCE (%)	20.3	20.3	20.5	20.5	21.3	14.0	13.2	15.3	20.4	20.0	18.3

Source: http://www.ril.com/html/investor/10_yearshighlight.html (accessed on 10 June 2010).

Textiles provided Ambani the future opportunity and quickly became the company's focus. Ambani was able to develop a thriving business, importing and exporting rayon and polyester. Reliance quickly identified the economic condition of the country and the buying power of the customers and forayed into businesses with high margins.

After a few initial years in trading yarns, the company set up its first factory in 1966, placing him in competition with his own customers. Success in the new venture came quickly with the launch of the highly popular Vimal fabric brand. By the end of the decade, Ambani was operating four factories. The company's success came from its determination to use only the most modern and highly efficient production equipment.

Into the early 1970s, however, India's economy remained dominated by a handful of families; between them, they controlled virtually every industry. This included the textile industry as well whose distribution side soon proved to be an obstacle in the growth of Ambani's fabric sales. In response, Ambani became determined to set up his own distribution arm, which later included not only the sale of raw fabrics, but also the company's own fashion clothings.

In 1981, Ambani received the license to construct a factory in Patalganga for producing polyester yarn.

Into the early 1980s, Ambani was joined by sons, Mukesh and Anil. Both had been sent to the United States for their education and, upon their return to India, played a prominent part in implementing Reliance's next phase of growth. Just as the company had moved from the sale of textiles to their manufacture, Reliance became determined to continue its backward integration in order to produce the chemicals from which the textile yarns were made.

After the death of Dhirubhai Ambani, his two sons not only parted ways but also ventured into unrelated businesses. The flagship company, Reliance Industries Ltd remained with the elder son Mukesh Ambani.

Key milestone

Reliance's vertical integration strategy naturally led to an interest in extending its operations to petroleum refining and even to exploration and production.

In 1993, it launched a public offering, which at that time, was India's largest ever IPO. The company began developing its petroleum products marketing and distribution operations, including a network of some 1,000 service stations.

Reliance continued to pioneer financing channels in India. For example, in 1993, the company became the first Indian company to raise capital on the foreign market.

In 1994, the company completed a second successful GDR issue. The company used the new capital, in part, to expand its petrochemicals wing, building the world's largest multi-feed at the Hazira site. The company also added production plants for ethylene and polyethylene. The new units launched production in 1998.

In 1997, Reliance announced a plan to build one of the world's largest and most modern petroleum refining complexes in Jamnagar, Gujarat, at a cost of some $6 billion. The government agreed to the plan and granted the company the right to import petroleum directly, rather than going through Indian Oil, which helped Reliance greatly drive down operating costs.

Constructed in record time, the Jamnagar site was commissioned in 1999. The site's production capacity was double that of any other Indian refinery and ranked among the top five in the world. The addition of the new facility also placed Reliance at the top rank of the country's private-sector companies.

Product portfolio

- Recron staple fibre and filament yarn
- Relab linear alkyl benzene
- Reon poly vinyl chloride
- Reclair linear low density polyethylene
- Relene high density polyethylene
- Repol polypropylene and PET
- Relpet PET
- Refinery product LPG, motor spirit, naphtha
- Vimal suitings and shirtings, dress materials and sarees
- Harmony furnishing fabric

- Slumberel fibre filled pillows
- Vimal RueRel Suitings
- Reance trousers, shirts and Jacket
- Crude oil and natural gas
- Trivera high-tech fibre and filaments and customised specialities

Change in strategic focus

After the death of Dhirubhai Ambani, his two sons ventured into non-related areas and diversified the business portfolio and subsequently separated the empire to be managed independently.

Reliance set up its own phone service, Reliance Infocomm, in that year, targeting the telecommunications sector, especially the fast-growing cellular phone market.

The diversification strategy has given them a wider platform in other core sectors and, therefore, the risk has also reduced.

The diversification strategy that Reliance adopted was conglomerate in nature as it diversified into those businesses which were totally unrelated to its existing businesses, for example, telecom and power.

It was used to capitalize on organisational strengths and to minimize weaknesses. It led to better management and utilisation of resources resulting in improved cash flows.

This change of focus in business also led to the breaking up of the conglomerate.

Breaking up in 2006

The company increased its dominance of the country's petrochemicals sector through its acquisition of the main private-sector rival, Indian Petrochemicals Corporation.

Yet, the petroleum industry remained the company's major growth focus.

Reliance's investment quickly paid off with the discovery of natural gas reserves estimated at some 14 million cubic feet, the largest natural gas field discovered in India in decades, in the Krishna–Godavari Basin in the Bay of Bengal.

In 2004, the company struck again, locating a new gas field in the Bay of Bengal, off Orissa coast.

Buoyed by its successful exploration efforts, Reliance unveiled an ambitious expansion program for the second half of the 2000s.

The company's plans included a $6 billion extension of the Jamnagar site, doubling it in size and making it the world's largest refinery by 2009.

The company also announced that it intended to spend $10 billion on further oil exploration efforts, targeting the international market.

At the other end of the petroleum market, the company launched a $1.5 billion expansion of its Reliance gas station chain, with the goal of 6,000 stations. The gas filling stations are required to compete with public sector undertakings like IOCL (Indian Oil Corporation Ltd), BPCL (Bharat Petroleum Corporation Ltd) and HPCL (Hindustan Petroleum Corporation Ltd.) which are selling petrol and diesel at a subsidized rate. Reliance petrol pump, therefore, had to stop marketing petrol and diesel through their own petrol pumps. Instead they preferred to export the products to have better realisation.

The company also expanded internationally, becoming the world's leading manufacturer of polyester yarn with the acquisition of Germany's Trevira. In addition to this, the company boosted its telecommunications wing, acquiring UK-based FLAG Telecom, an operator of a 50,000-kilometre underwater fibre optic cable network.

In the meantime, rising tensions between Mukesh and Anil Ambani came to a head in late 2005, when a long-simmering disagreement over company strategy broke out into an open and highly publicized feud. In the end, as was brokered by the brothers' mother (Kokilaben), who proposed a breakup of Reliance Industries into two roughly equal components, this change was effected. Mukesh Ambani remained as head of the company's petroleum and textiles operations and Anil Ambani regrouped the company's telecommunications, energy, capital finance and other operations into a new company. The breakup of the company took place in 2006.

As a result, Reliance Industries emerged as a focused and highly integrated petroleum and petrochemicals challenger to the global heavyweights.

New initiatives

- Telecom
- Power
- Engineering, procurement and construction
- Infrastructure
- Infocom
- Insurance
- Coal bed methane

Reliance now has many subsidiaries. Group companies include Reliance Industrial Infrastructure Ltd, Indian Petrochemical Corporation Ltd (a company acquired by Reliance which has a sales turnover now of $3 billion).

Key strategic drivers

EXPANSION THROUGH BACKWARD INTEGRATION

Dhirubhai remained focused on core business activities and on building the empire through backward integration which has given him not only the control of the business through its entire value chain but also a tremendous cost advantage.

In 1982, Ambani began the process of backward integration, setting up a plant to manufacture polyester filament yarn. He subsequently diversified into chemicals, gas, petrochemicals and plastics. This is a classic example where backward integration was used as a method of expansion (Figure 11.5).

The company's new strategy led it to enter the petrochemicals industry, building its first plant for the production of purified terephthalic acid in 1986. The following year, the company added a unit for the production of linear alkyl benzene, a key raw material for the detergent industry, followed by the opening of a paraxylene plant

FIGURE 11.5: RELIANCE DISINTEGRATION PROBLEM

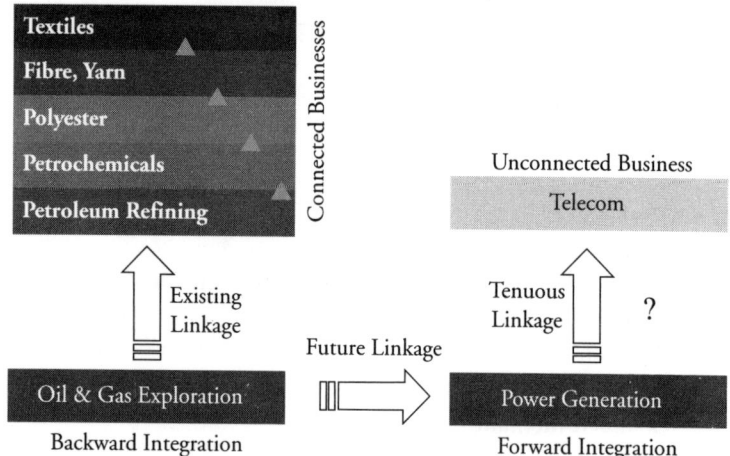

Source: Printed with the permission of The Information Company Pvt Ltd.
Note: While gas is an input for power generation as well as petrochemicals, a power transmission network can be used for carrying telecom message.

in 1988. The company then began developing a new petrochemicals complex at Hazira, which started production of vinyl chloride and polyvinyl chloride.

In this way, the company developed market leadership both in polyesters and in polymers. By 1992, the company had launched production of high-density polyethylene at the Hazira complex as well.

ACCESS TO CHEAP CAPITAL

Ambani took a major revolutionary step of turning to the stock market. It was judged that further expansion, especially into related sectors, would depend on access to a cheap source of capital. Rather than turning to the banking system, Ambani decided to tap Bombay stock exchange, pioneering an equity cult that was to transform the corporate financing system in India. Reliance went public in 1977 and it's initial public offering saw 58,000 investors buying shares. Currently the number of Reliance shareholders is more than three million. This cheap source of capital definitely saved them from high interest rates from banks and other financial institutions.

In 1977, Ambani launched Reliance Textile Industries' initial public offering (IPO). The IPO, of 2.8 million shares, raised $1.8 million, and was considered among the largest in India at that time. By circumventing the traditional system for capital investment, Ambani sparked a revolution in India and was widely credited for setting the stage for the country's emergence as a major regional industrial center.

SHAREHOLDING WIDELY DISTRIBUTED

As shareholding is widely distributed, the other benefit that they received was that they could not be manipulated by a single individual or institution. Their large number of small shareholders ensured that rigging of their shares was virtually impossible. This decision helped them become a thoroughly professional company as they were now accountable to their shareholders.

LARGE CAPACITY BUILDING AND GLOBAL SCALE OF OPERATION

Reliance has built global capacity, imbibing latest technology, giving them the economy of scale which helped them to compete globally. Speedy execution of the project also helped them to execute project within cost budget without overrun and a large capacity helped them to have a commanding position in the market.

CORE SECTOR BUSINESS PROVIDED READY MARKET

Dhirubhai entered the core sector with systematic backward integration which has helped him to be cost effective and have total control in the entire value chain. The market is ever growing and, hence, competing on cost efficiency against public sector was much easier for him.

Case IV: Biocon Industries Limited

Biocon is India's leading Biotechnology enterprise. Established in 1978, the company today is an integrated biotechnology enterprise focused on the development of biopharmaceuticals.

The company is headed by Kiran Mazumdar Shaw.

Kiran Mazumdar Shaw graduated from Mount Carmel College in Bangalore obtaining a B.Sc degree in Zoology after which she did her masters in malting.

Her professional career started with the position of trainee brewer in Carlton & United Breweries in 1974.

In 1978, she joined Biocon Biochemicals in Ireland as a trainee manager after which she collaborated with the same company to start Biocon India.

She is the second richest women in India.

She achieved this status after Biocon entered the stock market and went for an IPO in 2004. Biocon became the second Indian company to cross a market capitalisation of one billion $ on the first day of listing. Mazumdar-Shaw and her husband John Shaw own over 60 per cent of the company's stock.

To the wider public, Biocon is known as the largest biotechnology company in India, but at least 60 per cent of its turnover comes from pharmaceutical products. So it can be regarded as a biotech-turned pharmaceutical company.

Company history

Initially, the firm supplied simple enzymes to an Irish company, Biocon Biochemicals Ltd In 1978, Biocon India was incorporated as a joint venture between Biocon Biochemicals Ltd of Ireland and Kiran Mazumdar.

Biocon now already has two subsidiary companies, which proves that it had grown like a giant mammoth:

Syngene International Private Limited
Start up year: 1994
Area of operation: Biotechnology Research

and

Clinigene International Private Limited
Start up year: 2000
Area of operation: Clinical Research

Figure 11.6 shows the various constituents of the Biocon group of companies.

FIG 11.6: BIOCON GROUP OF COMPANIES

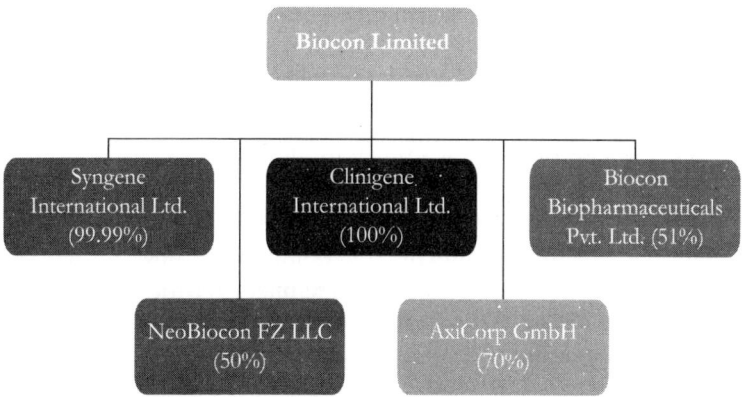

Source: http://www.biocon.com/biocon_invrelation_org_structure.asp (accessed on 10 June 2010).

Research and development at biocon

Biocon's R&D efforts are directed towards five principal domains:

1. Recombinant DNA Technologies
2. Bioprocess Development
3. Fermentation-based Small Molecules
4. Enzymes and Biotransformation
5. Clinical Development

Given below is a brief summary of what these domains are:

RECOMBINANT DNA TECHNOLOGIES
Research in early stage drug discovery, involving cloning and screening for potential drug target proteins, is conducted in collaboration with SYNGENE, to develop a range of recombinant products such as therapeutic proteins and enzymes.

BIOPROCESS DEVELOPMENT
Biocon continues to develop a wide range of technologies useful for the production of biological molecules. The company has innovated

in the area of fermentation development as well as post fermentation product recovery process development.

FERMENTATION-BASED SMALL MOLECULES

Biocon is continuously researching and developing a range of microbe-derived pharmaceutical products for disease areas spanning cardio-vascular, diabetes, immunosuppressants and onclology.

ENZYMES AND BIOTRANSFORMATION

It aims to substitute synthetic conversions with novel enzymatic routes, especially useful when producing pharmaceutically active advanced intermediate. Biocon also develops and markets a range of enzymes products for the food industry.

CLINICAL DEVELOPMENT

Their most recent research initiative is in the area of clinical development at their subsidiary, Clinigene. This effort aims to conduct longitudinal studies in select disease segments to discover new bio markets. Mapping clinical and genomic data on a web-based bioinformatics platform is the unique feature of this research activity.

Table 11.7 shows the financial performance of Biocon between 2004 and 2008.

TABLE 11.7: FINANCIAL PERFORMANCE OF BIOCON (2004–08)

	2004	2005	2006	2007	2008
Sales in Rs 10 million					
Bio Pharmaceuticals	435	557	603	728	787
Enzymes	67	90	85	95	46
Research and Technical Licensing Fees	39	66	100	163	220
Total	541	713	788	986	1054
Other Income	1	15	5	4	36
Total Revenues	542	728	793	990	1090
Expenditure					
Manufacturing & Other Expenses	362	488	557	697	748
Interest and Finance Charges	2	2	2	9	10
Depreciation	16	22	29	67	94
Total	380	512	588	773	852

(Table 11.7 continued)

(Table 11.7 continued)

	2004	2005	2006	2007	2008
Profit Before Tax	162	216	205	217	238
Income Tax	23	18	31	17	13
Profit from Operations	139	198	174	200	225
Exceptional Item, Net	–	–	–	–	239
Net Profit	139	198	174	200	464

Source: http://www.biocon.com/biocon_invrelation_key_over_profit.asp (accessed on June 10 2010).

Starting small

Using solid state fermentation for manufacturing enzymes and designing of fermentor, Biocon was born after it extracted two enzymes—papain and isinglass—started with the extraction of enzymes from papaya and catfish. After which, it started research and development (R&D) to manufacture enzymes through fermentation. Biocon focused on the difficult art of solid-state fermentation.

The company began with a clean slate. The R&D team had no idea whatsoever about the designing or manufacturing of the fermentor. The first blueprint for a fermentor was ready in 1989. Solid-state fermentation can give up to 20 times more yield than liquid fermentation, but is difficult to control. However, some microorganisms like fungi grow well in the solid state. Biocon had to work with fungi. So it had to learn solid-state fermentation. Biocon, thus, focused on fungal enzyme production in the initial years.

Along with learning solid state fermentation, it designed a new reactor wherein contents could be mixed while fermentation was going on. Things could be added and taken out without disturbing the fermentation process. It consumed less energy. Biocon called this novel reactor, the Plafractor.

Biocon's mastery of solid-state fermentation was a good strategic weapon. It got a US patent for plafractor. Solid state fermentation was extremely useful and profitable and drugs worth $20 billion were sold.

Kiran Mazumdar started the contract research firm Syngene in 1994. Syngene proceeded at a slow pace, but took off in 1998. It earned Rs 140 million in profit last year.

Biocon chose statins as a major focus area for research. Statins are a class of cholesterol-lowering drugs. Unlike the antibiotics, the statins are low-volume but high-value products. Biocon began with Lovastatin. The product was launched in 1997 in countries like Canada and Mexico, and regions like East Europe and South-east Asia. Merck's patent on this drug expired in 2001, giving Biocon the opportunity to sell in all countries. Biocon followed the product with other statins: Simvastatin, Provastatin and Atorvastatin. Astra Zeneca also launched a second generation statin called Rosuvastatin.

The statins form about 30 per cent of Biocon's pharmaceutical revenues. With the exception of Lovastatin, Biocon sells them only in countries that do not provide patent protection.

Unilever selling its shareholding to biocon

Quest International, a Dutch company, in speciality chemical businesses such as flavor chemical which has a holding in the Biocon Biochemicals Ltd of Ireland, a joint venture partner of Biocon India, was acquired by Unilever. Subsequently, Unilever inked a deal with ICI to sell its speciality chemicals division of which Quest International was a part. Unilever agreed to sell its shareholding in Biocon Biochemicals to the Indian promoters. Biocon became an independent entity.

Starting of a clinical research firm, Clinigene, in 2000

Clinigene conducts clinical trials for foreign companies by maintaining world class laboratory standards.

Biocon India decides to enter the stock market

Biocon creates a buzz in the stock market in March 2004 with its hugely successful Initial Public Offering (IPO).

Group companies

SYNGENE

Syngene is a world leader in gel documentation (gel doc) and analysis systems. These range from low cost entry level kits to fully computer controlled automatic analysers for fluorescence, chemiluminescence and proteomics workstations.

SYNGENE PRODUCTS

Gel Documentation and Analysis: Systems for the imaging and analysis of 1D DNA and RNA gels, 1D protein gels, spots, blots, films, plates, colony plates and a range of other media—now available for enhanced fluorescence.

Chemiluminescence: Specially designed high performance systems for the capture of chemiluminescence blots.

Chemiluminescence and Flouroscence: A range of chemiluminescence and fluorescence systems for the imaging and analysis of 1D DNA and RNA gels, 1D protein gels, spots, blots, films, plates, colony plates and chemiluminescence blots.

Proteomics: 2D protein gel generation, image capture and analysis systems.

Software: GeneSnap acquisition software, GeneTools analysis software and GeneDirectory database software for Syngene systems.

CLINIGENE

Cligene is a world-class clinical research organisation with strong clinical trial, regulatory and laboratory capabilities for drug development. Clinigene offers a wide range of comprehensive clinical research services including clinical studies and clinical trials and research.

A subsidiary of Biocon, Clinigene provides custom research services to pharmaceutical and biotechnology companies in the areas of R&D, drug discovery and development, and expansion of research capabilities. Clingene's clinical research laboratory is the first in India to be CAP (College of American Pathologists) accredited and NABL (National Accreditation Board Testing and Calibration

Laboratories) accredited as well as ISO 15189:2003 accredited for quality and competence

Table 11.8 shows the product portfolio of Biocon. Box 11.1 and Table 11.9 highlight some key facts about the human resources at Biocon.

Competition

In clinical research there are many other players with whom Biocon has to compete. These are:

- Wockhardt Limited
- Nicholas Piramal India Limited
- Sun Pharmaceuticals Industries Limited
- Dr. Reddy's Laboratories Limited
- Ranbaxy Laboratories Limited

TABLE 11.8: BIOCON PRODUCT PORTFOLIO

Product Category	Lead Brands/Products
Anti Diabetic agents	Acarbose
Anti Obesity Agent	Orlistat
Cardiovascular agents	Lovastatin, Atorvastatin
Digestive Enzymes	Amylase, Prooteases, Lactase
Industrial Enzymes	Oxidases, Cellulases, Esterases Pectinases
Haemeostatic Agents	Ethamsylate, Tranexamic Acid
Hepatoprotective Agents	L-Ornithine, L-Aspartate
Immunosuppressants	Mycophenolate Mofetil, Tacrolimus
Neutraceuticals	Chondroitin Sulphate, Glucosamine Sulphate
Gastro-Intestinal Agents	Prebiotics, Probiotics
Cardiology	Statix, Clasprin Telmistat H
Nephrology	Erypro Safe, Tacrograf, Rapacan, Renodapt
Diabetology	Insugen, Piodart, Zuker, Gabil, TriGPM
Oncology	BIOMAbEFGR
Anti inflammatory agents	Trypsin, Chymotripsin
Anti Oxidants	Alpha Lipoic Acid, L-Carnitine

Source: Complied by author from various product literatures and catalogues.

BOX 11.1: HUMAN RESOURCE AT BIOCON

In the words of Kiran Mazumdar Shaw, 'Biocon is a story of ordinary people who thought they could do great things'.

The intellectual profile of 2000 people working at Biocon in the year 2005 is given below:

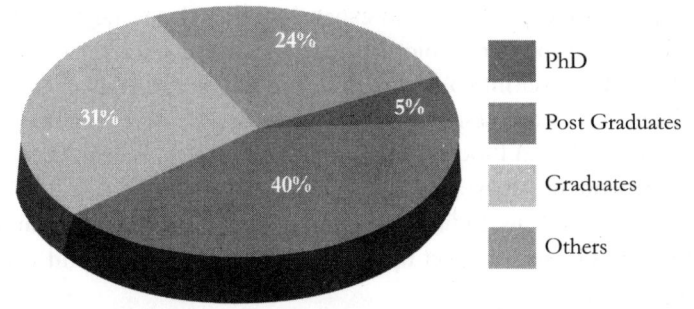

Biocon, Syngene and Clinigene together employ approximately 2,000 quali-fied personnel from biologists, chemists, computer scientists, medical practitio-ners, pharmacologists, engineers, finance, legal, marketing analysts to general administrators.

10% of the employees hold a PhD, 30% have a Masters degree in Science and the remaining are graduates with a Bachelors degree in Science, Commerce or Arts. 30% of Biocon employees are women. The employee attrition rate is less than 1% and the average age of the company employee is 28.

Source: http://www.dce.edu/jeev.

TABLE 11.9: NUMBER OF EMPLOYEES IN BIOCON

	31 March 2006	31 March 2007	31 March 2008
Biocon	1,225	1,643	1,634
Syngene	526	754	907
Clinigene	60	70	133
BBPL	28	75	98
Total Head Count	1,839	2,542	2,772

Source: http://biocon.com/biocon_invrelation_key_employee.asp.

Key milestones

1994: Biocon establishes Syngene International Pvt Ltd as a CRC to address the growing need for outsourced R&D in the pharmaceutical sector;

1996: The commercial success of Biocon's proprietary fermentation plant leads to a three-fold expansion. Biocon leverages its technology platform to enter biopharmaceuticals and statins;

1998: Unilever inks a deal with ICI to sell its speciality chemicals division of which Quest International is a part. Unilever agrees to sell its shareholding in Biocon to the Indian promoters. Biocon becomes an independent entity;

2000: Clinigene, India's first clinical research organisation and a subsidiary of Biocon, is set up to pursue clinical research and development;

2004: Biocon created a buzz in the stock market in March 2004 with its hugely successful IPO. Biocon closed day one of listing on the bourses with a market value of $1.11 billion to become only the second Indian company to cross the $1 billion mark on the day of listing.

Key achievements

- First Indian company to be approved by US FDA for the manufacture of Lovastatin, a cholesterol-lowering molecule.
- First company worldwide to develop human insulin on a Pichia expression system.
- India's largest producer and exporter of enzymes.
- First Indian company to manufacture and export enzymes to USA and Europe.
- First Indian biotechnology company to receive US funding for proprietary technologies.
- Second Indian company to cross the $1 billion mark on the day of listing.
- Launched India's first cancer drug BIOMAb EGFR and also won 'PRODUCT of the year' award for the same.

Again, in terms significant achievements, Kiran Mazumdar Shaw said, 'Our biggest achievement has been global recognition in the field of biotechnology through successful IPO'.

Key strategic drivers

- Significant innovation has helped Biocon create an Indian success story in the biotechnology sector. BIOCON India came to life at a time when no one even knew what biotechnology was.
- Focusing on solid state fermentation and producing fungal enzyme in the initial years, which had an assured and captive market for them, has provided the solid foundation for growth in the formative years. And then innovating a new design of solid state fermentor provided the additional impetus.
- Formation of Syngene has given Biocon added value to the brand BIOCON. Diversifying into biopharmaceuticals helped the company extend its boundary into the global biotechnogy business.
- Clinigene offered entry into world class clinical research activities. Both diversifications were synergistic and have added incremental value to Biocon.
- Entry into the stock market gave the company a kick start in addition to getting global recognition through the IPO which was the company's biggest achievement.
- Finally, being an early starter and having the right mix of strategy gave it an edge over others and also helped to create a successful business.

In an interview, the promoter, Kiran Mazumdar gave reasons for the remarkable success by saying,

The turning point was when Biocon leveraged its technology platform to enter biopharmaceuticals and statins in 1996. We progressed from discovering novel fungal enzymes to researching recombinant technologies and human therapeutics. The foray into biopharmaceuticals was a crucial strategic move that propelled the company's growth into a different league. While Biocon focused on developing a strong fermentation base for the production of enzymes, the advent of Syngene, stom Research Company (a Biocon subsidiary), introduced new skills in chemical synthesis and recombinant technologies for drug development. This expertise allowed us to leverage our fermentation knowledge from enzymes to drug molecules. (http://www.gurusonline.tv/uk/conteudos/mazumdar_shaw. asp [accessed on 10 June 2010])

Case V: Rasna Limited—A Case of Creating Your Own Category of Industry Which You Can Dominate

Introduction

Pioma Industries Ltd manufactures and exports beverages and processed foods from India. It was founded in 1973 and is based in Ahmedabad, India. The company has pioneered the powdered Soft Drink Concentrate (SDC) category for the first time in India, with a brand name called Rasna.

The company started as a proprietory organisation owned by Ariz Khambatta. Its product was initially launched as 'Jaffe'in 1976 and later its name was changed to Rasna in 1979. The product was initially distributed by Voltas Ltd, a Tata Group company but later on Pioma itself took over the distribution.The enterprise was started with a single office in Gujarat and subsequently expanded its operations in other states and even overseas. Today, the company has eight SDC manufacturing units of which five are located in Gujarat, two in Silvasa and one in the state of Punjab, respectively. The company opened its first Northern India manufacturing facility in Baddi, Himachal Pradesh with a production capacity of 350,000 cases per year. It also has a manufacturing facility in the United Arab Emirates to cater to the overseas markets.

The company has a dedicated R&D team in Ahmedabad to support its new flavors introduction in quick succession. The division is actually involved in monitoring new flavour developments, quality control and product innovation. In the initial year, Rasna was produced in all manual operations to save taxes. Controlling and managing the logistics in an entirely manual operation was in fact an uphill task. But Pioma did it well to keep the product cost low to compete with large players. This was also necessary to remain outside the tax net. In course of time, however, it has gone for mechanisation. Today, Rasna products are manufactured in a totally automated environment and uses advanced world-class technology for packaging.

Pioma undertook wide-spread promotional activities and participated in exhibitions, offering free samples and sponsoring tele-serials on prime time and literally ruled the market in the mid-1980s and 1990s and commenced its exports by 1993. By the end of 1999, the turnover had reached $650 million, of which Rasna International accounted for 15 per cent Pioma further diversified into the ethinic range of foods and beverages.

Pioma Industries saw a huge untapped potential in the market of SDC in the cola segment when Coca Cola was the only cola beverage in the market. During that period, there were no major players in the SDCs market, thus, creating an opportunity for Pioma to launch and offer the SDC product category in the Indian market under the brand name 'Jaffe' in 1976. Pioma was, thus, able to create a new category of business for them giving an option to middle and low income group population.

Brand Rasna and its proliferation

Rasna's SDC comprised of a powder sachet and a small bottle of thick, coloured liquid—while the powder provided the taste, the liquid gave the flavor. These ingredients had to be mixed with a specified amount of water and sugar. The resulting syrup could then be used over a period of time by mixing it with water. Though many analysts felt that Rasna's do-it-yourself concept would be cumbersome and, hence, would be unappealing to consumers, it became the very reason for its success. This was because Rasna was able to exploit the Indian middle class housewife's traditional distrust for food and drinks not made at home. Besides being easy to prepare, it was reported that it was the first brand in the country that provided consumers a real fruit-like flavour and taste. And at only 50 paise (Re 0.5) per glass, it was easily one of the most affordable drinks available in the market.

With many popular flavours such as pineapple, orange, mango and lemon-lime becoming runaway successes, Rasna soon established itself as an effective alternative to other products such as squashes, soft drinks and syrups. As a result, many new flavours were launched over the years. In addition to the standard fruity flavours, Rasna was made available in many local flavours such as *kala khatta* (tangy), *khus* and rose which became very popular.

Product portfolio

The product portfolio can be classified as follows:

- Rasna Foods and Beverages: The most popular product in this category consists of soft drink concentrate and instant drink powder.
- Products in the ethnic basket: This range of products consists of ready to eat authentic foods.

The various products in the portfolio of Pioma Industries are:

BEVERAGES AND FOODS
- Rasna Cola Cola
- Rasna
- Rasna Juc up
- Rasna fruit jams
- Rasna shake up
- Rasna fruit cordials
- Rasna instant drink
- Rasna Lite: 1/3 sugar
- Gofrut instant drink
- Rasna Juc fit
- Fruto instant drink
- Fruitplus
- Body Fuel: Health Drink
- Rasna International

ETHINIC FOODS
- Rasna Curry in A Hurry
- Rasna premium pickles and gherkins
- Rasna curry pastes and sauces
- Rasna instant curry mix powders
- Rasna chutneys
- Rasna syrups

The distribution set-up

The sales force is managed by the company's five regional offices, which ensured availability of Rasna products to consumers in the retail outlets nearest to them. One of the major factors responsible for Rasna's rapid sales growth was its well-entrenched, efficient sales and distribution network covering the entire country. The company operates an extensive distribution network throughout the length and breadth of the country. Its operations include 175 sales personnel, 24 warehouses and 2,000 stockists. These stockists served over 200,000 retail outlets directly and over 200,000 outlets indirectly through wholesalers.

The promotional initiatives

Every year, the company devised innovative methods to sustain the element of fun and surprise. In addition, Pioma participated in various exhibitions and fairs that provided an excellent opportunity for direct interaction with the consumers. The fairs also helped the company increase its visibility in the rural markets by distributing a large number of free product samples to consumers in the fairs. Above all, Rasna's advertisement campaigns helped it become a trusted and popular brand amongst the Indian consumers. Pioma was one of the few companies that went in for large-scale advertising on the state-owned TV channel, Doordarshan. Rasna also sponsored many programs on the channel, especially the ones that appealed to children, such as the animated series, 'Spiderman'.

The advertisements essentially revolved around cute and very-likeable children who were floored by Rasna's attractive colors, taste and fruity flavors. Eventually, Rasna's TV commercial featuring a small girl with the tagline 'I love you Rasna', was adopted as the brand's tagline for many more commercials over the next couple of years. As a result of all the above, Rasna virtually ruled the market during the 1980s and the early-1990s. For over 17 years, it remained the undisputed market leader in the Indian SDC market. This was aided largely by the fact that there was no serious competition in the market. Soft drinks, as a segment, were virtually stagnant and only a few syrups (Rooh Afza, Sharbet-e-Azam) and squashes (Dipy's and Kissan) were available in the market at that point of time. However, most of these products were priced higher. Besides, Rasna's product range was one of the world's largest distributed food brands at that time. In order to retain the interest and loyalty of its consumers, the company undertook various creative promotional activities. These included shop sampling, house-to-house calls, and live demonstrations on the method of preparation, retail window displays, gift offers to customers and other trade schemes.

Rationale for going global

Buoyed by its success in the Indian market, in 1993, Pioma also decided to market Rasna on the global platform. Besides the SDC, Pioma developed a whole new range of non-alcoholic beverages under the Rasna brand.

The company took special care to meet the specific requirements and preferences of global customers and leverage its own core competencies in terms of flavors and technology. By this time, Pioma also realized that it could tap the demand for ethnic Indian foods in global markets and cash in on the brand's strong image. This realisation led to the launch of products under two different categories: Rasna Beverages and Foods and Rasna Ethnic Basket. While the former comprised a range of drinks, the latter constituted a complete range of ready to cook authentic Indian foods.

Rasna faces new challenge from multinationals

Seeing Rasna's success, many global soft drink and food majors such as Coke, Pepsi, Kraft General Foods, Lipton and Unilever had introduced products in this segment covering many variants including iced tea. Rasna has withstood this onslaught by strategizing winning strategies. It has successfully extended the geographic boundaries and has started exporting to many other countries, competing with global brands such as Tang. In fact, both, Tang from Kraft General Food and Sunfill from Coke could not succeed against Rasna in India in spite of the fact that these MNCs have enormous financial muscle.

Seeing the shift in the consumer preference, Pioma Industries also introduced ready to serve fruit juices in tetra packs to compete with the plethora of brands both from local companies like Dabur Foods (manufacturer of Real-Juice) and Parle Agro Industries (manufacturer of the Frooti brand of beverages) as well multinationals like Coke and Pepsi (manufacturer of Tropicana brand of 100% juice).

Re-launch of the Rasna brand

The word 'Pioma' is perhaps not a familiar name for the average Indian consumer. However, the brand 'Rasna', from Pioma Industries Ltd, is well known to everyone in India. In fact, the name Rasna is almost a generic name for soft drink concentrates (SDC), a segment that had been created and nurtured by the company in the Indian beverages market. Rasna's extremely popular advertisements with the tagline, 'I love you Rasna', had become an integral part of the Indian advertising folklore. In March 2002, Pioma announced a radical overhauling of its strategies for the Rasna brand. This development was rather unexpected. Company sources revealed that these developments were in line with a restructuring programme that had been conceptualised in mid-2001. Keeping in line with this plan, Pioma launched two new brands, Rasna Utsav (Rasna Festive) and Rasna Rozana (Rasna Daily) in March 2002.

The launch was accompanied by a multi-media advertisement campaign, for which the company allocated Rs 160 million. The television campaign that ran across all major national and regional channels featured a 'song' exclusively composed for the new launches. A notable feature of this commercial was the fact that it was voiced by one of the country's most well known singer, Asha Bhonsle, who had never sung for any commercial before.

Pioma soon released music cassettes and CDs featuring remixes of old, popular Hindi songs and the new Rasna song. In addition to this, the company sponsored musical events across the country. Industry observers were, however, viewing the above developments as Pioma's attempts to infuse fresh life into Rasna.

Rasna wakes up to the challenge

Pioma decided to extend Rasna's brand portfolio and launched a pre-sweetened mix-and-drink product in 1996. Targeted at the upper end of the market, Rasna International was a nutritious and vitamin-enriched version of the regular Rasna SDC version.

This was followed by the launch of Rasna Royal, positioned as a vitamin-enriched version of Rasna. It was targeted at health-conscious consumers who did not prefer Rasna SDC on account of its synthetic image (that is, usage of synthetic colors and artificial flavors). These two products were priced at the higher end, as against the 'low price' policy followed by Rasna for other products.

Many analysts forecasted that Rasna's launch of product variants in the premium segment will put it in direct confrontation with the MNCs and, therefore, they are unlikely to succeed. Analysts' argument was that while consumers were willing to bear the inconvenience of preparing the SDC version on account of its lower cost, they will be unwilling to do so for a higher priced product. Commenting on the analysts forecasts that Rasna International might not succeed given the high pricing of the product, Khambatta said, 'Contrary to common perception, Rasna International has done exceedingly well and has created a market segment for pre-sweetened fortified soft drinks' (ICMR 2010). And, the fact was that Rasna International was yet another success story.

By 1999, Rasna International's sales accounted for an estimated 15 per cent of Rasna's total turnover of Rs 650 million, even as

SDC's contribution kept declining. During the same year, in summer, Rasna also went against its tradition of launching 'one-new-flavour per season' and launched two new flavours, Rasna Yorker and Rasna Aqua Fun. The company launched these products in order to exploit the World Cup Cricket fever. Kapil Dev (former Indian cricket captain) was roped in to endorse Rasna Yorker. Yet again, Rasna Yorker was a succees. Pioma's efforts at broadening its product portfolio continued with the launch of Oranjolt in 2000, an aerated fruit drink, available in 1.5 litre PET bottles. Considering the high rate of product failure in the food segment, Rasna's success story in terms of creating new brands is quite commendable.

Pioma began planning a three-year revamping program in mid-2001. The program aimed at overhauling all its operations and creating a new brand identity for Rasna. In the fiscal year 2001–02, Pioma Industries changed its name to Rasna Limited.

Pioma rebranding—2002: The second innings

In 2002 as part of a re-branding exercise, Pioma industries changed its name to Rasna Ltd. It started to focus on increasing its reach and creating brand awareness in rural India. As part of its affordability drive, it decided to increase the number of segments and varying price range from 80 paise to Rs 4. It launched the 'Rasna for one billion Indians' project. Explaining the company's new marketing strategy, Khambatta said:

> We are implementing a strategy through which we wish to make consumers drink more Rasna as well as get new people accustomed to the brand. We have come out with more product offerings to attract the new consumers. For those who are already used to the Rasna taste, we have brought out value-added products. We are aware than anybody else about the price-conscious behaviour of the Indian market and have accordingly positioned our products. (ICMR 2010)

According to its renewed distribution strategy, Rasna planned to reach an estimated 700,000 retailers annually. With its plans to reach the rural areas, the company began strengthening its distribution channels in order to cover villages with a population of up to 5,000. Following this, the company appointed 47 additional sales personnel, 350 cycle salesmen, and 145 pilot salesmen, in addition to new stockists, for the relevant areas. It also engaged 500 vans for the coverage of rural areas. However, Rasna was careful and cautious not to neglect the urban markets.

According to company sources, 'There are pockets with rural consumers even in the metros and they are large in number' (ICMR 2010). Hence, the company's advertisements also targeted the urban and semi-urban families. As a part of its new strategy, the company focused on multi-media advertising and promotion, wherein an effective marketing strategy was adopted to communicate the brand message, using different media such as TV, radio and print.

Mudra Communications, the leading advertising agency, undertook the advertising and promotional activities. Mudra developed an advertisement campaign constituting five television commercials, radio advertising and outdoor media campaigns. Special emphasis was laid on 'outdoor visibility' and over 45,000 bus shelters, 5,000 pole kiosks, 300 bus panels and over 200 billboards were used to display the brand message across the country. With a new, catchy brand tagline, 'Relish a gain', the campaign highlighted the affordability and easy availability of Rasna products. Speaking about the changed corporate identity and its reflection in the advertising campaigns, Khambatta said, 'Our aim is to reach out to the masses and we wanted a direct link between the brand and our advertising' (ICMR 2010).

Commenting on the advertisement campaigns, the accounts director of the agency said, 'We changed the advertising strategy to include every age group and every section of the society. "Relish a Gain" concept has been created in Hindi, as a song, which covers the total range of products to focus on Rasna's values in different moments of life' (ICMR 2010). According to company sources, the message expected to be conveyed through the advertisements was, 'Whenever you feel like celebrating, drink Rasna'. Special emphasis was laid on its affordability and value for money. Moreover, its product lines were categorized into two brands (Rasna Utsav and

Rasna Rozana) so as to effectively target different consumer segments in India.

While Utsav, an improvement over Rasna SDC, targeted the lower income group in rural markets, Rozana, a mix and serve powdered drink (no need to add sugar) targeted the convenience seeking semi-urban and urban consumers. Rasna re-launched Rasna International as well under the sub-brand, Rozana Fruit Booster. Fruit Booster was aimed at competing with Sunfill and Tang (both pre-sweetened powdered soft drinks), serving the upper end of the market. In addition, a completely new identity, a new 'leaf' symbol was added to the Rasna brand name. Commenting on this, Khambatta said, 'Apart from talking about the core values of Rasna, they also wanted a symbol for Rasna so that the product gets distinct visibility' (ICMR 2010).

Since the company planned to focus on rural markets, it felt that the product awareness could be best created by means of a symbol and hence the leaf (with red and green background) was chosen as the brand symbol. All the new brands were enriched with vitamins and ingredients to render instant energy.

Commenting on the launches, Khambatta said,

> With the launch of the Rozana line, we are reiterating our commitment to providing a health gain to our consumers. The products in the Rozana line contain Fruit Powder, Glucose/lactose, Vitamin A, C, B2, B6 as well as Niacin, Folic Acid, Calcium and Phosphorus, making it one of the healthiest and most refreshing soft drinks available. Cutting across all segments, Rasna has also ensured that the Rozana line is affordable to all sections of society. (ICMR 2010)

Rasna, in order to establish its Rozana line strongly in the market, priced Rozana Amrit sachets at Rs 2, while its major competitors, Sunfill and Tang sachets were priced at Rs 2 and Rs 5 respectively. This was expected to help Rasna beat competition as well as increase its reach among the lower-income groups. It also seemed to be more convenient compared to other product offerings of Rasna, as consumers were not required to add sugar to the mix. The launch of single-use sachets was expected to trigger the sales of powdered soft drinks in India expanding the market exponentially and increasing the share of powdered soft drinks in the total cold drinks market in India. Introduction of the sachet pack was also triggered by the increased competition from cola majors, namely Pepsi and Coke. Pepsi announced a significant policy change to foray into non-cola health drinks. The acquisition of Tropicana was intended for the same. While coke had its version of non-cola drink in the form of Sunfill.

Besides, there was a strongly felt need to revive the brand to a new level. The following actions were taken to rechristen the brand. The key actions taken include:

- Pioma changed its name to Rasna Ltd
- Focused on increasing the reach and creating brand awareness in rural India
- Increased the number of segments
- Launched the 'Rasna for one billion Indians' campaign
- Extensive media coverage and tie up with Mudra Communications
- New punch line 'Relish a gain'
- Multimedia advertisements campaign with a jingle
- Released cassettes with the Rasna jingle sung by Asha Bhonsle
- Emphasis on affordability and value for money
- Reinforcement of the message 'Whenever you feel like celebrating, drink Rasna'
- New leaf logo

Hoping for a sweet future

The entry of players like Coca-Cola, Kraft Foods and Hindustan Unilever Ltd and their financial muscle was expected to pose a tough competition for Rasna in the future. In 2002, Rasna reportedly finalized a joint venture with Del Monte, the largest producer of canned fruits and vegetables in the US to offer convenience foods.

While Del Monte wanted to leverage Rasna's vast and efficient distribution network, the latter planned to access Del Monte's technical expertise.

Focus on children had contributed significantly to Rasna's success. By broad-basing its target audience, and by extending its product to all the sections of the community, Rasna now has a much broader appeal. But in the SDC segment it is still the market leader. It survived the onslaught of many competitors such as Kraft General Foods, Dipys, Kissan, Best Foods International and, of late, from Coca Cola with its launch of Sunfill.

Rasna entered the middle-class homes by saying that one gests so many glasses from one pack, which worked out to so much per glass. There were three critical success factors in the SDC drinks segment—economy, taste and children's affinity. And with almost all the players focusing equally on all the three factors, Rasna indeed faced a tough challenge from MNCs to retain its leadership status. But they have faced it well and Pioma has enjoyed the category leadership for over three decades by occupying a unique segment that we can refer to as 'one minus concept' which it has occupied till date as the market leader. Rasna is seen to be a progressive and forward looking company adjusting constantly with time and introducing products in other segments as well to compete with the MNCs' onslaught in the pre-sweetened category of powder beverages. Pioma, therefore, has a creditable history of creating a category and then becoming the natural owner of that category.

Key strategic drivers

- Created product in a highly price conscious market from a simple concept of 'one minus'—one ingredient less which the consumer has to add.
- This has given it the first mover advantage in the market as well as category leadership.
- Highly efficient manufacturing, distribution and logistics management system which has helped it to retain cost leadership.
- Focused advertisement and promotional strategy—entering the household through the children, which worked well for many years.
- With the change in market and consumer behaviour, Rasna has changed and innovated new products as well as upgraded the original product to remain contemporary and contextual.

- Rasna could withstand the onslaught of multinationals that tried to make the category irrelevant by reducing the price of carbonated soft beverages like Cola drastically low. But when they found that the low price of Cola (Rs 5 a bottle) was driving the growth but was not profitable at all, they rolled back the price. Rasna, thus, became relevant once again.
- Rasna is the 'natural owner' of the category by ensuring that all new developments and innovations were first created by it.

Appendices

Appendix–I: McKinsey's Economic Reform Route for India

OVER A decade after the ushering of economic reforms in India, in 1991, the economic performance is far from satisfactory. Therefore, to continue with the reforms process, the union budget 2001–02 had proposed several reform proposals which were hailed as second generation of reforms.

However, these proposals came in for a very sharp criticism from the opposition as well as from some of the constituents of the ruling party. Against this backdrop, McKinsey Global Institute (MGI), an arm of the international consultancy, McKinsey and Company, presented to the prime Minister of India, on 6 September 2001, a report titled *India: The Growth Imperative* (MGI 2001), which consisted of an in-depth examination of 13 sectors which included two in agriculture, five in manufacturing and six in services. Overall, these 13 sectors accounted for 26 per cent of India's GDP and 24 per cent of its employment relevant at that time when this report was submitted.

Through this study, researchers have tried to identify barriers in the productivity growth and output growth in each sector, and then extrapolated these findings to the overall economy. Through this report, they had projected a GDP growth of 10 per cent per annum and doubling of real per capita income by 2010 (Table A1).

The MGI report identified three main barriers towards raising productivity and to grow faster, these were as follows:

TABLE A1: THE REFORM ROUTE TO FASTER GDP GROWTH

India (status quo)	5.5%
Product Market Barriers	2.3%
Land Market Barriers	1.3%
Government Ownership	0.7%
Others (Include poor transport infrastructure and labour market reforms)	0.35%
India (with complete reforms)	10.0%

Source: MGI 2001.

- Multiplicity of regulations governing product markets
- Distortions in the land markets
- Widespread government ownership of businesses

The barriers identified by the study together inhibit GDP growth by around 4 per cent per year. While the factors such as inflexible labour laws and poor transport infrastructure, though important for economic growth, their estimated impact on the GDP growth per year is less than 0.5 per cent. Hence, the report points out that it would be wise to focus on the main barriers of the GDP growth rather than focusing on the matters of general belief.

The MGI has identified 13 policy changes that the government should undertake as quickly as possible, so that the major obstacles to growth can be removed and India's economy can be set on the fast track of development. The proposals made by McKinsey are as detailed in Table A2.

TABLE A2: REFORM MEASURES REQUIRED

Category	Action	Key Sectors Directly Affected
Product Market	1. Eliminate reservation of all products for small-scale industry; start with 68 sectors accounting for 80 per cent of output of reserved sectors.	836 manufactured goods

(Table A2 continued)

(Table A2 continued)

Category	Action	Key Sectors Directly Affected
	2. Equalize sales tax and excise duties for all categories of players in each sector and strengthen enforcement.	Hotels and restaurants Manufacturing (e.g., steel, textiles and apparel) Retail trade
	3. Establish effective regulatory framework and strong regulatory bodies.	Power Telecom Water supply
	4. Remove all licensing and quasi-licensing restrictions that limit the number of players in affected industries.	Banking Dairy processing Petroleum marketing Provident fund management Sugar
	5. Reduce import duties on all goods to the levels of South East Asian Nations (10 per cent) over 5 years.	Manufacturing
	6. Remove ban on foreign direct investment in retail sector and allow unrestricted foreign direct investment in all sectors.	Insurance Retail trade
Land Market	7. Resolve unclear real estate titles by setting up fast track courts to settle disputes, computerising land records, freeing all property from constraints on sale and removing limits on property ownership.	Telecommunications Construction Hotels and restaurants
	8. Raise property taxes and user charges for municipal services and cut stamp duties (tax levied on property transactions) to promote development of residential and commercial land and to increase liquidity of land market.	Retail trade
	9. Reform tenancy laws to allow rents to move to market levels.	

(Table A2 continued)

(Table A2 continued)

Category	Action		Key Sectors Directly Affected
Govern-ment ownership	10.	Privatise electricity sector and all central and state government-owned companies in the electric-ity sector, start by privatising distribution; in all other sectors, first privatise largest companies.	Airlines Banking and insurance Manufacturing and mining Power Telecommunications
Others	11.	Reform labour laws by repeal-ing section 5-B of the Industrial Dispute Act; Introduce standard retrenchment-compensation norms; allow full flexibility in use of contract labour.	Labour-intensive manufacturing and service sectors
	12.	Transfer management of existing transport infrastructure to private players and contract out construc-tion and management of new infrastructure to private sector.	Airports Ports Roads
	13.	Strengthen extension services to help farmers improve yields.	Agriculture

Source: MGI 2001.

The MGI report suggests that if all these reform measures are im-plemented then the aim of productivity growth can be realized, led by the boost in labour and capital productivity, henceforth, achiev-ing the overall GDP of 10 per cent a year.

By removing all the productivity barriers, they have estimated that the labour productivity would almost double to 8 per cent a year over the next 10 years. Similarly, the capital productivity would grow by at least 50 per cent.

Some of the policy makers are apprehensive about the report sub-mitted by MGI as they feel it would take investment of more than 35 per cent of GDP to achieve a 10 per cent GDP growth rate. But MGI suggests that with the higher level of labour and capital pro-ductivity, the GDP growth rate of 10 per cent can be achieved with investment to only 30 per cent of GDP a year for a decade.

The report brings forth the point that although central government will have to take the lead but along with that, the state government would have to play a crucial supporting role, thereby, enabling the smooth implementation of policy changes. Thereby, enabling to harness the untapped potential of the Indian economy.

This was first published in the report *India The Growth Imperative*, prepared by McKinsey Global Institute, Copyright @ 2001 McKinsey & Company. All rights reserved. Reprinted by permission.

Appendix–II: Global Competitiveness Index 2008–09

Comparison of India's global competitive position with other countries

According to the *Global Competitiveness Report 2008–2009* (Porter and Schwab 2008), India is ranked at the 50th place, derives substantial advantages not only from its market size (ranked 4th for its domestic market size and 5th for its foreign market size) but also from its strong business sophistication (ranked 27th) and innovation (ranked 32nd). The country is endowed with strong business clusters and many local suppliers, and ranks an impressive 3rd for the availability of scientists and engineers and 27th for the quality of its research institutions. However, India's overall competitive position is weakened by its macroeconomic instability (109th) with the government running one of the highest deficits in the world (ranked 127th), unsustainable levels of government debt (ranked 113th) and fairly high inflation. Health and primary education is another area of concern, with poor health indicators (ranked 105th for both Infant mortality and life expectancy), related to the high prevalence of diseases such as tuberculosis and malaria. Educational enrolment rates also remain low at all levels, with the primary educational system in particular getting poor marks for quality. Certain labour market efficiency indicators are also poor, including female participation in the labour force (ranked 122nd) and the facility with which firms can hire and fire employees (ranked 104th). Table A3 compares the competitiveness of India with that of several countries worldwide.

TABLE A3: COMPARISON OF INDIA'S GLOBAL COMPETITIVE POSITION WITH OTHER COUNTRIES

| Country/Economy | Overall Index | | Subindexes | | | | | |
| | | | Basic Requirements | | Efficiency Enhancers | | Innovation Factors | |
	Rank	Score	Rank	Score	Rank	Score	Rank	Score
United States	1	5.74	22	5.50	1	5.81	1	5.80
Singapore	5	5.53	3	6.14	2	5.52	11	5.16
Japan	9	5.38	26	5.36	12	5.22	3	5.65
Hong Kong SAR	11	5.33	5	6.05	6	5.43	21	4.69
Korea Rep.	13	5.28	16	5.71	15	5.15	10	5.20
Taiwan, China	17	5.22	20	5.53	18	5.06	8	5.26
Malaysia	21	5.04	25	5.42	24	4.82	23	4.63
China	30	4.70	42	5.01	40	4.41	32	4.18
Thailand	34	4.60	43	4.97	36	4.45	46	3.91
Brunei Darus salam	39	4.54	29	5.30	77	3.84	87	3.35
India	50	4.33	80	4.23	33	4.49	27	4.29
Indonesia	55	4.25	76	4.25	49	4.29	45	3.98

Vietnam	70	4.10	79	4.23	73	3.94	71	3.59
Philippines	71	4.09	85	4.17	68	4.02	67	3.65
Sri Lanka	77	4.02	92	4.07	74	3.92	34	4.14
Mongolia	100	3.65	102	3.87	105	3.39	119	2.94
Pakistan	101	3.65	110	3.67	89	3.67	85	3.39
Cambodia	109	3.53	107	3.72	115	3.28	112	3.04
Bangladesh	111	3.51	117	3.57	97	3.48	115	2.98
Nepal	126	3.37	120	3.55	126	3.12	121	2.91
Timor-Leste	129	3.15	128	3.42	132	2.77	133	2.62
Chad	134	2.85	133	2.96	134	2.69	131	2.70

Source: Porter and Schwab 2008.
Note: Burma and Lao DPR not included.

FIGURE A1: THE 12 PILLARS OF COMPETITIVENESS

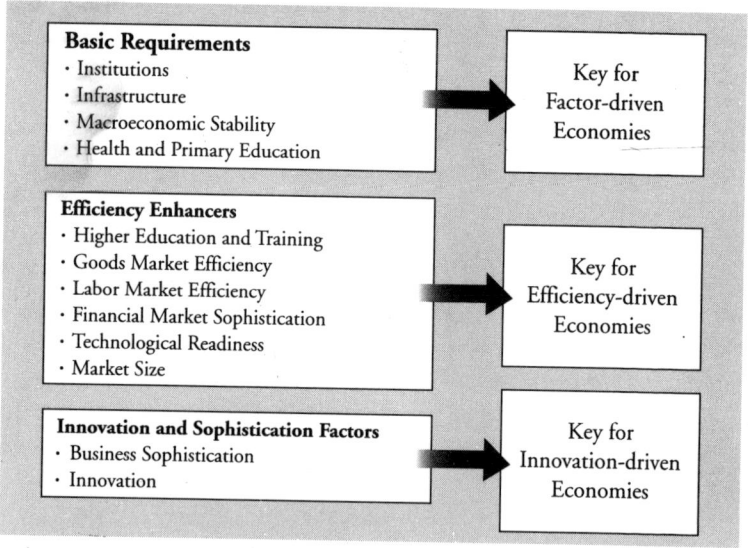

Source: Porter and Schwab 2008.

The Global Competitiveness Index is determined by the 12 criteria considered as the pillars of competitiveness (Figure A1).

Glossary

Activity-based Costing: The cost based on several activities and sub-activities performed to create a product and service.

Appraise: To assess the value of a property or of a person in-job performance.

Appraisal Cost: Includes the costs for conducting inspection and tests to find whether something is conforming to the set standards.

Assets: The items of value owned by a company or person and these include both tangible and intangible assets in a business.

Balanced Score Card: Balanced Score Card is a strategic management and organisation's performance measurement system first introduced by Robert Kaplan and David Norton in 1992 which takes into account a composite performance index covering financial, internal business processes, customer and growth and learning perspective of the business.

Bankrupt: Means insolvency or inability to pay one's debts.

Benchmarking: Comparison of operational and financial performance of the organisation with the market leader and also with the best in class performer.

Brand Assets: Assets of a brand based on market leadership, brand awareness and relevance, quality and brand loyalty.

Break Even Point: The level of sales or production that is required to break even or to reach a point of no profit or loss.

Brand Equity: Added value of the product attributable to the brand name and image.

Capital: Wealth that an organisation has to employ in achieving its objectives and aims.

Competitiveness: The ability of a business to score higher on key performance parameters in relation to its competitors in a sustained manner.

Consumerism: Continual expansion of customers' needs for goods and services. The social movement which insists that products and services have to be of standard quality without any harmful effect.

Core Competence: Introduced first by C.K. Prahalad and Gary Hamel (1990) describing those competences that the firm can exploit to provide differentiated consumer benefits which are not easily imitated and also can be leveraged across products and markets.

Cost of Capital: All associated costs attached to the capital employed in a business.

Cost Centre: The relevant cost assigned exclusively to the business as a whole or to the various business divisions.

Credit: Ability to borrow funds or quantum of funds borrowed.

Decentralisation: Disbursing decision making authority to multiple locations and levels rather than concentrating it at the top of organisation's hierarchy.

Demographics: The income, education, sex, age and other such factors of socio-economic class of population.

Dividend: Amount of profit per share returned to the owner for a given period.

Decision Theory: A set of analytical tools including logic, mathematical models using probability theory and diagrams to be used in decision making.

Depression: A period of extremely low business activity marked by high unemployment and extreme decline in demand.

Delegation: The process a manager uses to assign a task or part thereof to a subordinate.

Economic Value Added: Added value to the business net of interest, depreciation, taxes and cost of capital employed. It is a measure of a company's financial performance.

Effectiveness: Extent to which the desired result is realised.

Efficiency: Output per unit of input.

Entrepreneur: A person who starts and develops a business.

Enterprise Resource Planning: A business management system that integrates all functions of a business covering sales order processing, planning, manufacturing, marketing and distribution.

Failure Cost: The cost of rework and other product related liabilities and loss of market opportunity, etc.

Forecasting: Estimates projected into the future using one or more techniques to help management to cope with the uncertainty.

Fixed Cost: Costs that are incurred regardless of production.

Flexible Enterprise: Enterprises which are flexible in their approach and system making them capable of quick response to the fast changes of the market demand and environment including short term opportunities.

Functional Authority: Authority based on a business function.

GDP: Total value of production of manufacturing, agriculture and service goods of a country plus value of exports minus the value of imports.

GNP: The value of all the goods and services produced in an economy plus the value of goods and services imported, less the goods and services exported.

Globalisation: Increased mobility of goods, services, labour, technology and capital throughout the world. Its pace has increased with the advent of Information and Communication Technologies.

Innovation: Making significant improvement over the current products and practices followed.

Incentives: Items provided to motivate people to deliver incremental volume of output.

Just-in-Time: Activities are designed to happen just before they are required.

Kaizen: Small but continuous improvements.

Lateral Thinking: Seeking to solve problems by unorthodox or apparently illogical methods.

Liberalisation: Removal of or reduction in trade practices that thwart free flow of goods, services and capital from one nation to another by dismantling tariff and non-tariff barriers to trade and commerce such as license, permits, quotas and arbitrary standards.

Prevention Cost: The total cost attributable to activities undertaken to prevent defects in design, development, purchase, production, etc.

Productivity: The output per unit input such as total factor productivity and partial factor productivity (labour productivity, capital productivity and machine productivity).

Product Positioning: The way a customer perceives the features, benefit and value of a business's product with those of its competitors.

Profit Centre: Profits calculated in various subdivisions of the company which add up to the over all profit of the corporation and also compare with cost centers.

Return on Investment: Ratio of the amount earned per year to the amount invested in a particular project or business stated as a percentage.

Scientific Management: The approach to management fathered by Frederick W. Taylor. It deals with the organised study of work, the analysis of work into its simplest elements and systematic improvement of the worker's performance of each of these elements resulting into higher level of output per worker.

Shares: Unit of ownership of a corporation.

Simulation: An abstract replication of certain dynamics of a problem situation—usually involves manipulation of model function.

Social Responsibility: An organisation's obligation towards the society in which it exists.

Strategic Alliance: Formal relationship such as pooling resources between two or more parties to pursue a set of agreed goals or to meet critical business needs while remaining as independent organisations.

Sustainability: Living within limits through careful understanding of the interconnections among economy, society and environment.

Strategic Planning: Planning for company's long term future that includes setting of major overall objectives and deciding on the approach and action to achieve those including resource allocations.

Systems Thinking: Analysis that uses systems and their dynamics to examine problems and their possible solutions.

Task Force: A group assigned to accomplish a task. Task Forces are expected to perform a job or a specific assignment.

Theory X and Theory Y: Theories about Human behaviour formulated by Douglas McGregor. Theory X assumes that people are generally lazy, dislike and shun work, have to be driven and need both carrot and stick. It says that people are incapable of taking responsibility for themselves and have to be looked after. Theory Y assumes that people have a psychological need to work and that they desire achievement and responsibility and will find them under right conditions.

Variable Cost: Cost of production process that varies with the level of production.

Wholly Owned Subsidiary: Subsidiaries all of whose shares are owned by the parent company as contrasted with subsidiaries controlled by the parent company because of majority holding.

Zero-based Budgeting: Budgeting that assumes that each project or activity must justify against any expenditure.

Bibliography

Bloom, Paul N. and Philip Kotler. 1975. 'Strategies for High Market Share Companies', *Harvard Business Review*, November–December: 62–72.

Bossidy, Larry, Ram Charan and Charles Burck. 2002. *Execution: The Discipline of Getting Things Done*. London: Random House Business Books.

Boston Consulting Group (BCG). 1976. 'The Rule of Three and Four', *Perspectives*, No. 187.

Bowman, Cliff and Veronique Ambrosini. 2002. 'Value Creation Versus Value Capture', *British Journal of Management*, 11 (1): 1–15.

Cook, Jr Victor J. 1983. 'Marketing Strategy and Differential Advantage', *Journal of Marketing*, 47 (Spring): 68–75.

Cook, Jr Victor and John R. Page. 1987. 'Assessing Marketing Risk', *Journal of Business Research*, 15 (6): 519–30.

Cooper, Robert G. 1994. *Winning at New Products: Accelerating the Process from Idea to Launch*, Second Edition. Reading, Massachusetts: Addison-Wesley Publishing Company.

Crosby, Philip B. 1993. *Quality is Free*. New York: McGrawHill Inc.

———. 1995. *Quality is Still Free, Making Quality Certain in Uncertain Times*. New York: McGraw Hill Book Company—A division of McGrawHill Inc.

de Bono, Edward. 1980. *Future Positive*. New York, NY: Penguin Books.

———. 1991. *Conflicts: A Better Way to Resolve Them*. New York: Penguin Books Inc.

———. 1992. *Serious Creativity*. NY: Harper Collins.

Drucker, Peter F. 1964. *Managing for Results*. New York: Harper & Row.

———. 1973. *Management: Tasks, Responsibility and Practices*. New York: Harper & Row.

Drucker, Peter F. 1980. *Managing in Turbulent Times*. London: William Heinemann Ltd.

————. 1986. *Innovation & Entrepreneurship: Practices and Principles*. New York: Harper & Row.

————. 1992. *Managing for the Future: The 1990s and Beyond*. Oxford, UK: Butterworth Heinemann Ltd.

Gilder, George. 1984. *The Spirit of Enterprise*. New York: Simon & Schuster.

Goldratt, Eliyahu M. and Jeff Cox. 1993. *The Goal*. England: Gower Publishing Co. Ltd.

Hall, William K. 1980. 'Survival Strategies in Hostile Environment', *Harvard Business Review*, September–October: 75–80.

Hamel, Gary and C.K. Prahalad. 1994. *Competing for the Future*. Boston, MA: Harvard Business School Press.

Hammer, Michael and James Champy. 1995. *Reengineering the Corporation: A Manifesto for Business Revolution*. UK: Nicholas Brealey Publication.

IBS Center for Management Research (ICMR). 2010. 'Revamping Rasna—A Marketing Overhaul Saga.' Available online at http://www.icmrindia.org/free%20resources/casestudies/Revamping%20Rasna1.html (downloaded on 19 July 2010).

Infosys. 2008a. *Infosys Annual Report 2008*. Bengaluru: Infosys Ltd.

————. 2008b. *Enduring Values: Sustainability Report 2007–08*. Bengaluru: Infosys Ltd.

International Institute for Management Development (IMD). 2000. *World Competitiveness Yearbook 2000*. Lausanne: IMD.

————. 2002. *World Competitiveness Yearbook 2002*. Lausanne: IMD.

Kotler, Philip. 1980. *Marketing Management: Analysis, Planning and Control*, Fourth Edition. Englewood Cliffs, NJ: Prentice-Hall.

Lant, Theresa K. and David B. Mongomery. 1987. 'Learning from Strategic Success and Failure', *Journal of Business Research*, 15 (6): 503–17.

Levitt, Theodore. 1960. 'Marketing Myopia', *Harvard Business Review*, July–August: 26–37.

————. 1961. 'Marketing Intangible Products and Product Intangibles', *Harvard Business Review*, May–June: 94–102.

Lieberman, Marvin B. and David B. Mongomery. 1988. 'First Mover Advantages', *Strategic Management Journal*, 9: 41–58.

Mahajan, Vijay and Eitan Muller. 1979. 'Innovation Diffusion and New Product Growth Models in Marketing', *Journal of Marketing*, 43 (October): 55–68.

McCormack, Mark H. 1986. *What They Don't Teach You at Harvard Business School*. New York: John Boswell Associates/Bantam Books.

———. 1990. *The 110% Solution*. London: Chapmans Publishers Ltd.

McKinsey Global Institute (MGI). 2001. *India: The Growth Imperative*. San Fancisco, CA: McKinsey Global Institute.

Mitra, Ashok. 2008. 'Growth For Whom—Choice or Dilema,' 13th Prem Bhatia Memorial Lecture organised by Prem Bhatia Memorial Trust, New Delhi, 8 May.

Ohmae, Kenichi. 1982. *The Mind of the Strategist*. New York: Penguin Books.

Peters, Tom. 1987. *Thriving on Chaos: A Handbook for a Management Revolution*. New York: Alfred A. Knopf.

Peters, Tom and Nancy Austin. 1985. *A Passion for Excellence*. New Jersey: Wings Book.

Peters, Tom and Robert H. Waterman. 1994. *In Search of Excellence: Lessons from America's Best-Run Companies*. New York: Harper Collins Publishers.

Porter, Michael E. 1980. *Competitive Strategy: Techniques for Analysing Industry and Competitors*. New York: The Free Press.

———. 1985a. *Competitive Advantage*. New York: Free Press.

——— (ed.). 1985b. *Competition in Global Industries*. Cambridge, Massachusetts: Harvard Graduate School of Business Administration.

———. 1989. 'Industry Structure & Competitive Strategy: Key to Profitability,' in Victor J. Cook, Jean Claude Larréché and Edward C. Strong (eds), *Readings in Marketing Strategy*, Second Edition, pp. 43–52. Palo Alto, CA: The Scientific Press.

Porter, Michael E. and Klaus Schwab. 2008. *The Global Competitiveness Report 2008–2009*. Geneva: World Economic Forum.

Prahlad, C.K. and Gary Hamel. 1990. 'The Core Competencies of the Corporation', *Harvard Business Review*, 68 (3): 79–91.

Ries, Al and Jack Trout. 1982. *Positioning: The Battle for your Mind*. New York: Warner Books.

———. 1990. *Bottom Up Marketing*. New York: Penguin Books.

Schelling, Thomas C. 1960. *The Strategy of Conflict*. Cambridge, Massachusetts: Harvard University Press.

Töpfer, Armin. 1995. 'New Products—Cutting the Time to Market', *Long Range Planning*, 28 (2): 61–78.

Tzu, Sun. 1995. *The Art of War*. London: Hodder & Stoughton—A division of Headline Plc.

Ulaga, Wolfgang. 2001. 'Customer Value in Business Markets: An Agenda for Inquiry', *Industrial Marketing Management*, 30 (4): 315–19.

Womack, James, P. Jones, T. Daniel and Daniel Roos. 1990. *The Machine that Changed the World*. New York: Rowson Associates.

World Bank. 2005. *World Development Report 2005: A Better Investment Climate For Everyone*. Washington, DC: The World Bank.

Index

About the Author

Rajat Kanti Baisya is a Senior Professor of Marketing and Strategic Management and Chair Professor of Marketing Management Group at Department of Management Studies, IIT Delhi. He is also a Visiting Professor at ENPC International Business School, Paris and Northwestern Polytechnical University, Xian in China, where he teaches strategic management and marketing management.

He has worked with several multinational corporations and Indian groups including Reckitt Benckiser, United Breweries Group and Escorts at various senior management positions. He has been providing consulting services to many well known corporations such Airports Authority of India, Booker Group Plc, etc.

Rajat Baisya is the Founder President of Project and Technology Management Foundation. He is also on the boards of many leading Indian and multinational companies like Rajasthan Electronics and Instruments Ltd (also a Public Sector Undertaking), North Eastern Development Finance Corporation Ltd, Strategic Consulting Group Pvt Ltd, Frontier Agro Industries Pvt Ltd and Booker India Pvt Ltd (a wholly owned subsidiary of Booker Group Plc., UK).

He has written over 200 articles and research papers on various aspects of business and industry. He is an editorial board member of *Indian Food Packer, Process Food Industry, Journal of Scientific and Industrial Research, Journal of Food Science and Technology, International Journal of Asia Entrepreneurship and Sustainability, Project Management Today* and *Journal of Advances on Management Research*.

He is also the author of *Changing Face of Processed Food Industry in India* (2007) and *Aesthetics in Marketing* (SAGE, 2008).

He is the recipient of many awards including Gardner Award of AFST (I) for 1974 and Dr J.S. Pruthi Award for 2002 for making significant contribution to the industry.

Rajat Baisya is a Fellow of the Institute of Engineers (India) and Indian Institute of Chemical Engineers. He is also a member of the Research Management Board of International Project Management Association, Switzerland.